Community Safety:
Innovation and Evaluation

Community Safety: Innovation and Evaluation

Edited by

Elaine Hogard, Roger Ellis and Jeremy Warren

Chester Academic Press

First published 2007
by Chester Academic Press
University of Chester
Parkgate Road
Chester CH1 4BJ

Printed and bound in the UK
by the Print Unit
University of Chester
Cover designed
by the Graphics Team
University of Chester

The individual contributions © the respective authors
The design © The University of Chester, 2007

All Rights Reserved
No part of this publication may be reproduced, stored in a
retrieval system or transmitted in any form or by any
means without the prior permission of the copyright
owner, other than as permitted by current UK copyright
legislation or under the terms and conditions of a
recognised copyright licensing scheme

A catalogue record for this book is available from the
British Library

ISBN 978-1-905929-26-9

ACKNOWLEDGEMENTS

We would like to thank the Chester City Council, through their Service Manager, Community Safety, Peter Hartwell, for their support and funding for both this book and for the conference on which it was, in part, based. This support was a tangible expression of the partnership between the University of Chester, through the Social and Health Evaluation Unit, and the City Council, in the area of community safety.

We would also like to thank Professor Tim Wheeler, Vice Chancellor of the University of Chester, for his support for the conference which was a first event in the new University of Chester's calendar and for his sustained commitment to community safety.

We would like to give special thanks to Professor Ken Pease OBE, Visiting Professor of the University, who was instrumental in attracting contributors to the conference and this book.

Finally we would like to thank Peter Williams of Corporate Communications for his enthusiastic and meticulous assistance in producing this book.

Elaine Hogard
Roger Ellis
Jeremy Warren

CONTENTS

Editors' Introduction   1

Leadership, Community Safety and Delivery: 8
Evaluating the Effectiveness of Leadership
Within a Partnership Context
Stephen Brookes

Quick but Not Dirty: Rapid Evidence Assessments   50
(REAs) as a Decision Support Tool in Social Policy
E. Burton, G. Butler, J. Hodgkinson and S. Marshall

Appropriate Complexity: Capturing and Structuring   63
Knowledge from Impact and Process Evaluations of
Crime Reduction, Community Safety and Problem-
Oriented Policing
Paul Ekblom

The Trident: A Three-Pronged Method for Evaluating   109
Programmes and Initiatives
Roger Ellis and Elaine Hogard

Public Perceptions of Static and Redeployable CCTV   128
A. Rose, M. Gill, K. Collins and M. Hemming

Hands On or Hands Off?: Central Government's Role   148
in Managing CDRPS
Mike Hough

Community Intelligence in the Policing of   183
Community Safety
Martin Innes and Colin Roberts

Community Safety: Innovation and Evaluation

Crime and Disorder Audits and the Problems of Becoming Too Localised
R.I.Mawby — 206

Partnerships – Looking to the Future
Judith Million — 237

No Pain, No Gain: The Safer Derbyshire Research and Information Team Story
Kevin Pellatt — 250

Defining Deviant Lifestyles: Understanding Anti-Social Behaviour and Problem Drug Use Through Critical Methodologies
Craig Paterson and Allyson MacVean — 260

Back to the Future: Innovation, Evaluation and Reverse Survival Analysis
Kate Bowers, Shane Johnson and Ken Pease — 285

What Do We Mean by 'What Works?'?
Nick Tilley — 306

'Safer Homes': An Innovative Approach to Tackling Domestic Burglary
Jeremy Warren and Graeme Gerrard — 329

Mapping the Fear of Crime – A Micro-Approach
Chris Williams — 358

EDITORS' INTRODUCTION

Fifteen papers are collected in this book under the general title of *Community Safety: Innovation and Evaluation*. We will begin with some reflections on these three key concepts before introducing the individual papers.

What is community safety? It could be argued that the term is tautological. A concern with safety is surely axiomatic in the notion of community. Any community will be concerned with protecting itself from the enemy without and the enemy within. Defence looks after the enemy without; community safety is concerned with the enemy within. This internal enemy damages or misappropriates property and threatens the physical and psychological well-being of community members. Safety therefore requires the reduction or, ideally, the elimination of such criminal activities and of other behaviours which whilst not necessarily criminal are undesirable and anti-social.

Community safety is at the interface of material physical reality and socially constructed psychological reality. Broken windows and stolen cars are physically unambiguous although they are open to a number of psychological interpretations. Fear of crime on the other hand is a psychological phenomenon existing in the thoughts and feelings of individuals but with correlates in behaviour and physical events.

Given its complexity and constructed nature it is inevitable that there are definitional problems in the concept of community safety. One of us, Warren, is occupied at present in a Delphi survey of community safety practitioners to identify consensus and difference in the definitions that they hold. Pending the publication of his results we will have to rely on government statements and the practices that follow these. However, all the chapters in this book reflect to some extent on what we mean by community safety.

We can certainly expect community safety to be an abiding concern of both national and local government. A good starting point for a consideration of community safety in the United Kingdom is the Crime and Disorder Act (1998) implemented by the then newly elected Labour government. This gave community safety a new focus and priority. During the late 1990s there was a change in the political climate in the UK, particularly with regard to the management of crime. Uncertainty in the Conservative response to crime allowed New Labour to steal a march by adopting the principles contained within the Morgan Report into their own manifesto for the 1997 general election and into the new Act.

The Act was based largely then upon the recommendations of the Morgan Report, published in 1991, that had actually been commissioned by the previous Conservative administration. The report recommended the creation of Crime and Disorder Reduction Partnerships (CDRPs), recognising that crime reduction and prevention could no longer be seen as solely a police activity, but as an activity that only a multi-agency approach could hope to deal with in the long term. It also advocated the audit of crime and disorder in a local area and using the audit as a focus for consultation with local people. Finally it required the production of a Crime and Disorder Reduction

Introduction

Strategy, which would be based on the findings from the consultation.

The creation of CDRPs could be seen as something of a paradigm shift, requiring many different agencies to work together to reduce crime and disorder in a local area and to co-operate in addressing a shared agenda. The forcing of agencies to work together in this way created tensions and difficulties that took a long while to resolve, with many partnerships only starting to become effective after the second three year cycle had been completed. It could be said that part of this difficulty lay in the different ways that agencies construed and used the term 'community safety'. So clearly partnerships still require evaluation and development if they are to fulfil their potential.

The latest expression of government thinking in the UK is enshrined in the National Community Safety Plan published in 2005. The Plan reassures us that crime generally and violent crime in particular, together with the fear of crime, is on the decrease. Nevertheless a plan is required to make communities still safer. This plan has at its centre five themes which are expressed as aims. First, communities should be made stronger and more effective, placing the obligation for action locally rather than through central government. Second, and self evidently, there should be further reduction in crime and anti-social behaviour. Third, physical environments should be made safer. Fourth, the public should be protected and their confidence should be built. Fifth, people's lives should be improved so that they are less likely to commit offences or crimes. In order to achieve these aims the plan emphasises the importance of partnership, bringing a more holistic approach to local problems and initiatives.

How then do the papers in this book relate to the Plan and its themes? The Plan tries to be both reassuring regarding putative decreases in crime and fear of crime whilst at the same time ambitious to achieve further reductions. Both these statements, retrospective and aspirant, assume that there is a reliable database regarding both the incidence of crime and anti-social behaviour and the fear of crime. Without reliable and valid data it is impossible to operationalise and evaluate strategies and plans. The Act had recommended local audits but these have their limitations. Perhaps, as Dr Johnson said of Bible scholars, those who know their own area only, know not even their own area. Five chapters are concerned with such data gathering regarding community safety.

The Plan stresses the central importance of partnerships both between government and local communities and within local communities between the various agencies who should work together to achieve the five aims, including the police, social, education and health services and voluntary activists. Four chapters are concerned with such partnerships.

Statements of aims and methods are one thing; finding out whether they have been achieved and by what means is another. This is the role of evaluation. Evaluation is a complex but necessary enterprise and five papers address this topic.

Innovation is a relative term. One person's novelty is another's cliché. Historians remind us that conceptually there is nothing new under the sun; only the physical representations of concepts change and perhaps develop.

Introduction

On the other hand to the tyro everything appears new. We hope that all the papers in this book describe something innovative in their context. The reader will have to judge how innovative they are for themselves. The theme of innovation permeates all the papers but is brought to a more specific focus in the two operational innovations and evaluations described by Warren and Gerard, and by Rose et al.

The Social and Health Evaluation Unit is co-sponsor of this book and of the national conference on which it is based. The Unit has a slogan: No Innovation without Evaluation. Apart from its marketing value, this slogan does encapsulate an important truth. An innovation will only become known when it is disseminated with some evidence of its effectiveness. Such evidence is the business of formal evaluation. This has long been recognised in the area of community safety as both Ekblom and Tilley point out. Five papers consider approach and method in evaluation.

So the papers in this book can be considered as falling into four groups, concerned respectively with community safety data, partnerships, operational innovations and evaluation.

Mawby looks at the local community safety audits as a source of data but warns of the dangers of localism which make national or regional comparisons difficult. Whilst applauding their focus on local issues he points to the cost of the audits and their insensitivity to the mobility of both criminals and residents. Notwithstanding the difficulties inherent in local data gathering, Innes and Roberts propose a community intelligence methodology applicable not just for the police but for all the agencies involved in community safety work. Pellatt gives a case study of an initiative in one authority to gather data and Williams describes a micro approach to mapping the fear of crime. Paterson and MacVean look at anti-social behaviour but from the perspective of critical methodologies rather than conventional data gathering.

With regard to partnerships, Hough considers the reasons for underachievement in the CDRPs and the role of government in the management of CDRPs, suggesting possible alternative approaches to optimising local partnership work. Brookes considers the internal operation of partnerships and particularly the role of leaders. Million looks to the future prospects for partnerships in the context of the Community Safety Plan.

Two chapters are concerned with operational innovations to improve community safety and their evaluation. Gerrard and Warren describe the Cheshire Safer Homes Initiative which involved a business process approach to the reporting and follow up of domestic burglary. Rose *et al.* look at redeployable CCTV from the perspective of the public.

The evaluation of community safety is a major theme of this book and there are five chapters addressing this pervasive and vital activity. Tilley brings a sceptical view to the enterprise and questions whether we have really been able to answer the fundamental evaluators' question: 'What works?' Ekblom and Ellis & Hogard are concerned with the structure and design of evaluations. Ellis & Hogard present their Trident method that focuses programme evaluation on outcomes, process and multiple stakeholder perspectives. Ekblom argues that the

Introduction

complexity of community safety requires a commensurately complex evaluation design. The last two chapters link evaluation and innovation by proposing novel techniques that can be used in evaluation studies. Burton *et al.* describe rapid assessment technique used as part of evaluation. Bowers *et al.* advocate reverse survival analysis as an innovative approach to evaluation.

The chapters in this book are therefore contemporary in their focus: they relate to the key issues in the Community Safety Plan. They are, we believe, both reflective and practical, critical and committed. We hope they will prove stimulating and useful to practitioners and academics and will contribute, in their different ways, to safer communities.

LEADERSHIP, COMMUNITY SAFETY AND DELIVERY: EVALUATING THE EFFECTIVENESS OF LEADERSHIP WITHIN A PARTNERSHIP CONTEXT

Stephen Brookes

Introduction

Excellent leadership makes a difference to partnership performance and is arguably the most critical success factor for partnership working. Without it, partnerships would be ineffective. It is, however, perceived as a problematic issue for a number of reasons. First, traditional approaches to leadership have focused almost exclusively on individuals. Second, leadership is often seen as just one part of an organisational system rather than something which pervades the whole. Finally it is said to be difficult to measure and therefore supposedly hard to tell the good leadership from the bad.

This paper suggests that there is a need to change approaches towards leadership in the public sector in order to overcome these perceived problems. In suggesting an alternative model of leadership, it focuses on four main themes. First, it highlights that the traditional focus on individual leadership should be redirected to emphasise a model of collective leadership (both shared and distributive). Second, it emphasises that leadership pervades the whole of an organisation and that it is possible to take on board a model of public leadership which puts this collective style of leadership at the centre of an organisation. Third, it suggests that leadership can, in fact, be measured through a system of standards-based assessments. It concludes by setting a challenge to all in the public sector to accept that perhaps they are not very good at leadership and in so doing to look critically at their leadership styles and be prepared to improve their collective leadership. Why is this so important? Simply because it will: make for better partnership working; enhance ownership; improve accountability; and draw together what are currently perceived as disparate targets and objectives, thus highlighting the mutual benefits of partnership working to all those organisations involved.

First it is important to establish what is meant by leadership and why it is so important in the public sector context.

What is Meant by Leadership and why is it so Important?

Charles Handy (1985:92) once said of leadership:

> It is like driving a car or, perhaps, making love. Most of us do it at some time or other. Most of us do it at least adequately though perhaps we worry from time to time that we might do it better. But we are certainly not going to admit it openly, certainly not going to ask for lessons in it, hardly prepared to discuss it except in a jocular vein. For the management of people is something that all able-bodied men and women can take in their stride.

From the author's own experience and research an alternative definition of Public Leadership is offered as a form of collective leadership in which public bodies and agencies collaborate in achieving a shared vision based on shared aims and values which seek to promote, influence and deliver improved and sustained social, environmental and economic well-being within a complex and changing social context.

It is important at the outset to acknowledge that leadership can mean different things to different people at different times. As such it could be argued that there is no real understanding as to what leadership really is. Stogdill (1974) - in one of the most comprehensive reviews of leadership literature to date - concluded that an endless accumulation of empirical data has not produced an integrated understanding of leadership. To illustrate this point, let's imagine that the Police Commander of a Basic Command Unit or a Local Authority Chief Executive tells his/her Community Safety Officer to write an action plan to tackle anti-social behaviour and then says "get on with tackling the nuisance". This could be considered as leadership. Another Commander or Chief Executive however, may take an active lead in both influencing and approving the action plan and might also take personal steps in ensuring that it is delivered. This could also be considered as leadership. Other behaviours in between these two extremes may also be deployed and called leadership.

Leadership can also be vested in different people in different circumstances and for different reasons. Let's consider the role of Crime and Disorder Reduction Partnerships (CDRPs) in undertaking and publishing crime and disorder audits and strategies (which are required by legislation) and also the role of central government in influencing those strategies. The Prime Minister, supported by the cabinet, has a very clear leadership role in setting government priorities in relation to the electoral mandate. Let us continue with the anti-social behaviour

(ASB) theme. The PM delegates that responsibility to the Home Secretary through what are called Public Service Agreements (PSAs). These align central government funding to objectives and are led by the Treasury. By means of this agreement the Home Secretary (who 'owns' and thus leads the PSA for ASB) tasks Chief Constables and CDRPs with specific objectives to reduce anti-social behaviour and improve quality of life. However, the Home Secretary requires the support of his colleagues in other government departments. This would include the Deputy Prime Minister who ensures that local government plays its part. Similarly, at a local level the same would be true of the arrangements between police forces and local authorities working together to reduce anti-social behaviour; each would require leadership from the other. There is also an increasing call for local and community leadership. Local parish councillors can influence action locally and so can the population of those communities, but only if one of their number or a group takes a leadership role. All of these are examples of leadership *across* public agencies and groups. In addition to this is the need for leadership *within* these organisations as Chief Constables and Chief Executives provide corporate leadership to those charged with delivery.

In spite of this, it is probably true to say that leadership is often the ingredient most lacking in making partnership working a reality and, more worryingly, there is a reluctance to accept this amongst leaders. In a recent survey undertaken by the Chartered Management Institute (Charlesworth *et al.*, 2005), public sector managers delivered a damning assessment of the quality of their senior management. Two thirds felt that their leadership was so poor it threatened to derail the government's public sector reform agenda (which of course is at the centre of the government's approach to community safety).

We should not underestimate how important leadership is in driving up partnership performance. In the foreword to the CMI report (Charlesworth *et al.*, 2005:5), Sir Michael Bischard said:

> In most organisations leadership is the key which unlocks or blocks change. The public service is no different, so the consistently poorer ratings (when compared to the private sector) accorded to public sector leaders is a key cause for concern during a period of major reform.

This represents a major challenge for the public sector and it is to this challenge that this paper now turns with specific reference to the field of community safety. Innovative approaches to leadership are just as important as innovation within those activities that leadership seeks to influence. It is equally important to ensure that we 'know good leadership when we see it'.

Let us consider the 'average' community safety partnership which is illustrated in Figure 1.

The Police Commander, Chief Executives and other senior leaders from constituent partner agencies will normally form the leadership group (or responsible authority or other pseudonym for the statutory partnership). One of them will take the formal role of

Chairperson. The group will have shared aims (the strategy) and will clearly wish to achieve the objectives of

Figure 1. *Traditional Leadership Structures for Community Safety Partnerships.*

those aims. Most partnerships deliver the strategic aims through a 'shared' action plan. Not all would concentrate on doing this through shared values and even less, it is argued, may take into consideration either social or economic long term needs. The way in which the strategy is led in relation to implementation differs from partnership to partnership, but the focus on leadership invariably focuses on the personal leadership of the chair or the chief officers of each agency.

This paper suggests an alternative view in relation to public

public leadership, namely that public leadership can be viewed as the function of a system rather than the property of an individual. The resulting leadership style will thus seek to draw together and co-ordinate all elements of partnership activity. This is not to dismiss the importance of individual leadership, but rather to suggest that sustaining improvement in the delivery of public outcomes can only be achieved by what will be described as 'collective public leadership'. This involves sharing leadership across a number of constituent organisations and distributing it within each of those organisations.

Having established what is generally understood by leadership and why it is so crucial, it is important to address the problem of leadership being perceived as an individual rather than a collective issue.

From the Individual to the Collective

Stogdill (1974) describes how previous writers on leadership have suggested that it is an innate characteristic. This notion of a personal leadership style prompted Handy (1976:92) to ask the following question:

> Are leaders born or made? Can anyone be a leader, or only the favoured few? Is there a particular trick to it or a particular style, something that, if we could learn it, would transform our lives? Are there models we should imitate, great men we can learn from? Do you have to be popular to be effective? Or is it the other way round: is it impossible to be both well liked and productive?"

It has also been suggested that it depends on the particular circumstances in which a leader finds himself and that leaders will change at different times (Fiedler, 1967; Fiedler *et al.*, 1976). This approach to situational leadership would enable organisations to give careful consideration to the placement of people to positions of leadership within different contexts (Bull *et al.*, 1983), a concept that could prove useful in developing shared and distributed leadership.

Most of the theories on leadership were written during relatively stable times. We now live in a complex world where public leadership is a complex issue. Community safety and criminal justice provide a good example of this modern complexity. In his analysis of crime and social order in contemporary society, Garland (2001) made an interesting comparison between the strategies in the UK and the USA which address community safety on the one hand and criminal justice on the other. He described the former as a strategy of preventative partnership and the latter as traditionally one of punitive segregation. Garland's important point within the context of this paper relates to the notion of cultural and social support. Punitive segregation is a highly visible, highly politicized policy that could not operate in the absence of broad public commitment. Conversely, Garland argues that preventative partnerships are not as high profile as punitive segregation and can easily be implemented almost unnoticed by the public. Strong leadership is required to ensure that partnerships receive the attention of both policy makers and the public. An important point made by Garland - and one that is of direct relevance to leadership development - is that partnership working does involve the invention of new ways of thinking and acting. It is in this respect that a new approach to public leadership is needed, and that this may occur by creating the conditions that will enable new ways of thinking and acting to emerge to ensure that crime prevention is just as important in the eyes of policy makers and the electorate as other more punitive or criminal justice issues.

This paper briefly describes the notion of public leadership and how it is shared and distributed across and within a number of organisations and agencies using examples from community safety. The author's interest in the concepts of shared and distributed leadership was initially inspired through research in the field of school leadership although the two terms have tended to be used separately rather than in tandem. For example, Doyle and Smith (2001:1), in describing 'shared leadership', argue that "leadership can be explored as a social process – something that happens between people. It is not so much what leaders do, as something that arises out of social relationships. As such it does not depend on one person, but on how people act together to make sense of the situations that face them." In relation to distributed leadership a study undertaken on behalf of the National College for School Leadership (Bennett *et al.*, 2003) acknowledges that there are few clear definitions of distributed or devolved leadership and that those that do exist differ widely. The authors argue that distributed leadership includes leadership initiatives involving those in both formal and informal positions within the school community. For the purposes of this paper, the term distributed leadership is considered synonymous with that of devolved leadership and the author suggests that the two concepts of shared (relationships between a network of people) and distributed (relationships between different layers of the organisational hierarchy) leadership provide the two key dimensions of what can be classed as collective leadership.

Figure 2. Shared Leadership as One Dimension of Collective Leadership.

Shared and Distributed Leadership Within the Context of Partnerships

The role of individual Chief Executives and Police Commanders is clearly important in setting the initial vision and we can see this within existing partnerships. With collective leadership (illustrated in Figure 2), individuals influence one another during both the setting and development of the partnership's vision. As a result, the partnership moves toward its goals with unity and through shared values. This is the first key step in our public leadership challenge – to share the leadership across the relevant partnership players.

The next stage is to ensure that leadership is appropriately applied within each of the constituent organisations that make up a partnership. At the local level we know that police inspectors, assistant directors and similar people within organisations receive instructions from more senior colleagues in taking forward the strategy.

We would equally expect those people to share leadership at a more tactical level – and so it continues – until it reaches the beat officer, the housing officer and so on. This is what this paper describes as 'distributed' leadership. By distributing, as opposed to instructing, the commander or CEO retains overall leadership responsibility but distributes it to others in more distinct 'chunks'. By drawing together both shared and distributed leadership we thus start to get real meaning. This is illustrated in Figure 3

There are different layers of public leadership; hence the illustration in Figure 3 could equally be applied to Whitehall. If central government 'shares' leadership across Whitehall departments then there will be a much greater opportunity to create the 'joined-up approaches' that are so often spoken of but rarely applied. By then 'distributing' this leadership across local delivery public bodies (police forces/divisions, local authorities, etc.) the potential exists to deliver improved public services in a more collective or collaborative way. This paper is not the vehicle for exploring in detail the potential of this idea beyond traditional public bodies, but there is a real opportunity to develop leadership in a more structured way with, for example, the voluntary and community sector and other social entrepreneurs.

Figure 3. Shared and Distributed Leadership as both Dimensions of Collective Leadership.

It is important to identify *how* this model of public leadership could be both shared and distributed to achieve a shared vision and to describe how it can be assessed and evaluated. To this end, I want to suggest a model of public leadership which puts 'leadership style' at the centre. This leadership style would determine how the various elements of the public leadership model were brought together to achieve the shared aims, values and outcomes of the partnership.

Towards a Model of Public Leadership

The suggested model of public leadership is illustrated in Figure 4, and puts a collective public leadership style at its centre.

Figure 4. A Model of Public Leadership.

This leadership style draws together the collective efforts of the partnership in developing a shared vision based upon the needs and expectations of community members and other social and political stakeholders. This vision would be implemented through well-led delivery mechanisms in order to turn the strategy into action 'on the ground'. A clear role for potential leaders is the development of the capacity of the partnership and its people in order to turn the strategy into action. Excellent leadership is also about encouraging excellent management. This is important in relation to the management of change and in ensuring that the relevant organisations are effectively managing their processes in a collective and collaborative way. The final test of the model would clearly be the achievement of joint outcomes which – in the example used here – would result in improved and sustainable community safety. There are four elements to this particular model that merit further discussion.

1. Developing a Shared Vision
Taking due account of the political, social and environmental context within which it operates, the first priority of public leadership is to develop a shared vision at all levels. In relation to central government this is encapsulated through Public Service Agreements (PSAs) which are negotiated by Her Majesty's Treasury with individual government departments based upon the electoral mandate. At a more local level, the development of a shared vision for local authorities is a key part of its community leadership role in promoting the well-being of the 'community' (however defined) and in being accountable to the public bodies' key stakeholders which would of course include central government (through the Office of the Deputy Prime Minister [ODPM]). Taking a collective approach to public leadership may also have the potential to overcome some of the tensions which have dominated political debates in both central and local government for the last thirty years. Kingham (2004) argues that such debates have focused on the centralist versus localist dimensions. This tension is particularly evident in the balance between priorities identified locally and those determined by national government. Collective public leadership could mitigate a number of these tensions. One example is in relation to achieving a shared vision through which local authorities are viewed as central government's partners in providing services for the public, with local government and other public agencies having a role in both influencing and interpreting national policies and mobilising resources to enact them.

This notion of collective leadership can be shared and distributed further. Local government has a key responsibility to show community leadership through the development of a shared vision. The ODPM (2004:9) outlined this recently in its 10-year vision, giving a hint at the complexity of the local delivery landscape.

> There is leadership in decision-making and the accountability for what is delivered directly by the council. There is a role in leading local partnerships and bringing stakeholders together to help meet local needs and priorities, providing a focal point for local decisions. And there is a leadership role in enabling communities to lead themselves, developing social capital, fostering greater engagement in local decisions, and taking action to promote inclusion.

Arguably public leadership is needed at all levels and across many organisations. This starts from the premise of a shared vision which then determines the type of leadership required to turn this vision into action. To illustrate how the concept of public leadership can potentially make a difference in turning the vision into action across and within the various public sector bodies, this paper intends to refer to the government's *Together We Can* (Home Office, 2005) action plan. The shared vision that the action plan seeks to achieve is to bring people and government closer using a number of themes and objectives co-ordinated across twelve government departments but led by the Home Office. In the foreword to this document, the Home Secretary gave a clear indication of the extent to which the Home Office was taking a lead when he said (2005:3):

We want to transform the relationship between citizens and the state, to pass more power, control and influence from the centre to local communities. The Home Office has led the creation of the action plan and we are delighted that our colleagues across government – twelve departments in all – are taking part with us.

This action plan will be used to illustrate how public leadership can be distributed from Whitehall, through the regions and local government and eventually to the communities within the remaining three elements of the suggested model.

2. Leading Delivery

The second key element of public leadership is to lead delivery. Here, emphasis should be on the development and leadership of an action plan. The focus should be on quality services based on high expectations and in ensuring that delivery is monitored and the effectiveness of programmes evaluated and lessons learned. Leaders should be able to illustrate clearly how the shared vision is being implemented, for what purpose and with what effect.

Returning to the *Together We Can* initiative, the ambition and the scope of the programme is illustrated in Figure 5 which shows that this action plan outlines eight key public policy areas within four key strands as follows:

Figure 5. Scope of the "Together We Can" Cross-Government Initiative.

1. Citizens and Democracy:
   a. Ensuring Children and Young People have their Say;
   b. Strengthen our Democracy.
2. Regeneration and Cohesion:
   a. Revitalise Neighbourhoods;
   b. Increase Community Cohesion and Race Equality.
3. Health and Sustainability:
   a. Improve our Health and Well-Being;
   b. Secure our Future.
4. Safety and Justice:
   a. Build Safer Communities;
   b. Reduce Re-offending and Increase Confidence in the Criminal Justice System.

The action plan is carried out by the twelve government departments and delivered regionally and locally. Local bodies have a key role in the delivery of the action plan. The public policy areas are supported by a whole range of objectives. Government departments are given a lead role and for each key outcome, a range of success measures has been given. Space does not permit a detailed discussion of the range of outcomes and measures, but one outcome from the 'Build Safer Communities' theme is further illustrated in Table 1. This example also relates to the theme of anti-social behaviour and is thus of relevance to the leadership of Crime and Disorder Reduction Partnerships.

Having given a lead nationally, central government has set out what is expected of leaders locally in building safer communities. The example used requires local partners to work with local communities to address their concerns about crime, drugs and anti-social behaviour. Seven delivery objectives have been identified in total, including the example above, which require promotion of the government's anti-social behaviour strategy. Local leaders have a responsibility to engage with local community representatives and members, learn from and build upon good practice and encourage community members to 'take a stand'. One of the overall outcome measures is to assess change in community perceptions concerning anti-social behaviour and the direct engagement of the community in problem solving efforts.

Table 1. Example Outcome, Objective and Measure from "Together We Can" Action Plan.

Key Public Policy Area →	Together We Can Build Safer Communities
Outcome	Communities are safer and feel safer because

	→	the police, CDRP/DAATs, and other local partners work together to involve local people effectively in addressing their concerns about crime, drugs and anti-social behaviour.
What will be Done (one of 7 objectives)	→	Promote the messages of the Anti-Social Behaviour (ASB) Together campaign, that public agencies must respond to communities' concerns about ASB and that communities themselves have responsibility to tackle it, building on lessons learnt in the 10 Together Trailblazers and 50 Together Action Areas about involving neighbourhoods in making a difference; and promoting the third year of the Home Office Taking a Stand awards.
How Success will be Measured	→	Use BCS data to explore the relationship between perception of ASB, community cohesion and the willingness of people to get involved in tackling problems.

3. Building Capacity

The third element of the suggested model requires leaders to take responsibility for building the capacity of organisations and partnerships. This can be achieved, not only by building the capacity of those who undertake the day-to-day work, but also for leaders to accept responsibility for their own self development as leaders and that of the partnership more generally.

Arguably, building capacity is more about 'doing' than 'learning'. It requires a commitment to prioritizing relationships and shared dialogue ahead of processes and systems. In particular, it requires recognition of the development of human relationships rather than human resources. Referring again to the anti-social behaviour theme and the 'Together We Can' initiative a further illustration can be given.

The example illustrated in Table 1 requires effort by the partnership in encouraging communities themselves to take responsibility for tackling anti-social behaviour. The issue of noise nuisance serves as a good example. The partnership would need to call on strong leadership skills to tackle this issue. For example there is a clear role for the police in dealing with the immediate issues surrounding this very common complaint; there would also be an issue for the local authority in dealing with the enforcement of noise abatement. Finally there would be a responsibility for the community to take a lead in tackling the problem within their own immediate neighbourhoods. All of these activities would require capacity and capacity is not just about (more) human resources – it is about relationships and tackling problems together. Effective leadership prioritises the need to 'open up' the professions and engage in joint development for the overall benefit of the partnership and its aims, rather than for the benefit of individual organisations.

The real test for local public leadership is the extent to which leaders influence greater synergy amongst partnership members and their organisations, rather than simply protecting mainstream funding and pressing the right 'buttons' to get more public money. Local leadership can also take a more risk-based and initiative-taking approach. As Chesterton (2002:32) argued: "Local leadership is not waiting for the policy framework to become clear before you act; it is being willing to act in lots of small ways before the fog has lifted, so that new possibilities for policy integration can be discovered in the darkness". The test for national government (as part of their shared and distributed leadership role) is to provide the conditions for local partners to build this synergy and make a difference without unnecessary burdens and bureaucracies – something that the development of Local Area Agreements (LAAs), which align centrally allocated funding to locally determined priorities, seeks to achieve. For a more detailed discussion of the relevance of LAAs to community leadership generally and community safety specifically, see Brookes (2006).

4. *Managing the Organisation and Partnerships*
Excellent public leaders will recognise that change is constant and being responsive to that change should be a regular feature of managing the partnership. Having identified the capacity issues, the next important element of public leadership is the need to ensure that the day-to-day management of the partnership takes the identified capacity needs into account, along with identified priorities so that the organisation and partnership are managed appropriately. Effective management is about joined-up planning, honest and trusting dialogue and the creation of conditions in which mutual benefits are explored through challenge and support. The 'Together We Can' (TWC) initiative calls for a much greater involvement of the community in tackling the eight policy areas. This is in line with the wider Modernising Government Agenda, which seeks to reinforce more open, transparent and customer-focused government (Cabinet Office, 1999) with a view to increasing the trust of the public in the provision of public services.

Co-ordinated planning between constituent partners is critical to success. Cross-agency planning should be drawn into one framework. This requires closer linkage between Local Strategic Partnerships (LSPs) which have responsibility for a range of services provided by local partners (including health, education, employment, housing and the local economy, in addition to crime) and the sister partnerships which have specific responsibility for each of those strands such as the Crime and Disorder Reduction Partnerships (Brookes, 2006). The LSPs have a statutory responsibility to develop a community strategy based upon identified priorities in the same way that CDRPs have a responsibility to publish a crime and disorder strategy. The community networks which underpin these partnerships and their strategies should thus also be co-ordinated within a unified framework.

Two illustrations of the need for joined-up planning are offered. The first example concerns the Crime and Disorder Act 1998 and the Police and Magistrates Courts Act 1994 which require (respectively) Crime and Disorder Reduction Partnerships and Police Authorities to consult with the community in relation to crime and disorder priorities and the local policing plan. There is no statutory requirement for the emerging priorities to be co-ordinated although, in practice, BCU Commanders can do so by virtue of their membership of both partnerships and police forces. Consultation with the community is undertaken by other public agencies.

The second example concerns planning authorities. In 2004, the Government introduced changes to the development planning system, with the aim of making it faster and more responsive to change. Planning authorities are now required to produce a document known as the 'Statement of Community Involvement' within a Local Development Framework which sets out clearly how local authorities involve their communities. The policy statement for Local Development Frameworks (ODPM, 2004:16) states:

> Local planning authorities should involve the community at an early stage in the preparation of local development documents. This is essential to achieve local ownership and legitimacy for the policies that will shape the future distribution of land uses and development in an authority's area.

These requirements for community engagement are not routinely managed within the same timescale; this paper suggests that they should be. An example of the need to align these various consultations can be given. Using the 'Together We Can' action plan as an illustration, it highlights that a key objective is to revitalise neighbourhoods with an outcome that citizens "are able to play a successful part in guiding, directing and supporting effective deployment [and delivery] of local services" (Home Office, 2005:34). This has direct relevance to the need to engage citizens in both planning and crime reduction activity. A good practice guide exists for planners, architects and developers to help them make streets, homes, and parks safer places. It is aimed at encouraging greater attention to crime prevention principles and the attributes of safer places (ODPM, 2004c) but in reality, this is not routinely done (Moss, 2001) and planning decisions are often made in isolation from crime reduction imperatives.

Similar leadership qualities are needed at the national level. Lack of co-ordinated planning and implementation has been a feature of the various audit and inspection regimes. For example, best value and community planning have been described as being conceived of, managed and inspected as separate processes. As Demos (Chesterton, 2002) recently noted "Few links were made between them (inspections), and one of the consequences was that there was difficulty in getting community planning to 'bite'". Much the same can be said of the links between planning and crime reduction with the same consequence – that it is difficult to get crime reduction to bite. At a local level, section 17 of the CDA 1998 implies a statutory responsibility for relevant authorities (which include local authorities and police authorities) to consider the crime reduction impact of their decision-making but again, in reality, this does not occur (Moss & Pease, 1999). One of the key ways in which central government could display positive leadership is by making itself subject to the same section 17 principles, but it remains reluctant to bind itself by legislation in the same way that local government is bound.

The previous sections have discussed what public leadership is and how a model of public leadership could be used. The third key challenge that this paper now turns to is that contrary to popular belief, good leadership *can* be measured and that these measures can be identified through a system of standards-based assessments.

Evaluating Excellent Public Leadership

Having described a model of public leadership, it is now appropriate to move on to what this paper defines as 'Excellent Leadership' within the context of partnership working. A summary of what could be described as excellent public leadership standards and measures is offered. The components of this definition represent the standards and these, together with the underlying measures were developed on the basis of the author's own research and experience and are illustrated in Tables 2 and 3 respectively. These standards and measures have already been used in the assessment of high crime partnership areas in six of the nine government office regions, which allowed a subjective assessment of the importance of leadership and performance to be made.

Although this paper is not the vehicle in which to pursue the principles of evaluation, a realistic evaluation approach (Pawson & Tilley, 1997) can be suggested, which places importance on the interaction between contexts, mechanisms and outcomes. Realistic evaluation is supported elsewhere within partnership settings in relation to policing and crime and disorder partnerships (Brookes, 2004), health partnerships (Ansari *et al.*, 2001) and health interventions (Bowers *et al.*, 2003). It can also be used more widely across the public sector, with cross-sectoral comparisons, for example, in assessing the value of 'incentives' as a policy instrument in six domains: health; safety; corrections; transport; housing; and higher education (Pawson, 2001).

Realistic evaluation has the potential also to test the

theory underpinning the definition of public leadership suggested at the beginning of this paper. Using the Context-Mechanism-Outcome configurations at the three levels of public leadership (representing policy makers, practitioners and participants) the concepts of shared and distributed leadership could be tested. This approach could be particularly interesting if the evaluation took a programme – such as 'Together We Can' – and subjected this to rigorous evaluation of the programme leadership by using the standards framework outlined in this paper.

Table 2. Suggested Standards of Excellent Leadership.

Excellent Public Leaders ....

Display Community Leadership in all aspects of the role through active engagement with key stakeholders and, in particular, by both reflecting and engaging with community-led priorities. Excellent leaders will be open to the sharing of expertise and bring positive benefits to their own and other partnerships.

Secure accountability to and with key stakeholders in relation to clearly defined outcomes and readily engage in dialogue to secure further continued improvement.

Shape the Future through a shared vision which inspires and motivates.

Lead delivery through distributed responsibility, supported by regular monitoring and evaluation of the effectiveness of community outcomes.

Build Capacity through effective relationships between and within partners and by enabling others to achieve. Excellent leaders should be committed to the development of others as well as self development to enable leaders to deal with the complexity of the role.

Manage the organisation through the improvement of good communication, organisational structures, and functions based on a sound understanding of the need to respond to change.

Deliver Excellent Results.

Table 3. Suggested Measures of Excellent Leadership.

Display Community Leadership in all aspects of the role through active engagement with key stakeholders and, in particular, both to reflect and engage with community-led priorities. Excellent leaders will be open to the sharing of expertise and bring positive benefits to their own and other partnerships.

- Leaders are able to point clearly to evidence of their role as 'community champions';
- Leaders readily engage with local stakeholders in the delivery of the strategies aims and objectives;
- Leaders are fully open to giving and receiving examples of good practice and lessons learnt.

Secure accountability to and with key stakeholders in relation to clearly defined outcomes and readily engage in dialogue to secure further continued improvement.

- Leaders are fully open to and embrace their own accountability as leaders;
- Leaders demonstrably hold partnership members to account for turning the strategy into action;
- Leaders proactively influence and engage with continuous improvement reviews.

Shape the Future through a shared vision which inspires and motivates.

- Leaders proactively influence and drive the strategy;
- All partners share defined responsibility for the strategy;
- Strategy sets SMART targets which reflect national and local outcomes.

Lead delivery through distributed responsibility supported by regular monitoring and evaluation of the effectiveness of community outcomes.

- Leaders are able to show how the delivery arrangements are implemented 'on the ground' through effective distributed responsibilities;
- Leaders at all levels are able to display excellent results;
- Leaders at all levels are also able to show that they know why an impact 'on the ground' has/has not been achieved and the extent to which the partnership has been instrumental in this.

Build Capacity through effective relationships between and within partners and by enabling others to achieve. Excellent leaders should be committed to the development of others as well as self development to enable leaders to deal with the complexity of the role.

- Leaders are open to different and innovative ways of building capacity to deliver ;
- Leaders are able to show their own personal commitment to improving their roles;
- Leaders are clearly engaged in developing the partnership membership to improve performance.

Manage the organisation through the introduction of good communication, organisational structures, and functions based on a sound understanding of the need to respond to change.

- Leaders are open to and proactive in bringing about change;
- Leaders understand both the limitations and strength of current and future capacity needs;
- Leaders take an active role in communicating the work of the partnership.

Deliver Excellent Results

- Leaders deliver excellent results based on both national and locally determined goals;
- Leaders deliver excellent organisational developments and results.

Table 4. *Excellent Leadership and Excellent Delivery.*

Shaping the Future	Managing the Organisation
<ul><li>Clear Leadership from Chief Executives/BCU Commanders;</li><li>Good Member Involvement;</li><li>Clear Strategy;</li><li>Challenging Targets;</li><li>Performance Culture.</li></ul>	<ul><li>Crime and Drugs are within a unified structure;</li><li>Focus on continuous improvement through self assessment;</li><li>Good representation across Partner Agencies (i.e. good involvement of YOT/PCT).</li></ul>
Leading Delivery and Securing Accountability	**Community Leadership**
<ul><li>Effective tiered/thematic delivery group;</li><li>Good Analysis;</li><li>Progress Reports are routinely used;</li><li>Clear tactics delivered through good joint tasking and co-ordination;</li><li>Committed to Joint Commissioning.</li></ul>	<ul><li>Receptive to Change and new initiatives;</li><li>Good Community Engagement and Outward Facing Messages;</li><li>Prepared to Challenge; BUT</li><li>Relationships built on Trust.</li></ul>

Testing the Standards

The appropriateness of these standards has been tested since six of the nine government offices (GOs) undertook a rapid leadership audit of a sample of high crime partnerships using the standards as a framework. This leadership audit was focused on identifying the performance of the partnerships in terms of crime reduction and to identify those – in the view of GO staff – which displayed good leadership attributes based upon the standards and measures. Conversely, attention was also given to those partnerships which had not performed well and which had negative aspects of the standards. Table 4 shows a summary of the consistent factors that were perceived as being indicative of excellent leadership and delivery. Conversely Table 5 shows those partnerships where leadership was not as good and appeared alongside either poor or declining performance.

A total of 46 Crime and Disorder Reduction Partnerships were identified by six government offices as representing high-crime areas. Using the public leadership standards framework it was possible to identify some common features. In relation to 'shaping the future', the individual leadership of senior officers was considered critical alongside clear performance management arrangements. Relationships built on trust also came through as a critical success factor in relation to 'community leadership', as was the direct relationship between the vision and delivery arrangements through themed groups and formal tasking and co-ordination mechanisms in respect of leading delivery and securing accountability.

Community Safety: Innovation and Evaluation

Table 5. Areas for Development and 'Not So' Excellent Delivery.

Shaping the Future	Managing the Organisation
• Largely Police Driven; • Low profile of Elected Members; • Slow production of strategy and little strategic direction; • Performance Management Structures are lacking.	• Lack of Engagement across some areas (i.e. Health); • Slowness in vacancy filling; • No self-assessment.
Leading Delivery and Securing Accountability • Implementation Gap (strategy to implementation); • Thematic leads not clear; • Poor Commissioning; • No integration with National Intelligence Model.	**Community Leadership** • "We like the way we work now" (resistant to change/outside influence); • Lack of community engagement.

The common features identified in those partnerships considered to be poorly led and poorly performing tended to be the opposite of those shown in Table 4. Table 5 outlines these key factors. It was interesting to note that a number of the poorly-led partnerships were largely police

Evaluating the Effectiveness of Leadership

driven with a low profile of elected members. This could represent a further area for research as it may be indicative of a lack of shared leadership (as opposed to distributed). Lack of engagement of other potential key partners and lack of performance management processes were also prominent and might similarly offer further opportunities for research in respect of both shared and distributed leadership.

Shapes the Future through a shared vision which inspires and motivates					
Leaders proactively influence and drive the strategy based on good knowledge of trends, programmes and policies					
Red	Red	Amber	Amber	Green	Green
Leaders take no role at all in the strategy or activity of the partnership and leave it to the officers and have a very limited professional knowledge of the partnership environ-Ment.	Leaders take an interest in the strategy or activity of the Partnership through briefings and 'arms-length' direction but do not get actively involved and do not have an in-depth professional knowledge of the partnership environment..		Leaders take responsibility for chairing the partnership and manage the agenda through informed briefings and personal, professional knowledge.		Leaders take responsibility for all aspects of the partnership including the direction of activity between meetings in accordance with informed briefings and professional knowledge, and at frequent enough intervals, given the current challenge.

Figure 6. Example of Objective Measure in relation to Leadership.

Wider Applicability of the Public Leadership Framework

The audit described above was useful in testing the appropriateness of the suggested framework and in identifying further areas for development for individual partnerships alongside any further support that might be needed from the GOs. This paper suggests that there is real potential to use this public leadership framework in a more systematic and statistically defensible way across the public sector. With this in mind a range of objective statements are being developed alongside the suggested standards and measures to enable this to be achieved. An example is illustrated in Figure 6.

Similar criteria have been developed for each of the standards and measures. A good evaluation should be able to compare the actual style and results of leadership against the standards. For this to take place it is important that the defined measures should be **SMART**. This stands for (Home Office, 2002):

S pecific - all objectives should have specific outcomes;
M easurable - the outcome of an objective should be capable of being measured. Measurable objects will always contain a target;
A chievable - the objective should describe something that can be achieved within the timescale set for the preventive action;
R ealistic - objectives describe something that can actually be done;
T imebound - a timescale should be set for when the objective is to be achieved.

Each of the standards and measures should be subjected to the same level of objectivity and – once populated – the overall evaluation framework for public leadership standards would look like the illustration in Figure 7.

It would be important that such public leadership standards and measures were transferable across the public sector (at all levels) and provide a consistent description of excellent leadership. As well as providing consistency between partnerships, they could also provide consistency within and across central government in areas such as the alignment of planning processes and inspection regimes. There is also potential to use public leadership standards as an alternative to the myriad of assessment tools that currently exist. This aspect is also beyond the scope of this paper but is worthy of further exploration.

A starting point could be to align these leadership standards with what have been described as *The Good Governance Standards for Public Service* (OPM & CIPFA, 2004). The Office of Public Management points out that more than 450,000 people contribute as governors to a wide range of public service organisations and partnerships and that there is no common code for public service governance. This is also beyond the scope of this paper but suffice to say that the concepts of 'leadership' and 'governance' differ but are complementary. An alignment of the proposed standards of public leadership and good governance are illustrated in Figure 8.

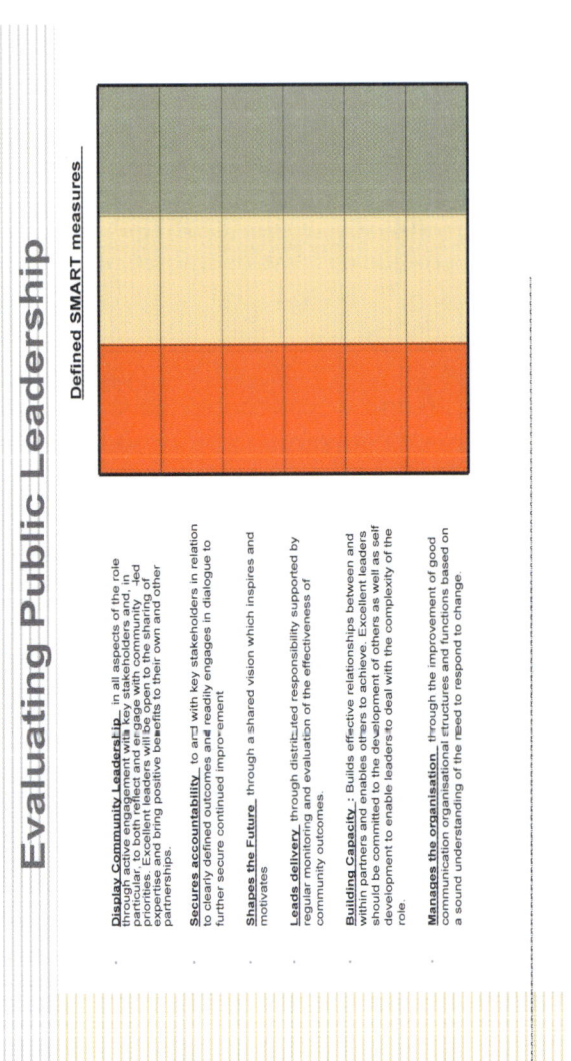

Figure 7. Evaluation Framework for Public Leadership Standards.

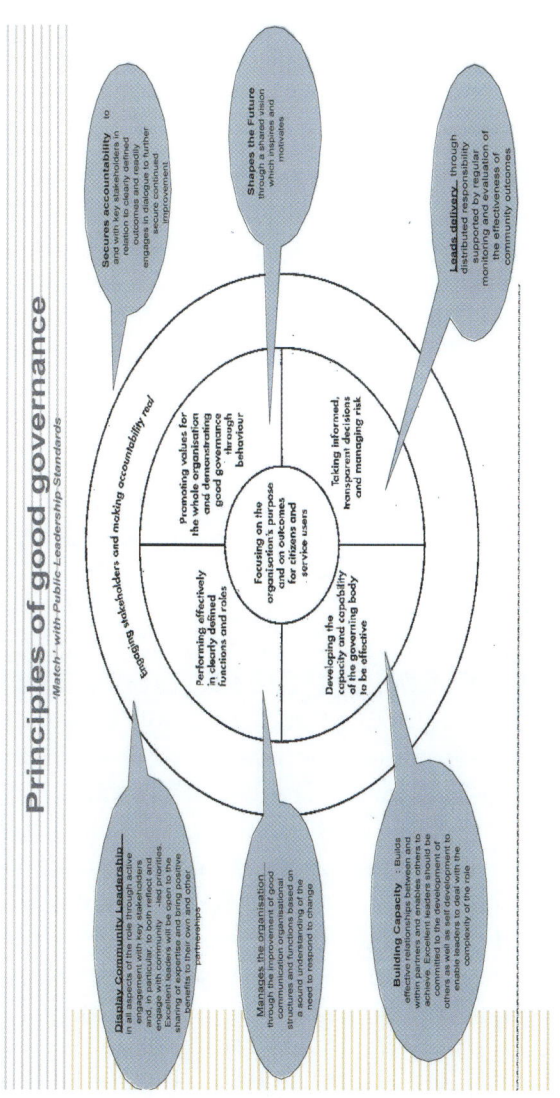

Figure 8. Alignment of Public Leadership and Good Governance Standards

Conclusion: Beyond the Power of One

Arguably the increasing complexity of public sector activity requires a different approach to public leadership. This paper has introduced the concept of collective leadership in both sharing (across) and distributing (within) organisations. It has defined what could be viewed as 'Excellent Public Leadership' and has suggested how this could be expressed within a series of standards supported by measures in order to evaluate leadership within a partnership context. The potential for further research has also been highlighted.

One challenge remains; those working in the public sector must accept that they are "not very good at leadership". Until such time there will not be an opportunity to improve public leadership skills. Therefore leadership development must be taken seriously. Leaders at all levels and across all organisations should be given the opportunity for development. There is a need to move away from the narrowly defined and restrictive meanings given to leadership and its development. In today's multi-disciplinary, multi-functional and multi-professional public sector world, multi-focused leadership development is a credible aim. This could include cross-professional development in which public sector leaders would share strengths and identify areas for development in a risk-free environment which encourages both organisational and individual leadership improvement.

If partnership leaders were to undertake an honest assessment of both the shared and distributed leadership within and across partner agencies the foundation would be set for sustained improvement. If it were possible to share and cross-tabulate these assessments across the sector, the theoretical basis upon which current leadership development programmes are based may also change. Further work should therefore be undertaken to make this challenge a realistic one, not least because of the benefits which would accrue if this public leadership challenge was tackled. For example:

i. The public sector could rise to the opportunities presented for partnership working in tackling the unprecedented demands of the 21st century.

ii. We could better identify 'what works for who and in what circumstances' through an evidence-based and shared understanding of what leadership styles and behaviours are needed in delivering today's public services.

iii. Based on the first two points, a stronger foundation for the better development of our leaders could be developed.

iv. A public leadership style in which leaders are 'free to lead' could be encouraged.

v. Leaders at all levels would be accountable to stakeholders for excellent delivery through consistent approaches to leadership against shared visions, aims and objectives.

In summary – and to use a well known problem-solving acronym (S.A.R.A) first coined by Eck & Spelman (1987) - the public leadership challenge is about;

S canning (the meaning of leadership);

A nalysing (the differing forms of leadership);

R esponding (to strengths and areas of development based upon a model of excellent public leadership); and finally

A ssessing (the extent to which leadership reflects the standards for excellence).

The notion that leadership should not be vested in one individual (no matter how charismatic that person may be) is not new - and the author seeks support for this contention from the highest authority:

> The thing that thou doest is not good. Thou wilt surely wear away, both thou, and this people that is with thee: for this thing is too heavy for thee; thou art not able to perform it thyself alone. (Exodus 18: 17-18).

References

Ansari, W., Phillips, C., & Hammick, M. (2001). Collaboration and partnerships: developing the Evidence Base. *Health and Social Care in the Community*, 9 (4), 215-227.

Bennett, N., Wise, C., Woods, P. & Harvey, J. (2003). *Distributed Leadership: Summary Report*. NCSL, Spring.

Bowers, H., Secker, J., Llanes, M., & Webb, D. (2003). *The Gap Years: Rediscovering Midlife as the Route to Healthy Active Ageing*. Health Development Agency, November, 2003.

Brookes, S. (2004). *Identifying the Conditions that Help or Hinder the Development of Community Policing*. Unpublished thesis, Nottingham Trent University.

Brookes, S. (2006). Local Authorities, Crime Reduction and the Law. In K. Moss and M. Stephens (eds), *Crime Reduction and the Law*. London: Routledge.

Bull, R., Bustin, B., Evans, P., & Gahagan, D. (1983). *Psychology for Police Officers*. Chichester: John Wiley and Sons.

Cabinet Office. (1999). *Modernising Government*. London: HMSO.

Charlesworth, K., Cook, P., & Crozier, G. (2005). *Leading Change in the Public Sector: Making the Difference*. Chartered Management Institute, June 2005.

Chesterton, D. (2002). *Local Authority? How to Develop Leadership for better Public Services*. London: DEMOS.

Doyle, M .E., & Smith, M. K. (2001). *Shared leadership*: the encyclopedia of informal education. http://www.infed.org/leadership/shared_leadership.htm - accessed 23 August 2005.

Eck, J., & Spelman, W. (1987). *Problem-Solving: Problem Oriented Policing in Newport News*. Washington: National Institute of Justice.

Fiedler, Fred E. (1967). *A theory of leadership effectiveness*. New York: McGraw-Hill.

Fiedler, Fred E. et al. (1976). *Improving leadership effectiveness: the leader match concept*. New York: Wiley.

Garland, D. (2001). *The Culture of Control: Crime and Social Order in Contemporary Society*. Oxford: University Press.

Handy, C. (1985). *Understanding Organisations.* London: Penguin.

Home Office. (2002). *Passport to Evaluation.* Home Office Crime Reduction College. http://www.crimereduction.gov.uk/evalgloss.pdf - accessed 27 October 2005.

Home Office. (2005). *Together We Can: a Government action plan led by the Home Office.* London: Home Office.

Kingham, Neil. (2004). *Interface between Central and Local Government,* Lecture delivered at the Tsinghua-Foxconn Nanotechnology Research Center, China on 25 October. http://www.britishcouncil.org/china-society-modernising-government-pavl-interface.htm - accessed October 2005.

Moss, K. (2001). Crime Prevention v Planning: Section 17 of the Crime and Disorder Act 1998. Is it a Material Consideration? *Crime Prevention and Community Safety: An International Journal,* 3 (3), 43-48.

Moss, K., & Pease, K. (1999). Crime and Disorder Act 1998: Section 17. A Wolf in Sheep's Clothing? *Crime Prevention and Community Safety: An International Journal,* 1 (4), 15-19.

ODPM. (2004a). *The Future of Local Government: A Ten Year Vision.* London: Office of the Deputy Prime Minister.

ODPM. (2004b). *Planning Policy Statement 12: Local Development Frameworks.* London: Office of the Deputy Prime Minister

ODPM. (2004c). *Safer Places: The Planning System and Crime Prevention*. London: Office of the Deputy Prime Minister.

OPM, & CIPFA. (2004). *The Good Governance Standard for Public Services*. Office of Public Management and Chartered Institute of Public Finance and Accountability.

Pawson, R. (2001). *Evidence Based Policy: II. The Promise of 'Realist Synthesis'*. Working Paper 4, ESRC UK Centre for Evidence Based Policy and Practice, University of London.

Pawson, R., & Tilley, N. (1997). *Realistic evaluation*. London: Sage.

Stogdill, R. (1974). *Handbook of Leadership*. New York: The Free Press.

QUICK BUT NOT DIRTY: RAPID EVIDENCE ASSESSMENTS (REAs) AS A DECISION SUPPORT TOOL IN SOCIAL POLICY

E. Burton, G. Butler, J. Hodgkinson and S. Marshall

Introduction

The demand for 'evidence' to inform social policy decisions is now widespread. Its prominence within the UK emerged in 1997 with the election of the New Labour government and their use of principles derived from 'new public management', with its emphasis on monitoring and control (Walker, 2000). In 1999 the UK Government called for "...better use of evidence and research in policy making..." and set out the sources of 'evidence' that policy makers should use, including: expert knowledge; existing domestic and international research; existing statistics; stakeholder consultation (Cabinet Office, 1999:16). Additionally, as Solesbury (2001:5) has pointed out: "Most research effort is expanded on new primary research and yet, on virtually any topic you can name, there is a vast body of past research that may have some continuing value".

This article describes a new approach to harnessing robust research evidence for policy makers in a more focused and timely way than many other secondary research methods, namely the Rapid Evidence Assessment (REA). An REA orders and filters research evidence in a similar way to a systematic review, but meets the urgent timescales of decision makers at national or local level.

Rapid Evidence Assessments

This article introduces the REA methodology. It then describes the second REA of two[1] so far conducted and considers the use the findings were put to by its commissioners. The article concludes by discussing challenges and future implications for the REA approach.

Background to REAs

Good practice in conducting research involves determining the extent of existing evidence relevant to the research question. Traditionally, a narrative or literature review would be undertaken to search the evidence. Typically in a literature review, reviewers seek to collate relevant studies and draw conclusions from them (Macdonald, 2003). However, there are limitations with this approach. Principally, literature reviews are susceptible to selection and/or publication biases. Furthermore, they are often opportunistic in that they review only literature and evidence that is readily available to the researcher (Macdonald, 2003).

Given the limitations of literature reviews, new techniques have been developed to try and overcome some of the issues. Systematic reviews of existing literature are increasingly being used as a valid and reliable means of harnessing existing research evidence. They differ from literature reviews by:

---

[1] The first REA was: Deaton, S., O'Shea, J., Campbell, S., Lower, C., Owen, N., Roe, S., & Smith, N. (2004), *The Effectiveness of Drug Treatment within a Criminal Justice System: An Assessment of the Existing Evidence.* (Unpublished)

- Being more systematic and rigorous in the ways in which they search and find existing evidence;

- Having explicit and transparent criteria for appraising the quality of existing research evidence, especially identifying and controlling for different types of bias in existing studies;

- Having explicit ways of establishing the comparability (or incomparability) of different studies and, thereby, of combining and establishing a cumulative effect of what the existing evidence is telling us.

(Davies, 2003:4).

Systematic reviews involve a methodical, rigorous and exhaustive search of all the relevant literature. Searches are conducted using electronic and print sources, by hand searching and identifying relevant 'grey' literature (i.e. unpublished studies or work in progress). This approach helps to remove the problems of bias associated with traditional literature reviews. The search criteria used in undertaking a systematic review and the criteria by which the literature is appraised and interpreted are clearly defined and recorded. This leads to greater transparency and allows future studies to be added to the review, enabling an interactive and cumulative body of sound evidence to be developed on a subject area.

Undertaking a systematic review however takes at least six to twelve months. Users of research and evaluation evidence often need quicker access to what the existing evidence can tell them. Consequently, Rapid Evidence Assessments (REAs) have been developed for use in public policy research and evaluation. REAs are based on the principles of a systematic review. The functions of an REA are to:

- Search the electronic and print literature as comprehensively as possible within the constraints of a policy or practice timetable;

- Collate descriptive outlines of the available evidence on a topic;

- Critically appraise the evidence (including an economic appraisal);

- Sift out studies of poor quality;

- Provide an overview of what the evidence is saying.

(Davies, 2003).

Like systematic reviews, they are based on comprehensive electronic searches of appropriate databases and some searching of print materials, but in order to complete an REA in a shorter time frame some concessions are made. As a result, exhaustive database searching, hand searching of journals and textbooks, or searches of 'grey' literature are not immediately undertaken. This shortened time frame is essential for policy-makers in order to meet deadlines, but does introduce some publication bias. However, searching may be continued beyond the time available for an REA until a comprehensive search of the available research literature has been completed and a full-blown systematic review is achieved.

All REAs carry the caveat that their conclusions may be subject to revision once more systematic and comprehensive reviews of the evidence-base have been completed. This is consistent with the important principle that systematic reviews are only as good as their most recent updating and revision allows (Davies, 2003).

Introduction to the Methodology

The exact approach undertaken in an REA will depend on the research question, but certain key stages need to be followed whatever the subject. These are:

- Identifying a clear research question;
- Developing a search strategy and establishing inclusion criteria for identifying relevant articles;
- Assessing the methodological quality and relevance of the identified articles. Articles are sifted using specified selection criteria. The case study described in this article employed a scoring system, based on the Maryland Scale (Sherman et al., 1997) and a 'Quality Assessment Tool' (QAT) developed by the authors of the first REA, (Deaton et al., 2004);
- Synthesizing the evidence across the different studies. Evidence may be synthesized in a number of ways, and it is necessary to adopt an approach most suitable for a particular review. One approach, for example, may be to undertake a meta-analysis[2], in which evidence from the studies is combined and summarized statistically.

---

[2] Meta-analysis is a statistical method of combining and summarising the results of studies that meets a minimum quality critieria.

However, this will be more problematic where outcome measures in studies are very different;
- Disseminating the messages. As REAs are aimed at practitioner and policy-maker audiences, it is important to consider what messages to disseminate to them and how to do this.

The following case study focuses on research utility and shows how the REA methodology has been used to produce research that is relevant and timely to policy-makers and practitioners.

Case Study: Evidence Based Approaches to Reducing Gang Violence[3]

In January 2003 two young women were killed in Birmingham, England, in shootings that formed part of an ongoing conflict between two criminal gangs in the city. As well as criminal investigations, the City Council, West Midlands Police Service and other statutory and voluntary sector partners formed an inter-agency group to combine and enhance efforts to reduce gang violence in the city. This group, which came to be known as Birmingham Reducing Gang Violence (BRGV) tasked the Regional Government Office[4] with advising on research and evaluation, notably the provision of advice on 'what works' in order to steer a course through conflicting options and proposals.

Although a range of literature reviews and other papers on gang violence were obtained, they were

---

[3] See Butler *et al.* (2004).
[4] Regional Government Offices represent the central Government Departments within nine administrative regions of England.

dominated by sociological explanations of cause and risk factors, or unsystematic accounts of programme evaluations without an explicit methodology. There was no readily available resource on effective approaches to reduction or prevention.

BRGV is a multi-agency, multi-disciplinary group made up of operational and strategic police officers, local authority regeneration and delivery managers, the head of the city's youth service, representatives from education, training and employment agencies, schools and youth offending services. A number of different professions were represented, and the individuals and agencies had a range of experiences and expectations in relation to research.

The Regional Government Office proposed the REA methodology to BRGV. The virtues of an REA were that it had a transparent methodology and could provide a means to focus on evidence of effectiveness, whilst taking significantly less time to complete than a full Systematic Review. Partner agencies in Birmingham also responded positively to the term 'rapid'.

The research question: "What is effective in preventing or reducing young people's involvement in gang and gun-related activity, as victims or offenders?" was framed in consultation with BRGV and a list of relevant terms was developed to inform the search strategy. The task of searching an agreed list of social science databases was given to an information management specialist at the Centre for Evidence-Based Policy and Practice at Queen Mary University, London, UK. This resulted in 311 abstracts being identified. These were reviewed by pairs of research team members, a filter applied, and 93 papers ordered via the Home Office library, with 69 being received in time to be considered for the review.[5] Those papers were reviewed using the QAT (Deaton *et al.*, 2004), leaving six papers for inclusion in the REA. These papers were then analysed for theories of change (what was the underlying hypothesis?) and critical mechanisms (what were the most important elements of the programmes and policies?), and emergent themes discussed and analysed.

The key findings were that effective approaches to reducing gang violence were:

- The co-ordination of a gang reduction activity through a multi-agency, multi-modal strategy, specific to one city or locality;
- Civil injunctions. These are civil actions that prohibit named individuals from engaging in specific problematic activities within a clearly defined area;
- Peer mentoring. This involved young people aged 14-21 mentoring children aged 7-13 through a programme of 12 violence prevention lessons over an 18 month period;
- School-based learning. This involved uniformed police officers teaching a nine-week gang prevention curriculum to students.

The findings were presented to BRGV as a comprehensive document that included a detailed account

---

[5] A subsequent review of the papers omitted by the use of a fixed cut-off date revealed that only one of them would have been considered for the REA. However, this 'project management bias', like any other form of bias in research, is a challenge to the validity of the findings.

of the methodology. Along with the report, the team made a one-page summary available and used presentations at local and national events to disseminate the findings.

The REA was delivered to a multi-agency partnership, and decisions made in light of the research are not always obvious. It is clear that some funding decisions have been made based on the REA. The REA has also been used to validate the local use of new interventions which have not been subject to robust evaluation, such as the use of Anti-Social Behaviour Orders (which are civil prohibitions on legal and illegal problematic behaviours, very like the Civil Gang Injunctions discussed in this REA) to disrupt gang activity in the city.

In order to continue to promote evidence-based approaches to gang violence, and the link between research and practice, the project team took the following steps:

- Forming a research sub-group with academic and practitioner input;
- Ensuring that one member of the REA team attends every BRGV meeting;
- Producing research updates for BRGV on relevant topics such as definitions of gangs and summaries of recent primary research;
- Advising the police and community groups on evaluation frameworks to generate UK evidence of effectiveness.

User feedback has been generally positive. A survey by the REA team indicated that one key message from the research ('target problematic behaviour rather than gang

Rapid Evidence Assessments

affiliation') was useful for the Prison Service, Learning and Skills Council and, especially, the police. Other agencies focused on the REAs ability to help them make defensible decisions on prioritising resources. At least one respondent criticised the methodology, reflecting the 'paradigm war' described by Tim Hope in McLaren (2002) between experimental criminologists and the 'realistic evaluation' school. There have been comments about the fact that all the papers analysed in the REA are primary studies from the USA, with attendant and understandable reservations about transferability. One outcome is that the REA has facilitated a range of debates about improving the evaluation of local programmes in order to develop UK research evidence in reducing gang violence.

Practical Considerations

Managers and practitioners needing high grade research evidence to inform a policy decision should consider whether an REA can address their needs. Practical elements to consider when commissioning such work would include:

- Resources - An REA should take six to twelve weeks; therefore it is important to be realistic about time commitments. Access to library resources and reference management systems to undertake the research also need consideration;
- Skills and knowledge - Those commissioned need to be familiar with research methodology and able to implement it. It is important that those reviewing papers for an evidence assessment have sufficient knowledge and experience in research methods to carry out the assessment;

- User involvement - Involving practitioners and policy-makers in undertaking an REA can be beneficial for all parties and increase ownership of the research findings.

Future Implications

The two REAs that have been completed to date have answered questions based on 'effectiveness'; however it is important to recognize that the methodology need not be restricted to this type of question. Leading organisations specialising in systematic review work, such as the Evidence for Policy and Practice Information and Co-ordinating (EPPI) Centre, UK, consider it perfectly possible to integrate a meta-analysis of data from controlled trials with a synthesis of findings from qualitative studies (Gough & Elbourne, 2002), and some systematic reviews have indeed managed this successfully (e.g. Thomas et al., 2004). As the methodology is applied to other questions, it will develop and this needs to be tracked. Precisely because the approach is developing, no standard methodology for REAs has yet been published. As the use of REAs increases, it will be important to have a standard REA methodology clearly set out so that the dilution of its focus and purpose can be avoided.

At times research can seem remote from front-line practice and policy decision making. The timeliness and rapid approach of REAs combined with practitioner involvement clearly provides a mechanism through which robust evidence can be presented and disseminated in a way that is policy friendly. Research utility is an area that generally warrants further investigation and as a result it is vital that the impact of this type of research on policy and practice is monitored.

Given the known limitations of REAs, it is important that they are completely transparent about the process adopted and stakeholders are made aware of the caveats. Systematic reviews are an established method for harnessing existing research evidence. REAs can be regarded as "interim" systematic reviews and have the potential to become a new method for applying research evidence to policy decisions, in an appropriate and rapid way which also effectively scopes the ground for a full systematic review.

References and Other Publications

Butler, G., Hodgkinson, J., Holmes, E., & Marshall, S. (2004). *Evidence Based Approaches to Reducing Gang Violence: A rapid evidence assessment of Aston and Handsworth Operational Group.*
Available online at:
http://www.gsr.gov.uk/downloads/rae/rea_gang_violence.pdf

Cabinet Office (1999). *Modernising Government.* London: The Stationery Office.

Davies, P. (2003) *The Magenta Book: Guidance Notes for Policy Evaluation and Analysis. Chapter 2: What Do We Already Know?* London: Cabinet Office.

Deaton, S. (2004). *Conducting an Evidence Assessment – Method and Lessons Learned.* (Unpublished.)

Deaton, S., O'Shea, J., Campbell, S., Lower, C., Owen, N., Roe, S., & Smith, N. (2004). *The Effectiveness of Drug Treatment Within a Criminal Justice System: An Assessment of the Existing Evidence.* (Unpublished.)

Gough, D., & Elbourne, D. (2002). Systematic Research Synthesis to Inform Policy, Practice and Democratic Debate. *Social Policy and Society,* 1 (3), 225-236.

Macdonald, G. (2003). *Using Systematic Reviews to Improve Social Care.* London: Social Care Institute for Excellence.

McLaren, V. (2002). In *Vista,* Volume 7 Number 2 (pp. 179-182). Birmingham: University of Birmingham.

Sherman, L., Gottfredson, D., MacKenzie, D., Eck, J., Reuter, P., & Bushway, S. (1997). *Preventing Crime: What Works, What Doesn't, What's Promising.* Washington, DC: US Department of Justice.

Solesbury, W. (2001). *Evidence Based Policy: Whence it came and Where it's Going.* London: ESRC Centre for Evidence Based Policy and Practice. (Working Paper 1).

Thomas, J., Harden, A., Oakley, A., Oliver, S., Sutcliffe, K., Rees, R., Brunton, G., & Kavanagh, J. (2004). Integrating Qualitative Research with Trials in Systematic Reviews. *BMJ, Volume 328.*

Walker, R. (2000). Welfare policy: tendering for evidence. In Davies, H.T.O., Nutley, S. and Smith, P.C. (eds.), *What Works? Evidence Based Policy and Practice in Public Services.* Bristol: The Policy Press.

APPROPRIATE COMPLEXITY: CAPTURING AND STRUCTURING KNOWLEDGE FROM IMPACT AND PROCESS EVALUATIONS OF CRIME REDUCTION, COMMUNITY SAFETY AND PROBLEM-ORIENTED POLICING

Paul Ekblom

Introduction

Many commentators have pointed to a history of implementation failure in crime reduction, community safety or Problem-Oriented Policing[1] (e.g. Bullock & Tilley, 2003; Homel *et al.*, 2004; Knutsson, 2003; Goldstein, 2003; Townley *et al.*, 2003; Scott, 2003; Hough, in this volume), and have attributed it to various factors such as deficient project management skills, short-term funding and over-centralised management, limited analytic capacity and unsupportive organisational context. (Resistance to evaluation itself among practitioners is also an issue but is not covered here.) In this chapter I focus on alternative, though not necessarily exclusive, diagnoses centring on the limitations of the kinds of *knowledge* collected by, and applied from, impact and process evaluations of community safety actions. These limitations constrain the performance of those responsible for decisions and actions ranging from strategic policy to tactical practice. Being aware of the limitations is particularly important because of the weight placed on building the body of case study

---

[1] Hereafter for brevity 'community safety' refers also to crime reduction and Problem-Oriented Policing; antisocial behaviour is included along with crime.

evaluations both by leading figures in Problem-Oriented Policing (Eck, 2003; Goldstein, 2003; Scott, 2003), and UK efforts to assemble knowledge for practice (www.crimereduction.gov.uk/ipak01.htm). One common underlying theme is the failure to handle the *complexity* of choice, delivery and action that creating and maintaining community safety requires.

This chapter first discusses the purpose of evaluation, the relationship between evaluation and knowledge, and the particular significance of *know-how of the process* of doing community safety. It then focuses on two aspects of that process: (1) the *strategic policy choices* made both nationally and locally in selecting interventions to roll out and implement; and (2) *replication and innovation*. In each case, limitations of evaluation and the knowledge to which it contributes are discussed, and specifications proposed to overcome these limitations and consequently improve performance. On the practice level particularly, existing knowledge frameworks, especially SARA and the Crime Triangle, are then reviewed and found wanting; and the 5Is and Conjunction of Criminal Opportunity are suggested as replacements. The chapter finishes with a discussion of complexity and the wider organisational context necessary to support more sophisticated policy and practice, and makes the case for a 'high investment, high yield' approach to community safety.

The Purpose of Evaluation

From an applied perspective, the immediate purpose of scientific evaluation in community safety (as in other fields) is systematically and rigorously to collect knowledge about the consequences of choices and actions in the *past* to help guide the choices and actions of the *future*, such that performance is consistently and sustainably optimised against some set of well-defined and measurable criteria.[2] This is true whether the choices and actions are at the level of *policy* (essentially strategy, whether national or local); *practice* (e.g. tactical details of how best to install alley-gates to reduce burglary); or the in-between zone of making it all happen commonly referred to as *delivery* (e.g. capacity building for community safety action, including training, knowledge management, organisational design and other infrastructural issues).

Other purposes of evaluation include contributing to *public affairs* – giving accounts of those choices and actions to funders and other stakeholders, including taxpayers; and *research* – testing theory through attempted manipulation of causes, and gleaning wider knowledge of the nature and context of the crime problems tackled in any preventive action. Other immediately practical tasks related to evaluation are *monitoring*, a mainly internal feedback and adjustment process to ensure implementation is on track; and *performance measurement*, which provides information to external bodies to guide the delivery process (as well as supporting accountability), but which does not normally scientifically investigate cause and effect.

The main emphasis in this paper is on the *applied* side of evaluation proper, but as will be seen theory plays a major role here too.

---

[2] The means to this end, the scientific/statistical process of causal inference and the economic process of assessing cost effectiveness are not covered here. See e.g. Ekblom and Pease, 1995; Sherman *et al.*, 1997; Bowles and Pradiptyo, 2004.

Evaluation and knowledge

Evaluations can contribute to a range of types of applicable knowledge about crime and its prevention (Ekblom, 2002a; Nutley *et al.*, 2003):

- *Know-about* crime problems, and their costs and wider consequences for victims and society – offenders' modus operandi, legal definitions of offences, patterns and trends in criminality, risk and protective factors ... and theories of causation;
- *Know-what* works – what methods work, against what crime problem, in what context, with what side-effects and what cost-effectiveness;
- *Know-who* to involve and how – contacts for advice, potential partners and collaborators who can be mobilised as formal or informal preventers; service providers, suppliers of funds and equipment and other specific resources; and sources of wider support;
- *Know-when* to act – knowing the right time to make particular moves – the climate must be right, other initiatives need to be coordinated with, etc.;
- *Know-where* to target and distribute resources;
- *Know-why* – covering the symbolic, emotional, ethical, cultural, political and value-laden meanings of crime and reductive action, including fairness and justice. Failure to address these issues can cause even the most rational and evidence-based actions to be rejected. The classic example is the public outrage sometimes caused by expensive sporting activities for young offenders which may be difficult to gain acceptance for even with (putative) evidence of cost-effectiveness;
- *Know-how* to put into practice – knowledge and skills of implementation and other practical processes, and methodologies for research and analysis.

Capturing and Structuring Knowledge

Know-how – the process of doing community safety

Know-how is, in effect, of a different order from the other kinds of knowledge in that it draws them all together in the *process* of doing community safety. From the perspective of the *users* of evaluation findings (whether practitioners, those responsible for directing delivery at a higher level, or those who formulate local or national policy) knowledge and technical skill are required to help:
- *Define* the crime/safety problem, if this is not already clear;
- *Select* intervention methods, which are evidence-based (i.e. derive from good quality evaluations already conducted); suitable to tackle the targeted crime problems in their particular contexts; and in line with the priorities and available resources of the responsible organisation/s;
- *Replicate* the methods – converting (usually) written accounts and instructions originating from evaluations into practical action, whether a single project or the roll-out of an entire programme built around a particular model or method.

There will, however, be many occasions when no direct evaluation finding fits, or can be generalised to supply the necessary information. This may be due to the paucity of evaluation material, especially that which is reliable (Sherman *et al.*, 1997); the marked context-dependency of crime reduction activity (Tilley, 1993a; Ekblom, 2002a) and the great variety of contexts to be adapted to; and the tendency of social and technological change and co-evolving offenders to render what once worked, obsolete (Ekblom, 1997, 1999 and 2002a). An incomplete evidence base is therefore inevitable, meaning that the knowledge we obtain and assemble through evaluation should also be deliberately designed to enable practitioners and policy-makers to:

- *Innovate* – a requirement more fundamental than might otherwise be thought because the context-dependency just described means that virtually every replication involves some measure of innovation followed, ideally, by monitoring, feedback and adjustment. Innovation in turn has to draw on two things:
  - High-level *principles of intervention* which can generate plausible new ideas where there is no specific evidence base. Such principles will usually derive from theories, or combinations of theories. To the extent that evaluation itself is able to test and refine these theories through the manipulation and attribution of causes, it can help build the theoretical platform for innovation.
  - Details of *practical methods* whose elements can be recombined in different ways to realise existing kinds of intervention in new contexts, or new kinds of intervention altogether. Capturing and assessing this information is another function of evaluation.

Evaluation, knowledge and performance are therefore intimately intertwined. To the extent that evaluations can draw on existing theory and knowledge of detailed causal mechanisms (Pawson & Tilley, 1997; Tilley, 1993b), they can pose sharper, more searching questions, and deliver tighter evidence that can better be applied. (In this respect, the relationship between theory and evaluation is less a one-sided affair and more like that between a river and its banks.) Both *impact* and *process* evaluation, however, have demonstrated quite serious limitations in the sorts of information they capture, which have, I believe, served to constrain their utility. A similar critique is advanced by the German-led Beccaria programme[3] for improving the quality of both crime prevention practice and its documentation. In the following two sections I review how both kinds of evaluation and the resultant knowledge are too narrowed-down and oversimplified respectively to inform policy and delivery, and to guide practice. The first section, on *selection* of action, gives greater emphasis to shortcomings of impact evaluation; the second, on *replication and innovation*, to those of process evaluation. These sections in fact correspond reasonably[4] closely to Tilley's (2006) distinction between 'What Works?' and 'What's To Be Done?', although Tilley presents these as alternative approaches rather than the complementary strategic choice and tactical realisation envisaged here.

Selecting Interventions – strategic choice

Depending on the range of evaluation results available to answer the basic question of 'What Works' against a given crime problem, the selection of what community safety action to implement can be guided in different ways – by:

---

[3] www.beccaria.de/Kriminalpraevention/en/Documents/Flyer_en_7.pdf

[4] Tilley's 'WTBD' guidance includes ethical issues relating to wider social values, utilities other than numbers of crime events and crime distributional consequences of different crime reduction strategies. The current chapter places them under strategic choice, though obviously they have to be revisited in practical implementation.

- Knowledge of *individual* solutions, like: 'Is CCTV effective?';
- *Comparative* knowledge, like: 'Is CCTV more cost-effective than street lighting?';
- *Portfolio* knowledge, like: 'What is the best mix of street lighting and CCTV to maximize cost-effectiveness, exploit synergy and avoid interference?';
- *Gap* knowledge, like: 'We have a good set of quick wins, but what effective long-term solutions are there?'.

All these alternatives should be further qualified by reference to context. They can be assembled at any level of detail, but there is a tendency for evaluations of community safety projects to compress the knowledge gleaned into just a few numbers reflecting impact, such as percentage reduction of crime or fear; or some more sophisticated equivalent such as effect size (based on odds ratios). The ultimate expression of this tendency is the Campbell Collaboration, a move to conduct systematic and rigorous reviews of evaluation of what works in specific fields of social research such as crime prevention. It is modelled on a similar programme in medical science.[5]

---

[5] Following the success of the Cochrane Collaboration in reviewing evidence for health care interventions, the Campbell Collaboration was founded in 2000 to produce systematic reviews of social, educational and criminological interventions. The aim of the Campbell Collaboration is to make the best knowledge about 'What Works' immediately available electronically (e.g. on the World Wide Web) to all interested persons, including scholars, practitioners, policy makers and the general public. These systematic reviews are subject to rigorous quality control, often draw on statistical techniques such as meta-evaluation (usually compressing evaluation results into uniform effect size measures), cover research throughout the world, are to

Capturing and Structuring Knowledge

Examples of these reviews, on the effectiveness of CCTV (Welsh & Farrington, 2002) and of street lighting (Farrington & Welsh, 2002) show what *can* be done through this approach. By default they also show what still *needs* to be done to fill the gaps in our ability to inform community safety action reliably.

The systematic review, and the compression of impact results more generally, have undoubted value in simplifying policy and delivery choices. Those choices are enhanced when *cost-effectiveness* information is included (for example the York University synthesis of cost effectiveness information on the burglary reduction projects in the UK Home Office's Crime Reduction Programme (Bowles & Pratipyo, 2004) and the Home Office's own use of this kind of information in guiding policy decisions (Home Office, 2004). But an essentially *one-dimensional* approach to 'What Works' has significant limitations, whether the relevant actions are being planned locally or nationally.

---

be regularly updated and revised. The Campbell Collaboration further aims to stimulate higher quality evaluations to feed the knowledge-gathering process in the future. Farrington & Petrosino (2001) describe the general background to Campbell and the aims of the Crime and Justice Group in particular. The general website is http://campbell.gse.upenn.edu and that of the Crime and Justice Group is www.aic.gov.au/campbellcj . It is worth noting in passing that strong disagreements exist over the issue of evaluation design and the 'Sherman Scale' of quality in particular (where best = randomised control trials) – see e.g. Hough (this volume); but this is not covered here.

Community Safety: Innovation and Evaluation

Knowledge framework for policy choice

The most appropriate framework for linking knowledge derived from evaluation findings to policy is one based on *performance*. Performance at a strategic level (whether national or local) can be assessed along a range of dimensions which are content-free. As such they complement the kind of performance indicators which reflect the state of particular policy problems such as Reassurance or Violent Crime. The dimensions are as follows:

- Obviously, selecting interventions that are *effective, cost-effective and whose benefit significantly outweighs cost*;
- Being *responsive* and *scalable* to crime/safety problems, which includes:
- *Prioritisation* of community safety action in terms of severity of *consequences* of crime/safety problems (and perhaps in line with wider policy targets);
- Accurate *targeting* on needs of victim and wider society – intervening universally or selectively as appropriate; and on causes of crime/safety problem – intervening at appropriate levels from local to international;
- *Coverage* on the ground, in terms of what *proportion* of a given crime problem the policy aims to tackle. Here, context knowledge is especially important. It may sometimes be most cost-effective to target only the worst-hit areas or the most serious crimes, but there are also benefits from interventions which can protect more targets of crime or influence more offenders, even if less efficiently. Ekblom (1998) illustrates this choice in relation to the evaluation of the Safer Cities Programme;
- *Scope*, in terms of the range of different crime problems that are tackled in the sphere of responsibility of the policymakers;

- *Adaptability* to changing circumstances (e.g. technological/social change or criminals' countermoves – Ekblom, 1997, 1999 and 2005a) and not locked into fixed conditions;
- Taking action over *appropriate timescales* – short, medium, long term;
- Pursuing policies that are *sustainable* in themselves over the desired timescales and do not jeopardise other community safety priorities through hunger for human/financial resources;
- Avoiding significant undesirable *side-effects* of action – such as stigmatisation of areas or people, and balancing or creatively optimising *trade-offs:* e.g. interference with other values and policy areas, such as privacy or environmental sustainability, inequity of provision or even displacement of crime on to more vulnerable victims;
- Maximising *legitimacy or acceptability* of preventive actions, within the wider population, within minority subgroups, or even among offenders themselves;
- Ensuring policies are *deliverable.* Although policymakers do not need to get immersed in details of delivery their decisions must take account of the *likelihood* of policy action successfully delivering appropriate action on the ground, and of that action then successfully producing the desired policy outcome.

If these are the dimensions of policy-performance, then evaluations, and the knowledge bases that organise the results of those evaluations, must reflect them in the features by which the evaluated actions are characterised. Table 1 suggests how this might be done. Column 1 lists the dimensions of policy performance. Column 2 lists the features of projects and programmes that evaluations should aim to measure and knowledge bases to capture and make available to policymakers.

Table 1. *Some Dimensions of Policy Performance, and Features of Knowledge of Community Safety Actions that can Inform Appropriate Policy Choices.*

Dimensions of policy performance	Features of projects/programmes that evaluations need to capture. In each case context-sensitivity and deliverability information are also important
Selecting interventions that are *effective, cost-effective and whose benefit significantly outweighs cost*	*Impact, cost-effectiveness, cost-benefit* information. *Range* of likely values – how *certain* is action to deliver desired result in terms of deliverability; impact once properly delivered?
Prioritisation of community safety action in line with values and targets	*Consequences* of crime/safety problems – individual and collective
Accurate *targeting* on needs of victim and wider society, and on *causes* of crime/ safety problem	<ul><li>The *ecological level* (WHO, 2004), such as individual victims, offenders, places or communities at which the intervention is targeted (relates also to Levels 1-3 crimes in UK National Intelligence Model);</li><li>Sherman *et al.*'s (1997) related concept of *institutional settings* for crime preventive action such as family, peer group or school;</li><li>Whether targeting is *primary* (directed to all people, places or objects), *secondary* (to those at heightened risk of offending or being the subject of crime) or *tertiary* (to those by whom/ against or in which crimes have already been committed) ; see</li></ul>

	Brantingham & Faust, 1976; Dijk & Waard, 1991.
Coverage on the ground	What *proportion* of a given crime problem can the programme or project tackle (cost-effectively, with acceptable risk of side-effects, etc.)?
Scope	What is the *range* of different crime problems that are tackled – are the interventions *narrow- or broad-spectrum*? (e.g. anti- domestic burglary versus tackling all crime motivated by drug-use)
Adaptability	How dependent is the action for successful delivery, impact and acceptability on certain conditions being maintained? How robust/flexible is the action if circumstances do change within a broad range of possibilities suggested by horizon-scanning? Is there risk of lock-in or can it be halted?
Taking action over *appropriate timescales*	What is the time needed to *plan and implement* the action, time for *action on the ground to have its preventive effect*, time for this *effect to be reliably demonstrable*?
Pursuing policies that are *sustainable* financially and in Human Resource terms, relative to competing priorities	How costly or difficult is the *implementation* of the preventive activity to maintain? (A recent example is the all-out war on street crime in certain UK cities which was successful while it lasted, but which was too demanding on resources to maintain.) How long does the *preventive mechanism* itself remain active? (for example, does CCTV act by merely (temporarily) frightening off

	offenders, or (more durably) substantively increasing the risk of arrest and conviction?
Avoiding significant undesirable *side-effects* of action and balancing or creatively optimising *trade-offs* with other policy values	e.g. to what extent does project/ programme *stigmatise, widen the net, displace crime, meet energy-efficiency targets and respect Human Rights*?
Maximising *legitimacy or acceptability* of preventive actions	What are nature, extent, risks and consequences of possible *legitimacy* issues surrounding programme/ project?

Some of the above features are 'value neutral' – for example, the timescale, the scope and the coverage of particular actions to realise a particular policy could, depending on circumstances, fall one way or the other. So sometimes it may be appropriate to select action that is long in timescale, narrow in geographical coverage, but broad-spectrum in scope of crimes tackled; at other times, and depending what else is in the portfolio, the best actions to select may be at the opposite ends of these scales. But other features tend consistently towards the positive (e.g. cost-effectiveness) or negative (e.g. adverse side effects), though these can be tolerated if wider priorities require it. In terms of measurement, some of the features are inherently quantitative, others could be converted to simple rating scales to aid choice: still others will remain resolutely qualitative and categorical, but no less important for that. Some of the knowledge derives from impact evaluation, and cost-effectiveness estimation, some from wider information describing the nature of the action and its context, and some from process evaluation. Portfolio-based policy performance especially requires additional knowledge of *trade-offs, synergies and contra-indications* among the features. For example, types of action that are especially cost-effective in high-crime areas may still be undesirable because legitimacy is hard to achieve there, or have a significant risk of causing a riot.

Coverage, scope and cost-effectiveness information were used in the UK Home Office's strategic modelling of the impact of various kinds of crime reduction activity (Home Office, 2004a). This approach was used to help set recent crime reduction targets (Home Office, 2004b). Such exercises are valuable, and target-setting is now far more rational than when based on the 'hunch' or 'predilection' approaches of previous occasions. But other dimensions were left out of the formal analysis.

Goldblatt & Lewis (1998) did attempt a richer portfolio-type assessment on the basis of the Home Office's comprehensive spending review of 'What Works', which set the scene for the 1998-2001 Crime Reduction Programme. But the exercise was not set up to assemble *systematically* information on features like those listed above. In many cases the necessary information was not available in the individual topic review chapters, nor, probably, in the original source evaluations.

Having systematic access to this array of information on community safety interventions would give decision-makers a kind of 'Consumers' Report' to guide their selection of types of action to implement.[6] Absence or inconsistency of this information must surely mean poorer policy decisions, whether these are made nationally or locally - e.g. by Crime and Disorder Reduction Partnerships, Local Strategic Partnerships or Strategic Tasking and Coordinating Groups acting within the UK National Intelligence Model.[7]

Knowledge for delivery

By *delivery*, I mean making community safety action happen routinely on the ground to a sufficient level of quality and appropriateness for crime problem and context, such that those intervention methods shown to work in *principle* (e.g. through demonstration projects) reliably do so in *practice*. Knowledge to inform deliverability obtained from evaluations would cover the prospects of successful *implementation* in mainstreaming of programmes and the corresponding risk of *implementation failure*. In particular:

- *Capacity building* (infrastructure, human resources and training to be supplied 'off the shelf'); *capacity development* (where that capacity first needs to be brought into existence perhaps through R & D); and *climate* (e.g. understanding and acceptance of a particular kind of

---

[6] For an example of a limited consumers' type review of situational crime prevention within the Goldblatt & Lewis report just cited, see Ekblom (1998).

[7] The latter currently applies to policing, but in future is likely to apply to community safety more generally (Home Office, 2005).

delivery organisation or community safety method on the part of the public, and/or of the practitioner culture);

- The appropriate *institutional settings* to support the action (cf. Sherman *et al.*, 1997) such as policing, justice, family or schooling; and the degree to which those institutions and organisations are designed to provide that support (for example, see Townley *et al.* [2003] on lack of institutional support for Problem-Oriented Policing).

This knowledge would not only help those planning the details of delivery, but would also feed back to guide policy: whatever the theoretical promise of impact on crime, nobody wants a policy whose delivery cannot be reliably guaranteed. But this sort of information currently does not feature in systematic reviews.[8] It may appear piecemeal in publications such as the Home Office's 'Development and Practice Reports' (for example the report of Gill *et al.* [2003] covering staff selection and training issues in CCTV control rooms), although the format does not necessarily highlight it or ensure its systematic collection, reporting and retrievability.

These failures of evaluators systematically to collect, and accessibly report, the kinds of knowledge described in the last two sections – or failures of those who commission

---

[8] Although in medicine there is at least one systematic review on methods of evidence on the effectiveness of the *processes* of transferring knowledge to practitioners (here, the outcome measures of the evaluations reviewed aren't reduced illness but improved performance of medics ... which hopefully does lead to reduced illness if the *impact* evidence base is also sound). See www.epoc.uottawa.ca/scope.htm

and use evaluations, to *ask* for them – mean that the people responsible for making policy or designing delivery are fed a patchy and thin gruel of knowledge of what works and how to deliver it. Clearly a richer, multi-dimensional diet is needed for nurturing intelligent decision-making and planning. And policymakers and delivery managers at all geographical levels need to be educated, encouraged and expected to partake of this nourishing fare.

Replication and Innovation for Community Safety Practice

The focus now moves to practice on the ground – to the design and execution of specific projects targeted on specific local crime/community safety problems. I have elsewhere (Ekblom, 2002a) identified further causes of implementation failure in terms of inadequate knowledge of good practice and a weak conceptual framework to organise it and impart it to practitioners. The argument applies mainly to process evaluations – with the additional focus on obtaining information on the causal mechanisms by which the intervention worked or was intended to work – and is summarised as follows.

Reviews of community safety projects (e.g. Bullock & Tilley [2003], Read & Tilley [2002] and Sutton [1996] on the Safer Cities Programme, and Goldstein [2003] on Problem-Oriented Policing) commonly reveal *superficial interventions* with no clear understanding of the causes of the crime problem and a lack of focus on either the fundamental principles of community safety or the detailed causal mechanisms by which the methods are meant to work (Pawson & Tilley, 1997). An example too often seen can be paraphrased as 'this project is about working with young people'. Now, this could equally be a good intervention or a poor one; it is certainly a poor description. What *exactly* is the project trying to do – and how exactly does it work? Both questions need answering before practitioners can reliably replicate.

Insufficient focus on causes and causal mechanisms additionally weakens the causal inferences made by impact evaluations and the replicability of their results. Sadly, therefore, we find many *cookbook replications* – which do not seek to copy the underlying mechanisms of a successful intervention, or the intelligent process of going from analysis to intervention to implementation.[9] Instead, they only copy its external form. They also fail to recognise that a method may work well in one social context, but not in others. Crime reduction methods are not like pesticide which can be sprayed uniformly over all the fields and have the same universal effect. A particular mechanism, such as deterrence of offenders by a CCTV system, may need a highly specific set of preconditions to be established among both offenders and crime situation before the desired mechanism is triggered, which then may or may not lead to the desired result.[10]

We also find *limited innovation* (cf. Sutton, 1996). Creativity too comes from an organised knowledge of principles and an ability to splice them together to suit

---

[9] The best-documented example is Tilley's (1993a) study of attempted replications of the successful burglary prevention project in Kirkholt (Forrester *et al.*, 1988, 1990).

[10] Tilley's (1993b) analysis of 10 possible mechanisms by which CCTV could protect a car park is a classic evaluation in this 'Scientific Realist' mode.

specific instances, rather than from a random idea generator or a fixed repertoire.

Under all these circumstances, we would do better to arm practitioners with a set of generic *principles* of community safety and knowledge of the *process*, rather than supply them merely with large numbers of fixed solutions which may not always fit, and may in any case become obsolete. More broadly put, we should help practitioners, when appropriate, to think less like technicians selecting a simple prepackaged remedy from a limited menu, like a service engineer with a broken washing machine; and more like expert consultants, using these principles to customise, to context, to innovate, design[11] and reconfigure their diagnoses and solutions as they go.[12] Tilley (2006) makes the case for both kinds of practice being valid in different circumstances, centring on the underlying simplicity or complexity of the crime problem being addressed.[13] Consequently, both kinds of supporting knowledge should be available in appropriate forms, albeit both tested against evidence as far as possible; but the focus in this chapter remains on the neglected, expert end of the scale.

---

[11] Ekblom (2005b) argues that community safety practitioners should 'draw on design', meaning not just incorporating in their solutions to crime problems the tangible *products of design* such as secure houses, but applying *design methods* to the entire process of generating community safety action.

[12] Interestingly, Hough (this volume), uses the very similar image of the plumber versus the social engineer.

[13] Tilley's 'What Works' and 'What's to be done?' correspond closely with 'Know what' and 'Know how' in this chapter.

Capturing and Structuring Knowledge

Knowledge requirements for practice – a design specification

To support the kind of expert-practitioner approach just described, the principles of knowledge management suggest that the knowledge gleaned from process and impact evaluations should meet certain requirements of *content, context, structure, terminology and conceptualisation:*

- *Know about crime and safety problems,* and *Know What Works* knowledge are as essential for guiding practice as they are for policy, of course. But for successfully sharing and replicating good practice lessons and supporting innovation, our knowledge base must also contain sufficient *Know How* to describe *process* in a way that promotes the *intelligent reconstruction* of community safety actions by describing every stage of developing and delivering them;
- The knowledge base must extract information on the original *context* of the project, and how that context was thought to contribute to successful analysis, intervention, implementation and impact. One important factor to capture in adapting to different contexts is what I call *Troublesome Trade-offs* (e.g. Ekblom, 2005b). By these, I mean the tricky balances that must be creatively resolved in designing any community safety activity (such as a surveillance strategy for a shopping centre) or designing a product (such as a crime-resistant car). How do we maximise security for reasonable cost, whilst also respecting convenience, privacy, aesthetics, environmental issues, social exclusion and sales figures? The general principles behind a new replication may be similar to the original project that is being copied. But the pressures, constraints and possibilities for realisation may be very different in new contexts, leading to rather different solutions in practice (ODPM & Home Office, 2004);

- The *structure* of the knowledge base must help practitioners to flip nimbly between thinking at several levels and from alternative viewpoints:
  - From an immediate, *implementation* perspective, we have to help practitioners think, and share information about practical, tangible *methods* – like installing CCTV, running particular activities in youth clubs, or fixing gates on the alleyways behind houses. Given the importance of process, we should be able to retrieve good practice *elements* of method derived from each stage of a project. For example, if a burglary scheme implemented a rather lacklustre intervention, it may still have developed an extremely useful and novel method of mobilising the local community – this is an element of good practice which could be used in a range of other circumstances such as in tackling car crime. Recombination of such elements contributes to the capacity for innovation;
  - From an *analytic* perspective we have to try to extract information on higher-level *principles* such as surveillance and on *theories* like social learning theory (theories are the ultimate in compressed knowledge), and very specific causal *mechanisms* – how principles actually combine and play out in detailed configurations in any given context;
- The knowledge base also requires a standard *terminology* (Ekblom, 2002a, 2002b, 2004). Its absence limits what can be described and retrieved in a knowledge base. This is especially a problem with international knowledge bases.
- Underneath the terminology, there has to be a clear *conceptual framework* to support the capture, storage, retrieval, transfer and application of knowledge. This is about supplying people with *precision tools for thought*. The

Capturing and Structuring Knowledge

development and widespread use of a strong conceptual framework has several important advantages for the performance of community safety. It:
- Facilitates communication and collaboration between diverse partners: the police may use one term, social workers a different one;
- Enhances clarity of planning preventive action, and quality assurance of implementation;
- Enables integrated, strategic thinking about causes and solutions – some people (and behind them, some occupational cultures) currently speak only a law enforcement language, others the language of civil reduction and community safety. And some people focus exclusively on situations, others just on offenders;
- Supports the analytic thinking specified above, and plays its part in a 'generative grammar' for creating plausible new ideas for community safety action;
- Supports education and training. Learning works best when practitioners have a complete mental *schema* (Bloch, 2000; Ekblom, 2002a) with which they can organise their knowledge, and assess and assimilate new facts, whether transmitted from above or from peers.

Existing practice guidance and knowledge frameworks

In contrast, say, to medicine, the practice guidance literature in the community safety field has no regularity of structure or precise and consistent terminology, and cumulation of knowledge is sporadic and inconsistent. Each of the Home Office Development and Practice Reports[14] covering community safety is entirely self-contained and independently structured; so are the

---

[14] www.homeoffice.gov.uk/rds/dprpubs1.html

toolkits in the Crime Reduction website – and the 'theory' section of that website can best be described as 'pick 'n' mix'. Earlier Home Office guides use a range of analogies and models, such as getting the grease to the squeak (Hough & Tilley, 1998), the chemistry of burglary reduction (Tilley *et al.*, 1999), not rocket science (Read & Tilley, 2000) and opportunity makes the thief (Felson & Clarke, 2004). Although centring on some common concepts, the reports in question have seemed partly to reinvent the terminology and framework with every publication.

The framework to capture and play back the process of community safety action that most commonly *does* appear in these and other publications in the English-speaking world is SARA (Scanning, Analysis, Response and Assessment). The framework for crime causes and interventions is the Crime Triangle (Offender, Place, Target/Victim). Both are well-described and illustrated in Clarke and Eck's guide for crime analysts (Clarke & Eck, 2005) and the American COPS publications,[15] a range of practice guides focusing on specific crime problems. But are SARA and the Crime Triangle up to the demanding specifications for a knowledge framework set out above?

SARA and the Crime Triangle are easily-grasped instant introductions to the problem-oriented approach to community safety. But once practitioners have understood the basics, they will rapidly find little depth to guide action further, let alone foster the development of expertise. Nor do these frameworks inspire or support the creativity vital to take community safety to new contexts and keep up

---

[15] www.cops.usdoj.gov/default.asp?Item=248

Capturing and Structuring Knowledge

with social change and adaptive criminals (Ekblom, 1997). SARA's 'Response' confuses several quite distinct activities (described in the next section). There is no consistent organisation of knowledge at more detailed levels. More recent alternatives such as PROCTOR ('PRObIem, Cause, Tactic or Treatment, Output and Result' - Read and Tilley, 2000) share the same limitations (and in this case, blow three letters of the acronym on just one concept!) The Crime Triangle offers incomplete coverage of the immediate causes of crime, especially under-representing the offender side.

A new framework – more fit for purpose?

The new framework that I have been developing since the mid-nineties has several elements which attempt to build on existing frameworks and overcome their limitations. It comprises:

- A suite of *definitions,* including crime reduction, crime prevention and community safety;
- A *map of the main crime reduction process*, the 5Is framework, which assembles know how and systematically captures and shares knowledge. 5Is was developed for the EU Crime Prevention Network (e.g. Ekblom, 2002b) and has been used in a number of 'What Works' conferences there; and also used, for example, by the Swedish National Crime Prevention Council.
- Finally, covering knowledge about crime and safety, and knowledge of what works to prevent it, we have the Conjunction of Criminal Opportunity framework. This maps out the *immediate causes of criminal events and the families of preventive intervention in those causes.*

Definitions

The following definitions are deliberately open-ended and inclusive of the widest range of theories and methods without reference to evidence of effectiveness. The latest versions are maintained at:
www.designagainstcrime.com/web/crimeframeworks

Crime reduction is simply about decreasing the *frequency* and *seriousness* of criminal events, by whatever (legitimate) means. *Crime prevention* is intervention in the *causes* of criminal and disorderly events to reduce the *risk* of their occurrence and/or the potential *seriousness* of their consequences.

Community safety is a wider *quality of life* issue going beyond individual events. It is a state of existence in which people, individually and collectively, are sufficiently free from a range of real and perceived risks centring on crime and disorder; are sufficiently able to cope with those they nevertheless experience; and where unable to cope unaided, are sufficiently well-protected from the consequences of these risks. In all cases this is achieved to a degree which allows people: to pursue the necessities of their cultural, social and economic life; exercise skills; to enjoy well-being and receipt of adequate services; and to create social capital (i.e. trust and collective efficacy) and cultural and commercial wealth.

5Is

In 2002 (Ekblom, 2002b) I set out a version of the above design specification for a framework for knowledge. In parallel I developed a framework intended to meet that specification: the 5Is. In effect, this centres on the 'know how' of community safety, serving both to capture knowledge of existing good practice and to specify a

Capturing and Structuring Knowledge

methodology for doing the practice itself, in a series of tasks that replay the 'Preventive Process' (Ekblom, 1988).

- *Intelligence* is about gathering and analysing information on crime problems and their causes, participants and consequences;

- *Intervention* is about action to block, disrupt or weaken those causes and risk factors, in ways which wherever possible are evidence-based and appropriate to the crime problem and the context;

- *Implementation* involves converting the in-principle interventions into practical methods, and putting them into action on the ground;

- *Involvement* covers *mobilising* other agencies, companies and individuals in the community to play their part in implementing the intervention; the more symmetrical *partnership*; and *climate-setting*;

- *Impact*, cost-effectiveness and the dimensions of policy performance and delivery discussed above. *(Process evaluation can be covered under the relevant tasks – Intelligence to Involvement.).*

5Is obviously builds on SARA. But it reorganises the tasks and in particular, it breaks the crude task of Response into three distinct aspects. One could say that SARA supplies the action words – the verbs – whilst 5Is comprises the nouns of the knowledge produced or used by that action.

- Scanning and Analysis for Intelligence;

- Response through Intervention, Implementation and Involvement;

- Assessment of Impact.

As will be seen, the noun structure allows expansion into much more detail.

The 5Is tasks are linear, but not rigidly so: as researchers in Problem-Oriented Policing acknowledge (e.g. Knutsson, 2003; Weisel, 2003), doing community safety involves a great deal of iteration, zooming in and out between tactics and strategy, and passing the responsibility to other organisations and individuals to carry out particular tasks or adopt particular roles. It is worth also noting that by posing the question, 'What are the necessary organisational and infrastructural conditions to support each task?', there is a ready framework to distil evaluation implications for delivery.

To help organise and communicate the framework, 5Is has three levels of detail:

- The 5Is themselves are the *Message*. This is an easily remembered slogan which communicates the basic concept in everyday language to a wide range of users;
- The next level is the *Map* – a detailed list of standard headings under each of the 5Is. This is suitable for managers and supervisors to be familiar with;
- The final level is the *Methodology*. This is the detailed guidance and knowledge for professional practitioners that appears, or will appear, under each of the headings of the Map.

Conjunction of criminal opportunity
Where SARA is usually accompanied by the Crime Triangle, 5Is uses by preference the *Conjunction of Criminal Opportunity* framework (CCO). It appears as Methodology under the *Immediate Causes of Crime* (Map level), which in turn comes under *Intelligence* (Message level). CCO reappears as Methodology under *Intervention principles* (Map level), which comes, unsurprisingly, under *Intervention* (Message level).

CCO incorporates the Crime Triangle, Routine Activities Theory (RAT – Cohen & Felson, 1979), Rational Offender theory (Cornish & Clarke, 1986), General Theory of Crime (Gottfredson & Hirschi, 1990), wider offender-oriented approaches and more. CCO is deliberately inclusive – theory-friendly but not adherent to specific theories. It has the added advantage of extensions into organised crime and terrorism (Ekblom, 2003; Roach *et al.*, 2005); it is designed to switch between a **structural** perspective of simply mapping the proximal causes of criminal events to **dynamic** perspectives covering how these causes interact to generate and shape the event, and how higher-level **emergent** factors at various 'ecological levels' beyond events (such as criminal careers, communities, networks or markets) bring the proximal causes together.

Limited guidance material for 5Is and CCO is on the UK Crime Reduction website at: www.crimereduction.gov.uk/learningzone/.

An up-to-date list of project descriptions, publications and guidelines applying both frameworks and associated definitions is at: www.designagainstcrime.com/web/crimeframeworks

An illustrated example of 5Is and CCO in action together, recording a project aimed at reducing anti-social behaviour fuelled by underage consumption of alcohol, is on the 'Together' website.[1] As that example shows, 5Is deliberately reflects the complex structure of community safety action discussed above, in that it specifies the recording of both methods and underlying principles.

Table 2 shows the summary sheet for the anti-social behaviour project, which also includes one of the other 'elements' of action centring on Involvement. This summary (in the original document) gives hyperlinks to separate sections for each of the 13 intervention methods.

---

[1] www.together.gov.uk. Search for 'Eastleigh' or go to the formal project description at:
http://www.together.gov.uk/cagetfile.asp?rid=892 .
A slide-show presentation on the same project is at:
www.crimereduction.gov.uk/gpps05.htm.

Table 2. 5Is Summary sheet of Intervention and Involvement, antisocial behaviour project.

	Intervention Method	Intervention Principles	Involvement
1:	Modification of carrier bags to identify the origins of alcohol purchase	Reducing readiness to offend (removing supply of alcohol); incapacitating crime promoters (shopkeepers), mobilising preventers (parents); empowering preventers (police)	Police; deterring and Retailers
2:	Targeted high visibility police patrols	Deterrence and discouragement; Reassurance; Removing offenders from crime situation/dispersing groups of offenders	Police; Community wardens
3:	Antisocial behaviour contracts considered for persistent offenders	General and specific deterrence and discouragement; Removing offender from crime situation; Cracking down on promoters (parents) and converting to preventers	Police; Local councils
4:	Target hardening of a retail store to stop alcohol theft	Perimeter/access security; Target hardening; Environmental design; Conversion of crime promoters to crime preventers	Police; Retailers

5:	Removing a flowerbed from in front of a row of shops	Environmental design; Restricting resources from crime; Deflecting offenders from crime situation; Reassurance	Police; Retailers; Landowner
6:	Community clean up of litter in local streets	Reassurance; Deterrence; Motivating preventers	Police; Community wardens; General public
7:	Youth shelter	Removing offenders from crime situation and from alcohol; Reducing readiness to offend by meeting needs legitimately	Police; Local Authority; Crime Reduction (HO grant)
8:	Mobile recreation unit	Removing offender from the crime situation	Police; Local authority
9:	Arresting/Cautioning of ASB offenders	Removing offenders from the crime situation; Giving offenders resources to avoid offending (education); Deterrence and discouragement; Mobilising preventers (parents)	Police; Parents; Local authority
10:	Drop in centre	Removing offender from the crime situation	Police; Local

	youths	authority
11:	Healthy living centre for youths	Removing offender from the crime situation; Police; Local authority Reducing readiness to offend by meeting authority offenders' needs
12:	A forest location as alternative place for youths to gather	Removing offender from the crime situation; Police; The Conservation Volunteers Group Rule setting; Reducing readiness to offend by meeting offenders' needs
13:	Disrupting a possible drugs market targeting youths	Removing offender from the crime situation; Police; CJS Resources to avoid offending (drugs education)

Source: Interview with Hampshire Police Project Team (2004).

Complexity

Undoubtedly, the above specifications for the structure and content of knowledge needed to support high standards of policy, delivery and practice make for some complexity. There are, though, many proponents of simplicity. A prominent figure in the UK community safety field once advised me to simplify my ideas in order to get them across. With practitioners, he went on, we would be lucky to have them remember just one or two simple slogans. Is this a valid argument, albeit put rather patronisingly? After all, the basic premise of crime prevention is extremely simple (cut the causes to cut the crime). My own view is that it is wrong: reliance on simplicity alone has plainly neither delivered successful community safety, nor Problem-Oriented Policing. The answer to this particular aspect of 'Life, the Universe and Everything' is clearly not '42'.

To a large extent, the specification for knowledge, and thus for the evaluations needed to feed that knowledge base, themselves embody the case for complexity – yes, community safety is that complex.[17] However, to place things in context, architectural or medical students would surely scoff at complaints that CCO and 5Is are complex relative to the knowledge structures *they* have to assimilate and apply; likewise the knowledge that police have to apply to interrogation or rules of evidence.

Whatever the case, leading proponents of the Problem-Oriented approach such as Knutsson (2003), Eck (2003) and

---

[17] One is reminded of the story of the king who said, 'Yes, I'm paranoid – but am I paranoid enough?'

Tilley (2006) now also acknowledge that undertaking this approach is more complex and demanding than originally thought. But – by remaining with SARA and the Crime Triangle they are building on too narrow a base for policy, delivery and practice; equally serious, it is too narrow a base to support the leading edge of *research*. Ashby's Law of Requisite Variety (Ashby, 1957), a cybernetics principle that has had wide currency in the organisational world, articulates the problem. To paraphrase: *our mental frameworks must reflect the complexity of the problems they are intended to tackle or understand; it takes complexity to deal with complexity.* In more everyday language: given the complexity of community safety practice, it is futile dumbing down community safety knowledge into slogans and rapid-read case studies to aid communication to practitioners, and one-dimensional guidance for the choices of policymakers, if these cannot inspire actions that are sophisticated enough to do good and avoid harm. And on the receiving end of those communications, it is equally futile if practitioners are not endowed with the expertise to understand, critique and assimilate that knowledge so they can operate at that same level of sophistication.

Any complexity we introduce must, however, be *appropriate*, and *deliberate*. An *unnecessary* layer of complexity masquerading as simplicity is added by criminologists' failure to integrate theory (Ekblom, 2002a). In the criminological literature fragmentary part-models of causation abound. Each individual model (e.g. Routine Activities Theory [Cohen & Felson, 1979]) is indeed simple, and often excellent in itself. But in both research literature and practical guidance they are all dumped in a heap,[18]

---

[18] This calls to mind the TV series 'Scrapheap Challenge' www.channel4.com/science/microsites/S/scrapheap/ in which

leaving each reader to figure out afresh how to combine them and cope with gaps, overlaps, competing explanations and possible emergent causes linking individual criminal behaviour to area crime patterns. How, for example, does RAT relate to Rational Offender (Cornish & Clarke, 1986)? Where does self-control (Gottfredson & Hirschi, 1990) fit? How do criminal career, network or market processes emerge from the interaction of elementary causes? The CCO and Wikström's (2004) Cross-Level Situational Action Theory are among the few systematic attempts at integration.

Another complexity-related issue is the appropriate level of *detail* of practice to capture. Such detail can be extensive, as the full 5Is case study shows – but to a significant extent this is necessary to harvest the rich *tacit* knowledge of experienced practitioners (Tilley, 2006). The structured headings and concepts of 5Is facilitate extraction of such knowledge in an orderly way to make it more explicitly transferable. Deliberately capturing tacit knowledge also exposes it to quality assurance – as Scott (2001) notes, a tradition of purely 'oral transmission' of knowledge from peer-to-peer imparts limited and perhaps inaccurate information, and constantly draws practitioners back into their own occupational culture. Tilley (2006) also argues however that there is an *inappropriate* degree of detail to be rigidly adhered to in the 'programme fetishism' that characterised various recent police and correctional initiatives and was seen as diminishing discretion. Ekblom

---

teams compete to assemble functional objects such as mobile cranes from junkyard materials. However, as Nick Tilley (in conversation) pointed out, the teams include engineers who combine both strong professional discipline and practical nous – so may be better placed than many current crime preventers.

Capturing and Structuring Knowledge

(2002a) makes a similar point against copying with excessive fidelity. By its focus on process and its twin perspectives of principles and methods, 5Is is intended to support the 'practitioner as consultant' rather than 'as technician', with an appropriate blend of discretion and detail.

Conclusion - philosophy

Making complexity work for policy, delivery and practice of crime prevention and community safety requires a well-structured knowledge base populated with good quality, detailed evaluations reflecting a sophisticated conceptual framework. But these necessary, but insufficient, conditions must be accompanied by: a completely refurbished *delivery system* of supportive organisations and working culture; career structure of practitioners (currently too limited) and policymakers (currently too generalist and comprising short-lived stints in community safety); and training in knowledge, skills and techniques.[19] As I have argued before (Ekblom 2002a, 2002b) nobody expects or desires the training of medics or architects to be built on a few slogans or elementary diagrams. (I certainly wouldn't want to be treated by the former, in a hospital designed by the latter, based in both cases on the work of academic researchers whose models are equally limited or fragmented!) Little wonder, then, that the Problem-Oriented approach is now seen by its proponents as hard to make happen, and likely to take a long time (Knutsson, 2003) to bed in.

---

[19] Knutsson (2003) and his contributors make a still wider set of suggestions for making Problem-Oriented Policing happen.

The philosophy behind 5Is, CCO and the whole approach advocated here is that a high level of *investment* in concepts, capturing of knowledge through evaluations, and sharing of knowledge and skills through training, guidance and other infrastructure is necessary for a high *yield* in terms of successful *performance* in crime reduction and community safety.

To make this happen clearly requires a change of attitude towards complexity. Fear prevails in policymaking and delivery circles that practitioners can't be prised from their comfort zones of SARA and Crime Triangle to accept something more fit for purpose, if initially more challenging. But things are finally beginning to move in this direction in both Problem-Oriented Policing and wider community safety, as the importance of knowledge and the existence of complexity is recognised throughout the English-speaking world and in continental Europe. But we cannot proceed far without the leading academic proponents and implementers of crime reduction, community safety and Problem-Oriented Policing programmes grasping the nettle of improving the frameworks for capturing and transferring knowledge, and the research and evaluation that feeds it.[20]

References

Ashby, W. R. (1957). *An introduction to cybernetics*. London: Chapman & Hall Ltd. Retrieved May 2 2005 from: http://pcp.vub.ac.be/books/IntroCyb.pdf

---

[20] For further discussion of the drive to oversimplify and what lies behind it, see Ekblom (2006).

Bloch, M. (2000). A Well-Disposed Social Anthropologist's Problems with Memes. In R. Aunger (ed.), *Darwinizing Culture: The Status of Memetics as a Science*. Oxford: Oxford University Press.

Bowles, R., & Pradiptyo, R. (2004). *Reducing Burglary Initiative: an analysis of costs, benefits and cost effectiveness.* Home Office Online Report 43/04. Retrieved from: www.homeoffice.gov.uk/rds/pdfs04/rdsolr4304.pdf

Brantingham, P. J., & Faust, F. (1976). A Conceptual Model of Crime Prevention. *Crime and Delinquency*, 22:130-146.

Bullock, K., & Tilley, N. (2003). The Role of Research and Analysis: Lessons from the Crime Reduction Program. In J. Knutsson (Ed.), *Mainstreaming Problem-Oriented Policing*. Crime Prevention Studies 15. Monsey, New York: Criminal Justice Press.

Clarke, R., & Eck, J. (2005). *Crime Analysis for Problem Solvers in 60 Small Steps.* Center for Problem-Oriented Policing. Retrieved from: www.popcenter.org/Library/RecommendedReadings/60 Steps.pdf

Cohen, L., & Felson, M. (1979). Social Change and Crime Rate Changes: A Routine Activities Approach. *American Sociological Review*, 44: 588-608.

Cornish, D., & Clarke, R. (Eds). (1986). *The Reasoning Criminal: rational choice perspectives on offending.* New York: Springer-Verlag.

Dijk J. van, & Waard, J. de. (1991). A Two-Dimensional Typology of Crime Prevention Projects: with a bibliography. *Criminal Justice Abstracts*, 23:483-503.

Eck, J. (2003). Police Problems: The Complexity of Problem Theory, Research and Evaluation. In J. Knutsson (Ed.), *Mainstreaming Problem-Oriented Policing*. Crime Prevention Studies 15. Monsey, New York: Criminal Justice Press.

Ekblom, P. (1988). *Getting the Best out of Crime Analysis*. Home Office Crime Prevention Unit Paper 10. London: Home Office.

Ekblom, P. (1997). Gearing up against Crime: a Dynamic Framework to Help Designers Keep up with the Adaptive Criminal in a Changing World. *International Journal of Risk, Security and Crime Prevention*, 2/4: 249-265.

Ekblom, P. (1998) Situational Crime Prevention. In Goldblatt, P. & Lewis, C. (eds) (1998). *Reducing Offending: An Assessment of Research Evidence on Ways of Dealing with Offending Behaviour*. Home Office Research Study No. 187. London: Home Office.

Ekblom, P. (1999). Can we Make Crime Prevention Adaptive by Learning from other Evolutionary Struggles? *Studies on Crime and Crime Prevention*, 8/1: 27-51.

Ekblom, P (2002a). From the Source to the Mainstream is Uphill: The Challenge of Transferring Knowledge of Crime Prevention Through Replication, Innovation and Anticipation. In N. Tilley (ed.) *Analysis for Crime Prevention*. Crime Prevention Studies 13: 131-203. Monsey, NY: Criminal Justice Press/ Devon, UK: Willan Publishing.

Ekblom, P. (2002b). Towards a European Knowledge Base and The Five I's: Experimental Framework for a Knowledge Base for Crime Prevention Projects. In *European Crime Prevention Conference 2002*, vol. 1: 62-97. Copenhagen: Danish Crime Prevention Council. Retrieved from: www.crimprev.dk/eucpn/docs/EUCPNAalborgReport200210.pdf

Ekblom, P. (2003). Organised Crime and the Conjunction of Criminal Opportunity Framework. In A. Edwards & P. Gill (eds), *Transnational Organised Crime: Perspectives on Global Security*, pp. 241 - 263. London: Routledge.

Ekblom, P. (2004). Le Cadre des 5I. In P. Bruston & A. Haroune (éds). *Réseau européen de prévention de la criminalité: (REPC) Description et échange de bonnes pratiques*. Paris: Délégation Interministérielle à la Ville. Also in English.

Ekblom, P. (2005a). How to Police the Future: Scanning for Scientific and Technological Innovations which Generate Potential Threats and Opportunities in Crime, Policing and Crime Reduction. In M. Smith & N. Tilley (eds), *Crime Science: New Approaches to Preventing and Detecting Crime*. Cullompton: Willan.

Ekblom, P. (2005b). Designing Products against Crime. In N. Tilley (ed.), *Handbook of Crime Prevention*. Cullompton: Willan.

Ekblom, P. (2006). Good practice? Invest in a framework! *Network News* Spring. Chester: National Community Safety Network.

Ekblom, P., & Pease, K (1995). Evaluating Crime Prevention. In M Tonry & D Farrington (Eds), *Building a Safer Society: Strategic Approaches to Crime Prevention. Crime and Justice,* 19:585-662. Chicago: University of Chicago Press.

Farrington, D., & Petrosino, A. (2001). Systematic Reviews in Criminology and the Campbell Collaboration Crime and Justice Group. *Annals of the American Academy of Political and Social Science,* 578: 35-49.

Farrington, D., & Welsh, B. (2002). *Effects of Improved Street Lighting on Crime: A Systematic Review.* Home Office Research Study 251. London: Home Office.

Felson, M., & Clarke, R. (2004). *Opportunity Makes the Thief: Practical theory for crime prevention.* Police Research Series Paper 98. London: Home Office.

Forrester, D., Chatterton, M., & Pease, K. (1988). *The Kirkholt Burglary Prevention Project, Rochdale.* Crime Prevention Unit Paper 13. London, Home Office.

Forrester, D., Frenz, S., O'Connell, M., & Pease, K. (1990). *The Kirkholt Burglary Prevention Project, Phase 11.* Crime Prevention Unit Paper 23. London: Home Office.

Gill, M., Smith, P, Spriggs, A, Argomaniz, A, Allen, J, Follett, M., Jessiman, P., Kara, D., Little, R., & Swain, D. (2003) *National Evaluation of CCTV: Early Findings on Scheme Implementation – Effective Practice Guide.* Development and Practice Report 7. London: Home Office. Retrieved from: www.homeoffice.gov.uk/rds/pdfs2/dpr7.pdf

Goldblatt, P., & Lewis, C. (eds). (1998). *Reducing Offending: An Assessment of Research Evidence on Ways of Dealing with Offending Behaviour.* Home Office Research Study 187. London: Home Office.

Goldstein, H. (2003). On Further Developing Problem-Oriented Policing: The Most Critical Need, the Major Impediments, and a Proposal. In J. Knutsson (ed.), *Mainstreaming Problem-Oriented Policing.* Crime Prevention Studies 15. Monsey, New York: Criminal Justice Press.

Gottfredson, D., & Hirschi, T. (1990). *A General Theory of Crime.* Stanford, CA: Stanford University Press.

Home Office. (2004a). *Modelling Crime Reduction for the Home Office's Strategic Plan.* Home Office Online Report 38/04. Retrieved from: www.homeoffice.gov.uk/rds/pdfs04/rdsolr3804.pdf

Home Office. (2004b). *The Home Office Strategic Plan 2004-08.* Retrieved from: www.homeoffice.gov.uk/documents/strategicplan.pdf

Home Office. (2005). *Review of the Partnership Provisions of the Crime and Disorder Act 1998 – Report of Findings.* Retrieved from: www.crimereduction.gov.uk/partnerships60.doc

Homel, P., Nutley, S., Webb, B., & Tilley, N. (2004). *Investing to Deliver: Reviewing the Implementation of the UK Crime Reduction Programme.* Home Office Research Study 281. London: Home Office.

Hough, M., & Tilley, N. (1998). *Getting the Grease to the Squeak: Research Lessons for Crime Prevention.* Crime

Detection and Prevention Series, Paper 85. London: Home Office.

Knutsson, J. (2003). Introduction. In J Knutsson (Ed.), *Mainstreaming Problem-Oriented Policing.* Crime Prevention Studies, Volume 15. Monsey, New York: Criminal Justice Press.

Nutley S, Walter, I., & Davies, H. (2003). From knowing to doing: a framework for understanding the evidence-into-practice agenda, *Evaluation*, 9(2): 125-148.

ODPM, & Home Office. (2004). Reconciling evidence of what works, knowledge of crime reduction and community safety principles, and values. Annex 2 of *Safer Places: The planning system and crime prevention.* London: Office of the Deputy Prime Minister.

Pawson, R., & Tilley, N. (1997). *Realistic Evaluation.* London: Sage.

Read, T., & Tilley, N. (2000). *Not Rocket Science? Problem-solving and crime reduction.* Crime Reduction Research Series Paper 6. London: Home Office.

Roach, J., Ekblom, P., & Flynn, R. (2005). The Conjunction of Terrorist Opportunity: A Framework for Diagnosing and Preventing Acts of Terrorism. *Security Journal*, 18 (3): 7-25.

Scott, M. (2001). *Problem-Oriented Policing: Reflections on the First 20 Years.* Washington DC: US Department of Justice Community Oriented Policing Services.

Scott, M. (2003). Getting Police to take Problem-Oriented Policing Seriously. In J. Knutsson (ed.), *Mainstreaming*

Problem-Oriented Policing. Crime Prevention Studies 15. Monsey, New York: Criminal Justice Press.

Sherman, L., Gottfredson, D., Mackenzie, D., Eck, J., Reuter, P., & Bushway, S. (1997). *Preventing Crime: What Works, What Doesn't and What's Promising. A Report to the United States Congress.* Washington: US Department of Justice.

Sutton, M. (1996). *Implementing Crime Prevention Schemes in a Multi-Agency Setting: Aspects of Process in the Safer Cities Programme.* Home Office Research Study 160. London: Home Office.

Tilley, N. (1993a). *After Kirkholt: Theory, Methods and Results of Replication Evaluations.* Crime Prevention Unit Paper 47. London: Home Office.

Tilley, N. (1993b). *Understanding Car Parks, Crime and CCTV: Evaluation Lessons from Safer Cities.* Crime Prevention Unit Paper 42. London: Home Office.

Tilley, N. (2006). Knowing and doing: Guidance and good practice in crime prevention. In J. Knutsson & R.V.G. Clarke (eds), *Putting Theory to Work: Implementing situational prevention and problem-oriented policing.* Crime Prevention Studies. 20. Monsey, New York: Criminal Justice Press.

Tilley, N., Pease, K., Hough, M., & Brown, R (1999). *Burglary prevention: Early lessons from the Crime Reduction Programme.* Crime Reduction Research Series Paper 1. London: Home Office. Retrieved from: www.homeoffice.gov.uk/rds/prgpdfs/crrburg1.pdf

Townley, M., Johnson, S., & Pease, K. (2003). Problem Orientation, Problem Solving and Organizational Change. In J. Knutsson (ed.), *Mainstreaming Problem-Oriented Policing*. Crime Prevention Studies 15. Monsey, New York: Criminal Justice Press.

Weisel, D.L. (2003). The Sequence of Analysis in Solving Problems. In J. Knutsson (ed.), *Mainstreaming Problem-Oriented Policing*. Crime Prevention Studies 15. Monsey, New York: Criminal Justice Press.

Welsh, B., & Farrington, D. (2002). *Crime Prevention Effects of Closed Circuit Television: A Systematic Review*. Home Office Research Study 252. London: Home Office.

Wikström, P.-O. (2004). Crime as alternative: towards a cross-level situational action theory of crime causation. In J. McCord (ed.), *Beyond Empiricism: institutions and intentions in the study of crime*. New Brunswick, N.J.: Transaction.

WHO. (2004). *Handbook for the Documentation of Interpersonal Violence Prevention Programmes*. Geneva: World Health Organisation. Retrieved from: www.who.int/violence_injury_prevention/publications/violence/handbook/en

THE TRIDENT: A THREE-PRONGED METHOD FOR EVALUATING PROGRAMMES AND INITIATIVES

Roger Ellis and Elaine Hogard

Introduction

There is no doubt that evaluation is big business for social researchers. At the recent (2006) combined annual conference of the UK Evaluation Society and the European Evaluation Society, more than 300 papers gave what was probably no more than a sample of the evaluation activities carried out by private and public evaluation units and individuals in the fields of education, social and health care, regional policy and, of interest to this paper, community safety. A substantial area of applied social research involves evaluating the success of such occurrences as social, educational or health programmes or interventions (Bryman, 2001). Interestingly, Bryman does not include community safety in his list, but it is arguably one of the major areas for evaluation activity. As an aspirant discipline, evaluation has spawned numerous theoretical and practical models. However, our experience with contractors through the Social and Health Evaluation Unit led us to the conclusion that there was room for one more and this chapter describes our approach and its application to community safety initiatives. Our aims were to devise a structure which was comprehensive, gave a focus to evaluation questions and data gathering, was intelligible to contractors, and allowed for analysis, leading to recommendations.

Community Safety: Innovation and Evaluation

Developing the Trident

We devised the Trident for our first evaluation contract in 2000 and since then have used it in over 30 evaluations. It is usually clear from funders' documentation that they are interested primarily and understandably in whether their money has been well spent. Was the programme meeting its objectives in a cost-effective manner? Was the scheme working as it promised? Nothing new here: evaluations, we gathered from a selection of textbooks (Herman *et al.*, 1987; Ovretveit, 1998) typically focus on outcomes and measurement of their accomplishment. This was the first prong of our Trident, addressing outcomes, determining whether the scheme had met its stated objectives.

However, our knowledge of professional interaction and its relatively light literature (Ellis, 1988) led us to believe that it was also important to capture what had been happening. What did the programme providers actually do? How could we describe their work in such a way that others could emulate it or at least learn from it? This concern to find out what actually happened in the delivery of the scheme pointed to a second prong of the evaluation strategy: that is, a focus on process.

Our first project, for which the Trident was developed, evaluated the work of a new category of staff in the health service known as clinical facilitators. Clinical facilitation was a term coined to describe the support and supervision that was offered to nursing students when they undertook their placement in medical and surgical wards of general hospitals. The facilitation was of their clinical skills, which were being acquired, developed, practiced and evidenced on placement in the medical and surgical wards of general hospitals. These placements involved a number of individuals, arguably stakeholders, in addition to the clinical facilitators themselves. There were the students whom they taught, the nurses they worked with, the college staff they were supposed to link with and the clinical and educational managers responsible overall for their work. What did all these individuals and groups think of the clinical facilitators and their work? This seemed to us a separate set of questions from whether the outcomes of the scheme were achieved and from a description and analysis of the process. We called this area multiple stakeholder perspectives and this was the third prong of our approach.

So this paper describes an approach to evaluation which seeks to address three main questions regarding a scheme. The first is the obvious one: did the scheme work, did it meet its stated objectives? The second question is what happened in the scheme: who did what to or for whom? what were the processes involved? The third question is: what did the various participants and stakeholders in the scheme think of the scheme? This threefold approach might be likened to a trident, each prong of which probes into the scheme to gather data. The three prongs of investigation can be characterised as concerned with outcomes, process, and multiple stakeholder perspectives.

We concluded that a programme evaluation meets three main objectives. First, it demonstrates accountability. An objective external evaluation shows that the scheme is prepared to be scrutinised and the findings communicated to its funders and the public at large. Second, evaluation can provide useful intelligence and feedback for those delivering the scheme to improve or maintain performance. Third, evaluation and particularly its final report is useful to disseminate what has been learned from the project and how it might be replicated. It also provides good publicity for the scheme. The Trident gives an intelligible structure to all these activities and makes clear the kind of questions and data gathering the evaluators are undertaking.

The Trident and Methods of Data Gathering

Evaluation is essentially a process of data gathering to answer questions that make sense to contractors, participants and evaluators. Each of the evaluative prongs of the Trident and their characteristic questions pose distinctive problems with regard to the validity, reliability and feasibility of data gathering. The use of this model leads to a multi-method approach to data gathering with distinctive research questions, design, data gathering and analysis for each prong of the Trident.

Outcomes

Outcome measurement must be based on the agreed objectives for the scheme. At best, social interventions have their outcomes specified in terms of a change in behaviour for the recipients of the intervention, or at least as a change in learning or attitude which must be expressed in behavioural terms if is to be measured. The way in which this behaviour will be specified will vary according to the scale and nature of the intervention. The consideration of instruments to measure behavioural outcomes is essentially a psychometric problem. A measure has to be found which will provide a valid and reliable indication that the objectives have been met.

In our experience, the objectives of schemes may not be sufficiently precise in principle to allow valid and reliable measurement. A first task for the evaluator should be to agree objectives with the participants and contractors and also agree indicators that will be taken as evidence of the objectives having been met. Valid and reliable measures may already be available (if you are lucky) or, more usually, may have to devised by the evaluator. It may be that data are already being gathered for some other purpose, but may be taken as sufficient to indicate that outcomes are being met.

Outcomes may be likened to concentric circles. At the centre may be a change in the behaviour or attitudes of the primary recipients. However, this behaviour change may be only a means to an end, which is the impact of the changed behaviour on a contingent variable, such as detection rates or reduction in crime. So outcomes come in different forms and the evaluation must be sensitive to those which are intended for a particular programme and by which it should be judged.

In the clinical facilitator scheme, outcomes were expressed in such general terms that it was unclear what evidence would be sufficient to indicate that they were being met. We therefore had to agree with both the contractor of the evaluation and the clinical facilitators themselves a more precise specification of objectives linked with outcome measures and valid and feasible data that would be gathered. In the 'Safer Homes' Initiative described by Warren and Gerrard, a set of objectives were available, some relatively precise in themselves, others more general in nature. Discussion was necessary to agree the indicators that would be deemed sufficient to demonstrate that the objectives had been met. In both cases, this discussion took place when the pilot of the scheme was almost complete. Ideally agreement about outcomes and evidence should be reached at the outset of the evaluation.

Of course, the satisfaction of participants may be considered to be a key outcome for a scheme. However, we would argue that it is preferable to keep stakeholder perspectives separate from outcome measurement. This is not to diminish the significance of user views. But to make user views the prime outcome measure is in effect to abrogate the responsibility for determining if outcomes have been met to those individuals affected by the outcomes. Thus, in the example of the 'Safer Homes' scheme, victims will have legitimate views on the effectiveness and acceptability of the service provided for them, but they should not be expected to be the sole judges of whether their competence has been enhanced. This requires some more external and objective measurement. This separation of stakeholder perspectives from objective outcome measurement is one advantage of the Trident approach.

Assuming that measures are available or can be devised, the next problem is the attribution of causality for the outcomes measured. How do we know the measured behaviour or impact can be attributed to the intervention being evaluated? Perhaps the behaviour change would have occurred anyway or perhaps there are other causes than the intervention. Ideally, the evaluation will follow an experimental design with an experimental group who have received the intervention being compared with a control group who are identical in all respects other than the receipt of the intervention. The randomized clinical trial (RCT) is the gold standard for this part of an evaluation.

Process

Separate from outcome measurement, describing and analysing the process of intervention requires a different approach. The central component of many schemes consists of interactions between professionals themselves and with recipients of the scheme. How can this be captured, described and modelled? Ideally, there should be systematic observation, recording and analysis of the key features of the intervention with data gathered from a representative sample of interactions between provider and recipient. Unfortunately, such an approach is usually impracticable in the time scale and with the resources available and may also be precluded by the nature of the intervention.

When an intervention involves, centrally, interaction between client or recipient and a professional or trained volunteer, there are three main approaches possible in principle to establishing what has happened. The first, naturalistic or participant observation, is usually ruled out for the reasons already mentioned. The second method, usually employed, is to assume that best practice is being followed and that the profession concerned has codified this best practice. As it happens, this is rarely the case. In nursing, for example, the question of what constitutes professional competence and hence effective interaction with clients is still problematic and lacks a comprehensive or conclusive research base. A third approach relies on tapping the recollections of participants and has been described by Caves (1988) as constitutive ethnography. Essentially, this method involves in-depth interviews with participants so that they can recall and reconstruct events through focusing on critical incidents. These recollections are recorded by the researcher, who than feeds them back, ideally in categorised and modelled form to the participants for verification.

Whatever approach is adopted, we would argue that capturing the processes of an intervention or programme is a vital part of an evaluation, but logically and methodologically discrete from outcome measurement and stakeholder perspectives. Without an adequate record of the processes of a programme it is impossible to relate outcomes to their causes. Further, it is impossible to replicate a programme or learn from the experiences of an innovation. Yet many evaluations neglect this component by concentrating on outcomes and merging these with the perceptions of stakeholders. Here again the Trident is useful in identifying process description and analysis as a discrete component of the evaluation.

Multiple Stakeholder Perspectives
Identifying the perspectives of the multiple stakeholders in a scheme again requires a distinctive approach, which is fit for its purpose. First, the key stakeholders must be identified. The evaluators should identify with the contractors the whole range of individuals, groups and organisations who are involved in or affected by an intervention or programme. The starting point will of course be the providers and primary recipient, but a comprehensive stakeholder analysis will include partners of the providers or alternative providers whose functions are being complemented or even replaced, together with secondary recipients and managers of providers and recipients. Then an appropriate method must be determined for identifying their views. This is likely to be a combination of interviews, focus groups and questionnaires focusing on predetermined questions, but also allowing for less predictable individual views to emerge. Where possible common questions should be

The Trident

included to allow for comparison and contrast between participants and, for example, between providers and recipients.

The Trident approach thus ensures that logically discrete perspectives on a scheme are covered and that appropriate data gathering methods are employed. A danger of an approach of this kind might be to compartmentalise data or to force questions and data into one category to the exclusion of the others. Thus, for example, the kind of client satisfaction indicators addressed as part of the multiple stakeholder perspectives might have been expressed as an outcome in the first place. Certainly, it is important to try to relate aspects of the process to outcome measures: it is not only what happens in the intervention, but the effect this process has on the outcomes.

Since we devised this Trident approach, it has proved remarkably robust in structuring evaluations of interventions within different timescales and scope. The remainder of this paper describes the recent use of the approach in two evaluation studies covering, respectively, the pilot scheme for clinical facilitators of student learning on clinical placement and the 'Safer Home' Initiative of Cheshire Constabulary. The application of the model in these contrasting settings is now described briefly. Further details may be obtained from published reports and articles.

The Trident in Context

Of course, the Trident has not emerged fully formed with no antecedents. In a sense there is nothing new under the evaluation sun. The three aspects of evaluation addressed by the Trident, outcomes, process and stakeholder perspectives, each have a background in the evaluation literature, although process is comparatively neglected in comparison with outcomes and stakeholder views (Ovetreit, 1998). The Trident itself is representative of so-called mixed method approaches to evaluation which employ both quantitative and qualitative methods (Bryman, 2001). A number of theorists have aimed to balance the quantitative, experimental traditions of evaluation research with an in-depth exploration of the diverse views and constructions of stakeholders (Greene, 1994; Pawson & Tilley, 1997). Concentrating on the reality constructed through the views of participants has been described as a fourth generation of evaluation (Guba & Lincoln, 1989) and is conceived as replacing the previous positivist concentration on measurement, description, and evaluation, all undertaken from a supposedly objective external perspective.

The Trident allows for a mixture of external and would-be objective measures of outcomes, with the charting of reality as perceived by stakeholders, together with a description and analysis of process from both external and internal perspectives.

The Trident in Use

Evaluation of Clinical Facilitators

The clinical facilitators were trained and experienced nurses who were appointed to work with student nurses on the medical and surgical wards of six major hospitals. The key objective for the clinical facilitators was to enhance the clinical competence and confidence of the student nurses. Finding an outcome measure for this objective proved unexpectedly difficult. Our first thought was to use the assessment data on the students from the college where they were enrolled. Surely, we anticipated, students training to be nurses would have to be assessed validly and reliably to determine their fitness to practise. We envisaged a kind of *post hoc* clinical/educational trial, in which the results of students who had received clinical facilitation would be compared with those who had not. If clinical facilitation was adding value to the students' learning, this should be apparent in their results.

However, our expectations were not fulfilled. The assessment schedules of the colleges concerned were 'pass/fail' only, which was insufficiently differentiated for research purposes. Only a small proportion of students failed and the interesting data, which we had expected regarding degrees of competence, were masked, if they had ever existed, in the global pass category. This precluded the anticipated comparison of students who had received clinical facilitation with those who hadn't through the analysis of their records. We therefore had to develop a new form of assessment to gather data that would be considered indicative of the enhanced competence that the clinical facilitators were expected to bring about. We found in the literature that so called Objective Structured Clinical Examinations (OSCEs) had been developed and widely used in medical education. The examinations, clinical in focus, were structured in that they were built round a specified performance in controlled circumstances and objective through their associated assessment schedules, employed by independent trained examiners. These practice-based examinations were based on component clinical and communication skills known to be relevant to medical practice. OSCEs had been demonstrated to be valid, reliable and feasible and, incidentally, were given a high rating for relevance and fairness by students, educators and clinicians (Hodges *et al.*, 1996; Carraccio & Englander, 2000).

We therefore developed a small battery of OSCEs relevant to basic nursing practice, covering such competencies as temperature-taking, blood pressure measurement, and hand-washing. In the first two cases, students were given clear instructions regarding the measurements they should carry out on (simulated) patients and their performance was assessed independently by two examiners using an assessment schedule. Comparable instructions were given regarding hand-washing at an appropriate wash basin and a similar assessment took place against predetermined criteria. These were used as measures of competence for groups of students who had and had not received clinical facilitation. The development of these instruments was for pilot purposes only and was intended to be indicative of the approach that should be adopted in future evaluations of educational innovations. Ideally, they should have been developed at the beginning of the scheme and used systematically throughout.

The difficulties and tentative solution to outcome measurement in this evaluation are exemplary in several ways. First, it is important to ensure at the beginning of the evaluation that objectives and outcomes have been specified in measurable terms and that reliable and valid data gathering instruments are available. Second, it is important that outcome measurement should be objective and separate from the interesting but subjective impressions of participants. Before the evaluation strategy was agreed for this scheme, it had been assumed that the views of students and the clinical facilitators themselves would be sufficient evidence that the objectives had been achieved. Recognition that these views were important as stakeholder perspectives, but not the same as outcome measures, was an immediate benefit of developing and employing the Trident. Third, the existence of valid and reliable outcome measures allowed in principle for further studies identifying cause and effect, not just with clinical facilitation as a whole, but with aspects of clinical facilitation identified through the process studies.

Since clinical facilitation was an innovation (Rowan & Barber, 2000), little information was available on how clinical facilitators should fulfill their role. It was therefore particularly important that the process part of the evaluation should be pursued in depth. The constitutive ethnography approach described above was employed to establish a catalogue of critical incidents of successful clinical facilitation practice. Two in-depth interviews were held with each clinical facilitator to enable them to reflect on their practice and, crucially, to highlight incidents when they believed it had been successful in bringing about student learning. These incidents were then analysed to produce models of clinical facilitation, which were then verified or modified by the clinical facilitators. Clearly, this method is not the same as sustained observation of practice. In the absence of such an observed ethnography, constituting a description by interviewing the key participants is advocated as the best feasible method. At the end of this part of the evaluation, descriptions of practice were available, which now enable replication of the scheme and further research and evaluation to link aspects of practice with outcomes.

To elicit stakeholder perspectives on the scheme, a combination of individual interviews, focus groups and questionnaires were employed with students, ward staff, college staff, managers and the clinical facilitators themselves. The questionnaires were able to refer to features of clinical facilitation that had emerged from the process analysis and invited participants to place these six features of clinical facilitation identified in the process models in rank order. Common questions allowed comparison of views on the extent to which CFs had met their objectives, the relative contribution of CFs to student learning, and the relative value of the teaching methods identified in the process stage.

This combination of outcomes, process and perception measures enabled the researchers to produce a balanced evaluation and a set of recommendations for future practice (Ellis & Hogard, 2001).

Evaluating the Safer Homes Initiative
Our second example of the use of the Trident is in the area of community safety and concerns the 'Safer Homes' Initiative described in another chapter by Warren and Gerrard. Applying the Trident in the evaluation of this scheme yielded a number of research questions. First, the outcomes had to be addressed. What were the main objectives that the initiative had been established to meet? What evidence was there that these objectives had been met? Second, it was necessary to focus on the process whereby the scheme had been delivered. What exactly were the activities, based on a putative business process analysis, whereby the initiative was delivered? Thirdly, attention had to be paid to the views of the various stakeholders affected by the initiative including, of course, burglary victims and also the officers involved in delivering and managing the scheme and also the partners involved through the local CDRP.

The Trident

Intended outcomes included the delivery of a better quality of service to victims of domestic burglary. Better, of course, implies baselines against which improvement can be measured and these were not available in this case. The best that could be achieved was to check that the service provided reflected the best practice in the guide which informed the scheme and that the victims assessed the service they received positively. A comparison of the new with the old could, in principle, have been made by repeat victims, but this was not possible.

A second intended outcome was a reduction in the overall number of domestic burglary incidents across Cheshire. This was achieved, but reflected a similar reduction nationally and in the family of constabularies with which the location of the scheme compared.

A third anticipated outcome was a higher quality of investigation, leading to a higher domestic burglary detection rate. In fact the detection rate in Cheshire improved at a faster rate than the national trend and the trend in the comparable family of constabularies.

A fourth aim was that there should be an improvement in the relationships between crime reduction agencies in Cheshire. This was assessed through the views of partners in the CDRP and proved inconclusive.

Finally, the effectiveness of the Force Burglary Coordinator and the sustainability of the coordination he initiated was to be assessed. This last outcome would, in the Trident framework, be considered more a facet of process; that is, a means by which the principle outcomes would be achieved.

Evaluation of the process of the initiative was in large part an audit of compliance, to confirm that the procedures set out in the Good Practice and Tactical Options Guide (Home Office & ACPO, 2003) had been applied. Second, as mentioned above, the role of the Force Burglary Coordinator was assessed, as was the likely sustainability of the scheme in his absence. The process evaluation described the establishment and operation of the project implementation scheme and liaison with partner agencies. The process part of the evaluation was largely descriptive of these activities, with stakeholder views on them comprising the third prong of the evaluation.

Multiple stakeholder perspectives were solicited from victims through a focus group and telephone interviews, from constabulary staff through a questionnaire, and from senior officers, departmental managers and community safety partners through interviews. Views within the force were, as might be expected, wide-ranging, with an appreciation of the intelligible and practical nature of the initiative balanced with an awareness that staffing the scheme to the specified levels had an opportunity cost in other services.

The application of the Trident to this scheme ensured a comprehensive evaluation which was able to: address statistical and behavioural outcomes; describe and analyse the processes involved in delivery; and sample the views and perceptions of a wide range of stakeholders. Clearly these three bodies of evidence are related, but usefully discrete in focus and methods.

The Trident

Conclusion

We began as admitted tyros in the evaluation business and had to decide how we would approach bidding for and undertaking contracts. We have found our so-called Trident, with its emphasis on distinctive questions regarding the outcomes, process and stakeholder perspectives in a scheme, to be of conceptual, methodological and practical value. For us, it has balanced the usual and appropriate concern with measuring outcomes with an exploration and enhanced understanding of process and a rounded picture of perceived reality deriving from the views of participants and stakeholders. The Trident has helped us to win contracts, to structure our data gathering and to facilitate both the formative and summative functions of evaluation. It has generated material that serves what seem to us to be the three main purposes of evaluation: the demonstration of public accountability; the provision of information to improve delivery; and the dissemination of information to enable others to replicate or learn from the scheme.

References and Other Publications

Bryman, A. (2001). *Social Research Methods.* Oxford: Oxford University Press.

Carraccio, C., & Englander, R. (2000). The objective structured clinical examination: a step in the direction of competency-based evaluation. *Archive Pediatric Adolescent Medicine.* Baltimore: University of Maryland School of Medicine.

Caves, R. (1988). Consultative methods for extracting expert knowledge about professional competence. In R.

Ellis (ed.), *Professional Competence and Quality Assurance in the caring Professions* (pp. 199-229). London: Chapman and Hall.

Ellis, R. (ed.). (1988). *Professional Competence and Quality Assurance in the Caring Professions.* London: Chapman and Hall.

Ellis, R., & Hogard, E. (2001). *An Evaluation of the Pilot Project for Clinical Placement Facilitation.* Chester: Chester College of Higher Education.

Greene, J.C. (1994). Qualitative programme evaluation: promise and practice. In N. K. Denzin & Y.S. Lincoln (eds), *Handbook of Qualitative Research, second edition.* Thousand Oaks, CA: Sage Publications.

Guba, E.G., & Lincoln, Y.S. (1989). *Fourth Generation Evaluation.* Thousand Oaks, CA: Sage Publications.

Herman, J., Morris, L., & Fitz-Gibbon, C. (1987). *Evaluator's Handbook.* London: Sage Publications.

Hodges, B., Turnbull, J., Cohen, R. Bienenstock, A., & Norman, G. (1996). *Evaluating Communication Skills in the OSCE Format: Reliability and Generalisability.* Medical Education, Department of Psychiatry, University of Toronto, Canada.

Home Office, & Association of Chief Police Officers. (2003). *Domestic Burglary: National Good Practice & Tactical Options Guide.* London: Home Office Police Standards Unit.

National Evaluation of Sure Start (NESS). (2004). Available at: http://www.ness.bbk.ac.uk/ (site visited: 22 November 2004).

Ovretveit, J. (1998) *Evaluating Health Interventions.* Buckingham: Open University Press.

Pawson, R., & Tilley, N. (1997). *Realistic Evaluation.* London: Sage Publications.

Rowan, P., & Barber, P. (2000). Clinical facilitators: a new way of working. *Nursing Standard,* 14 (52), 35-38.

PUBLIC PERCEPTIONS OF STATIC AND REDEPLOYABLE CCTV

A. Rose, M. Gill, K. Collins and M. Hemming

Introduction

This chapter presents findings on public attitudes from an evaluation of redeployable CCTV conducted on behalf of the Home Office[1]. Redeployable CCTV differs from traditional ('static') CCTV in that a redeployable system can be temporarily deployed in specific areas ('hotspots') where crime problems are identified. If offenders are displaced or the problems move, redeployable CCTV can quickly be relocated to follow the problem, whilst if they are deterred, the system can be redeployed at another hotspot. The new technology appears particularly suited to tackling transient crime problems such as drug dealing.

Previous and current research on public opinions of static CCTV showed that, rather than being concerned with issues of civil liberties, the British public appear to approve of the concept and its use (Bennett & Gelsthorpe, 1996;

---

[1] The authors are very grateful to the Home Office for sponsoring the research. A range of people offered advice at various stages of the research and the authors would like to thank them all. In particular: John O'Mahoney, John Boff, Dave Gwynne, Martyn Triggol, Matt Gibbs, Ron Armitage, Jon Laws, Tricia Jessiman, and Nicola Douglas and Emmeline Taylor.

Gill & Spriggs[2], 2005). This has facilitated CCTV's rapid expansion in the UK over the last decade, despite the concerns of those who have argued that the degree of public acceptance has been overstated (Ditton, 2000). This chapter presents findings on whether the public are as favourably disposed to redeployable CCTV, and whether they see the differences between the two technologies as advantageous or disadvantageous. What would be the attitude of the public, in town centres and residential areas, to CCTV cameras being installed and then removed? Would they understand and accept the rationale of redeployable CCTV systems?

Public opinion is crucial, as we cannot assume that people will approve equally of different types of CCTV with different functions. Public acceptance of and support for what is being installed, particularly in residential areas, is desirable. This chapter is an opportunity to investigate some of these previously neglected issues, including the importance of engaging with the public to manage their expectations of redeployable CCTV.

Redeployable CCTV in Perspective

Previous research on redeployable CCTV undertaken at approximately the same time as the Home Office study

---

[2] The authors are very grateful to the Home Office for supporting the National Evaluation, to Kate Painter for commissioning it, to Chris Kershaw for support and guidance, and to Peter Grove for statistical advice. Jenna Allen, Jane Bryan, Martin Hemming, Patricia Jessiman, Deena Kara, Jonathan Kilworth, Ross Little, Polly Smith and Daniel Swain worked on and made important contributions to the National Evaluation.

reported here (2002-3) has painted a somewhat disappointing picture of its effectiveness. For example, Gill & Spriggs (2005) found that redeployable CCTV was not only not that effective at reducing crime, but also suffered from a range of technical problems. Indeed, in one case the technical difficulties were so great that the cameras were rendered useless for live monitoring. More recently, Walpes & Gill (2006) explored this issue in greater depth and discussed how cameras were not deployed frequently, not interlinked with other cameras, and potential cost savings in having fewer cameras were not realised. Moreover, redeployable camera systems did not meet their main objectives, which were to tackle and displace drug markets and drug related crime in areas not covered by static CCTV systems. Overall, the technical problems undermined the potential effectiveness of redeployable CCTV, but so too did a lack of clarity concerning how they could and should be used. Similarly, Gill *et al.* (2006) have outlined how redeployable CCTV has been used in the fight against drug crime (in the evaluation sites discussed in this study) and again found that effectiveness was compromised by technical failure. Although the police were able to identify some successes, overall redeployable CCTV was a disappointment, failing in most deployments to deliver on the supposed advantages. There is a definite need to be realistic about what redeployable CCTV systems might be able to achieve. Before examining the evaluation's findings, the context of the participatory sites and the methodology employed are briefly explained.

Perceptions of CCTV

Site Context and Methodology

The evaluation was conducted at three sites in England where Drug Action Teams (DATs) had purchased redeployable CCTV systems under the Home Office's local Community Against Drugs (CAD) initiative to tackle open drug markets and drug related crime. The three sites varied demographically and geographically. Site A was located in a London Borough, site B in a largely rural area in the South West of England and site C in a predominantly urban part of the North East of England. The evaluation was undertaken between July 2002 and August 2003, resulting in the Home Office's publication of a good practice guide for the implementation of redeployable CCTV (Gill *et al.*, 2005). The aims of the evaluation were two-fold: firstly to consider the impact of redeployable CCTV in addressing drug markets and related crime; secondly to identify transferable lessons concerning the implementation of this new technology. In total, 25 deployments were made across the three sites, a much lower number than originally anticipated, with many of these aborted due to technical failure. As a result, the evaluation was predominantly concerned with process. However, redeployable cameras were deployed in a variety of settings, including outside railway stations and night clubs, on residential estates and in local parks. As part of the evaluation, the public's views on redeployable CCTV were canvassed at the three sites. The resulting data form the basis for this chapter.

To measure public perceptions and acceptance of redeployable CCTV, a street survey was conducted outside a railway station at site A, and at sites B and C residents were surveyed in their homes. The survey sample comprised 430 respondents at site A, 401 at site B and 399 at site C, giving a total survey sample size of 1230. Respondents were asked, amongst other questions, about their knowledge of crime levels in the area and of redeployable CCTV systems, including its perceived impact, advantages and disadvantages. In addition, focus groups were conducted at all three evaluation sites with separate groups of residents, young people, and drug users. The main objectives of the focus groups were to establish public perceptions of local drug markets and drug-related crime and public knowledge of, and opinions on, the use of both static and redeployable CCTV to tackle the aforementioned crimes. In total, fifteen focus groups were conducted, with sample sizes varying from five to fourteen, of mixed ages and gender. Participants were predominantly white at all three sites, but a substantial minority, six per cent, were non-white at site A, reflecting this demographic within the local population. Clearly, this data is limited in that there was not the scope for assessing control areas. However, these findings might best be assessed in the context of other studies that have also focused on redeployable CCTV (see especially Gill & Spriggs, 2005; Gill *et al.*, 2006; Walpes & Gill, 2006).

Findings

Survey respondents in the residential areas were asked about their level of support for CCTV in general by being invited to agree or disagree with a number of statements. The proportions stating that they agreed or agreed strongly with each statement are given in Table 1.

Perceptions of CCTV

Table 1. Proportion of Respondents Agreeing with Statements about CCTV.

Statement	Agree or agree strongly
CCTV will decrease the number of crimes	78.0%
CCTV will decrease the level of anti-social behaviour	74.1%
CCTV will move the problems elsewhere	72.8%
CCTV will decrease the fear of crime	66.7%
CCTV will increase the number of arrests	62.1%
CCTV will increase the number of crimes reported	58.3%
CCTV will increase police activity	48.0%
CCTV will have no effect on crime	21.1%
CCTV will stop the problems altogether	13.1%

Whilst over three-quarters of respondents thought that CCTV would have a beneficial impact on crime rates, they were less inclined to agree with statements suggesting specific mechanisms by which it might produce an effect, and fewer than half agreed that the erection of cameras would increase the level of police activity. Few respondents thought that cameras would stop crime problems completely, and almost three-quarters agreed with a suggestion that CCTV would displace crime to other locations.

When asked how much they knew about redeployable CCTV, the majority of respondents (an average of 74% across the sites) professed to know little or nothing about it. Moreover, despite the fact that the surveys were conducted in areas where CCTV was advertised by signs (although not specifically stating that the CCTV was redeployable), only about a third of respondents said that they were aware of their presence. Clearly, this needs to be borne in mind when interpreting the finding, although, as the national evaluation found, it is not uncommon for large parts of some communities, at the time of the research, to be unaware of CCTV (Gill & Spriggs, 2005). As might be expected, residents were more aware of cameras operating in their neighbourhoods (an average of 38% being aware) than were the respondents at the railway station (27%). After respondents were asked if they knew anything about redeployable CCTV, but before they were asked whether they knew it had been operating in the area, the following information was given to survey respondents:

> Traditionally, CCTV is put up in one place and left there. But redeployable CCTV can be put in an area where there is a problem and removed when it is no longer needed. It can be put back if the problem returns.

Focus group participants were informed in similar terms. This was to allow researchers to assess public perceptions of the potential of redeployable CCTV as a tool to disrupt drug markets and related crime, including its advantages and disadvantages when compared to static CCTV. Respondents were invited to cite as many advantages or disadvantages as they wished.

Even after the characteristics of redeployable CCTV were explained, using the statement above, an average of 31% of respondents across all three sites could not name a single advantage relating to the technology. While the remainder did attempt to cite an advantage of redeployable cameras, only 29% of the respondents mentioned a feature possessed specifically by redeployable CCTV, and only 14% gave a redeployabilty-related feature as their first response. Table 2 opposite shows the results:

Table 2. Advantages of Redeployable CCTV Identified by Survey Respondents.

Advantages related to redeployability	Nos.	%	Other advantages	Nos.	%
Transportable, redeployable, move to different places, mobile	175	14.2%	Target specific areas, keep eye on troublesome areas	181	14.7%
Keep criminals, people unaware, won't know where they are next	87	7.1%	Stop crime, gets rid of, combats crime, lowers, lessens crime	167	13.6%
Cost effective, more economical, cheaper	59	4.8%	Deterrent, people know they are being watched	117	9.5%
Can be quickly deployed, moved, quick response to crime area	31	2.5%	Catch more people, catch culprits, offenders, vandals	108	8.8%
Can follow crime/criminals around, move, put where needed	26	2.1%	Watches wider area, whole area	87	7.1%
Help police, police can't be everywhere	17	1.4%	Feel safe, make areas safer, more security	76	6.2%
Put in areas where static CCTV can't be used	16	1.3%	Good idea, helpful	53	4.3%
More versatile, flexible	11	0.9%	Stop anti-social behaviour, make people more civilised	51	4.1%

Save buying more cameras, buy fewer cameras	9	0.7%	Other answers (including don't know)	43	3.5%
All right to use in small areas	8	0.7%	Give, use as evidence, assist in getting prosecution	28	2.3%
Recycling, can be used again and again	7	0.6%	Check, look at different areas, different angles on cameras	23	1.9%
Monitored 24 hours, constantly watched	2	0.2%	Conditional answers (so long as watched etc.)	19	1.5%
Less likely to be damaged, vandalised	2	0.2%	Get a better idea of crime averages, help monitor crime	8	0.7%

Focus group respondents saw the mobility of redeployable cameras as their main advantage:

> A portable camera [redeployable CCTV] breaks patterns, keeping them [offenders] on their toes and guessing.
> *(Resident)*

> It would be better if they [redeployable CCTV] could be moved around because the element of surprise may stop them [offenders] in their tracks and make them think twice.
> *(Resident)*

> It would be good for using in places where there are lots of crime, say on estates or in parks and you could remove them [the cameras] when the problem has gone.
> *(Drug user)*

When asked to cite disadvantages of redeployable CCTV, more than half (57%) declined to cite any at all. However, those who did express concerns tended to cite concerns related to the logistics of redeployability rather than general issues with the cameras. Again, people were free to cite as many disadvantages as they wished. The most frequent concern was the prospect of cameras being removed: 16% thought that offenders would return when the cameras were redeployed somewhere else, 8.5% said that redeployable cameras were not a permanent solution, and 5% stated that offenders would notice that the cameras were no longer in place. A small number of respondents made statements such as 'it makes no sense to remove cameras from a crime area', 'people no longer feel safe once the cameras have been removed' and 'cameras are no longer a deterrent after they have been taken away'.

One focus group respondent pointed out that the process of erecting and taking down cameras draws attention to them and undermines their effectiveness:

> Some of the younger ones said it [the operation] was comical. It was like watching Del Boy ... all these police putting it [redeployable CCTV] up and taking it down. And the kids, the ones that burglarised, they were stood there laughing and watching, they thought it was hilarious. It was ridiculed from start to finish.
>
> *(Resident)*

Concern about the redeployability of the cameras was more graphically expressed when respondents were asked whether they agreed or disagreed with specific statements about how they might feel if redeployable cameras were erected in their street and later removed (see Table 3, overleaf).

Table 3. Proportion of Respondents Agreeing with Statements about Removal of Redeployable CCTV Cameras.

Statement	Agree or agree strongly
I would worry that the problem would reoccur	79.4%
I would be unhappy because I would not feel as safe as when the cameras were here	72.4%
I would be glad to see the cameras go because I feel that they are always watching me	9.2%
I would be happy to see the cameras go but only if they were replaced with permanent CCTV cameras	72.2%
I would be happy that the cameras could be used elsewhere	66.4%

While respondents generally accepted that redeployable CCTV cameras might be useful elsewhere, a substantial majority were concerned enough about what might happen after cameras are removed to demand that permanent cameras be erected. This scenario occurred during the evaluation at site C, resulting in a low number of camera deployments. If such demands were acceded to, then any cost savings resulting from the use of redeployable cameras rather than static would be negated. This finding is supported by similar enquiries about redeployable CCTV in the National Evaluation - see Walpes & Gill (2006). In some cases, cameras were put up and left there for several months, losing many of the qualities of being redeployable and became more like static cameras.

Thus, despite the fact that they had only just had the concept of redeployable CCTV explained to them before being asked to think about its advantages and disadvantages, far more people wanted static than redeployable cameras. This last point is more strongly illustrated by responses to a specific question on whether respondents would choose static or redeployable CCTV to deal with the particular problems they were aware of in their area and are listed in Table 4.

Table 4. Given the Local Problems You are Aware of, if Choosing a CCTV System for this Area, Would You Choose?

Static	53.1%
Redeployable	24.2%
Neither of them	3.2%
Don't know / don't mind / either	19.5%

Those respondents who appeared most knowledgeable about redeployable CCTV, and who could cite as advantages features of the system that were related to redeployability (see Table 2), were significantly more likely to prefer redeployable cameras as a solution to the problems in their area ($x^2 = 48.14$, $p<0.05$). However it is telling that even these respondents preferred static CCTV by a narrow majority.

The effectiveness of CCTV (both static and redeployable) was also compared to other crime prevention activities in the residential surveys and focus groups. Survey respondents were given a list of six crime reduction measures and invited to choose which three of them, in priority order, they thought would do most to reduce drug dealing and drug related crime. The results, averaged across both sites, are tabulated in Table 5.

Table 5. Public Preference Between Measures to Reduce Drug Dealing and Drug Related Crime.

Crime reduction measure	Ranked 1st	Mentioned in top 3
More police on the street	37%	77%
More activities for young people	21%	51%
Static CCTV	19%	46%
Redeployable CCTV	8%	39%
Wardens on the street	4%	33%
Better drug treatment facilities	3%	22%
Don't know	4%	-
None of these	3%	-

Table 5 puts public approval of CCTV systems into context, and shows that, despite the evidence in Table 1 showing most respondents thought CCTV results in more arrests and more reporting of crime, when offered a choice only 27% of respondents prefer CCTV to the presence of more police officers on the street or the provision of activities for young people as a means of reducing drug dealing and drug related crime. The surveys did not ask people's reasons for preferring more officers to CCTV, but taken together, the findings in Tables 1 and 5 lend some support to Ditton's (2000: p. 692) suggestion that 'respondents believe that CCTV is better than the police at detecting crime, but that police patrols are more effective than CCTV in making people feel safer.'

Focus group drug users concurred with the view that police are a more effective deterrent than CCTV cameras:

Perceptions of CCTV

More police would make me more worried about doing a crime than CCTV.

People would be much happier if they had more police officers on the street. When I see one [a police officer] I do think twice, if a camera's there I sometimes think there is no one manning that and any way they will never catch me.

Focus group members generally were concerned that CCTV (of all kinds) was not in itself enough, as the quality and amount of monitoring of the images was important too:

CCTV is only as good as who mans it.
(Resident)
Most people around here don't think that cameras are linked up to anything because even in areas where there are cameras nothing gets done.
(Drug user)
If they [redeployable CCTV] are monitored properly they are good.
(Young person)

Focus group residents also doubted the ability of CCTV to deter drug users:

I don't think they [offenders] are bothered by the cameras, they do it anyway.
(Resident)
I mean, if they [offenders] were on drugs then it [redeployable CCTV] wouldn't make any difference anyhow.
(Resident)

Focus group drug users gave some useful insights on how redeployable cameras might be viewed by dealers. There were encouraging statements, such as:

Redeployable CCTV would have a big effect on dealers as they are all paranoid anyway, so the possibility of cameras would make them very wary.

On crack it makes you paranoid and higher so you take notice of the cameras.

Supporting the findings of Gill & Loveday (2003), those with experience of having been caught by CCTV were particularly impressed with its capabilities:

You only worry about it [CCTV] when you get nicked.

More and more are convicted through CCTV. Its strong evidence, if you snatch a hand bag and you're on CCTV you can't deny it.

Yeah the evidence is good and it makes you more wary.

However a more typical view was that dealers and users, especially those involved with heroin, were too committed to drugs to care very much about cameras, static or redeployable.

When you are on drugs you don't care, you don't know what you are doing when you are on heroin.

If you are on heroin it doesn't matter what is in your way you just don't see it. All you see is your next fix and that is it. It won't make any difference if you have a camera following them twenty-four hours a day.

The drug dealers just work around them. People are clued up, you know where they are, how they work and just work around them.

Dealers will still find a way of getting the gear to you, you just have to move around more and change the way you deal.

People [dealers and users] use their mobiles to get in contact with people so what are you going to charge them [dealers] with, making a phone call?

The cameras didn't stop me [in the past]. I knew they'd be being monitored but I didn't care. It was the drugs, they take over, you need your fix. Redeployable CCTV still would not have bothered me because I would have been so desperate for the drugs.

It doesn't matter if there are redeployable CCTV cameras or not, people will just carry on doing what it is they are doing. The need for gear [drugs] is so strong that it doesn't matter what is in front of you, or who is watching you, you just want the gear.

Conclusions

The findings echo previous studies showing broad public support for CCTV although less support for redeployables. Nevertheless, as the national evaluation noted, there are often unrealistic expectations placed on CCTV. Focus group drug users - particularly those who had previously been caught by CCTV - were more impressed by the quality of the evidence and said that they would give the cameras respect. However the general view, particularly of heroin users, was that dealers and users were committed and would always find a way of conducting their transactions. This is broadly what the public also thought. When cameras are offered as the only option, people want them, but when offered a choice between CCTV and other potential crime-reducing options, their enthusiasm is less marked. Asked to prioritise CCTV with other measures to reduce drug related crime, the public preferred more police on the streets and better facilities for young people to CCTV, and the redeployable version was less popular than the static.

The surveys discovered little public knowledge of redeployable CCTV and limited enthusiasm for it, even after its chief features were explained. Few respondents identified advantages in using redeployable cameras and an equal number were able to point to disadvantages. Respondents worried that offenders would simply return after the cameras were removed, and most considered that any redeployment should result in the installation of static cameras. The national evaluation also found one of the major issues for the public concerning redeployable CCTV was their removal, finding that '...people liked them where they were and wanted more, not fewer.' (Gill & Spriggs, p.119).

The chief suggestion to be gleaned from this evidence is that, despite their general approval of CCTV, many members of the public have little idea how it is supposed to prevent or detect crime. The public's support for the use of cameras cannot, on this evidence, be regarded as informed. Perhaps as a result of this lack of understanding, there is likely to be a marked resistance to removing cameras once they have been installed. The main advantage of redeployable cameras – that they can follow problems around – appears lost on most of the public.

One of the implications of these findings is that local authorities expecting to reduce costs by buying redeployable CCTV cameras as an alternative to static are likely to find themselves under pressure from residents determined that redeployable cameras should stay put until or unless permanent systems are put in their place. Further, there is a need to ensure that the latest developments in technology have overcome the technical problems of redeployable CCTV systems that have been highlighted by studies in different areas.

References and Other Publications

Armitage, R. (2002). *To CCTV or not to CCTV? A Review of Current Research into the Effectiveness of CCTV Systems in Reducing Crime.* London: NACRO.

Bennett, T., & Gelsthorpe, L. (1996). Public Attitudes Towards CCTV in Public Places. In *Studies on Crime and Crime Prevention,* Volume 5, No. 1, National Council for Crime Prevention.

Cohen, L.E., & Felson, M. (1979). Social Change and Crime Rate Trends: A Routine Activity Approach. In *American Sociological Review,* 44, pp. 588-608.

Cornish, D.B., & Clarke, R.V.G. (eds) (1986), *The Reasoning Criminal: Rational Choice Perspectives on Offending.* Springer-Verlag.

Ditton, J. (2000). Crime and the City: Public Attitudes Towards Open-Street CCTV in Glasgow. In *British Journal of Criminology*, Volume 40, No.4, pp. 692-709.

DrugScope. (2001). *Annual Report on the UK Drug Situation 2001*. Retrieved from: www.drugscope.org.uk

Gill, M., & Loveday, K. (2003). What do offenders think about CCTV? In Gill, M. (ed.) *CCTV*. Leicester: Perpetuity Press Ltd.

Gill, M., Rose, A., & Collins, K. (2005). *A good practice guide for the implementation of redeployable CCTV*. Home Office Online Report 16.05 . Retrieved from: http://www.homeoffice.gov.uk/rds/pdfs05/rdsolr1605.pdf

Gill, M., Rose, A., Collins, K., & Hemming, M. (2006). Redeployable CCTV and drug related crime: a case of implementation failure. In *Drugs: Education, Prevention and Policy*, 13 (5), 151-160.

Gill, M., & Spriggs, A. (2005) *Assessing the Impact of CCTV*. London: Home Office Research Study 292. Retrieved from: http://www.homeoffice.gov.uk/rds/pdfs05/hors292.pdf

Lupton, R., Wilson, A., May, T., Warburton, H., & Turnbull, P. (2002). *A Rock and a Hard Place: Drug Markets in Deprived Neighbourhoods*. Home Office Research Study 240.

Nelson, A. (1997). Public Perceptions of the Electronic Eye. In *Crime and Security*, July / August, pp 196-197.

Site C Community Safety Partnership. (2003). *Crime and Disorder Audit Update*. Site C Community Safety Partnership.

Smith, P., Spriggs, A., Argomaniz, J., Allen, J., Jessiman, P., Kara, D., Little, R., Swain, D., Follet, M., & Gill, M. (2003). Lessons in Implementing CCTV Schemes: An Early Review. In M. Gill. (ed.), *CCTV*. Leicester: Perpetuity Press.

Walpes, S., & Gill, M. (2006). The Effectiveness of Redeployable CCTV. In *Crime Prevention and Community Safety: an International Journal*, 8.1, pp. 1-16.

HANDS ON OR HANDS OFF? CENTRAL GOVERNMENT'S ROLE IN MANAGING CDRPs

Mike Hough

Introduction

This chapter examines reasons for the underachievement of a crime reduction strategy involving local partnerships that was introduced into England and Wales by the incoming New Labour government shortly after winning power in 1997. This was one of the new administration's most welcomed crime reduction measures. The 1998 Crime and Disorder Act required local police and councils to set up Crime and Disorder Reduction Partnerships (CDRPs). They were required to be in place in 1999. They were intended to be coalitions of senior managers from:

- Local authorities[1];
- Local police;
- Local Health authorities (now Primary Care Trusts);
- Probation;
- Fire service;
- And other relevant statutory, voluntary and commercial bodies.

The underlying principle in establishing CDRPs was that the criminal justice system can exercise little direct control over many of the main 'drivers' of crime, and that other parts of the local state are better placed to do so. For example, local planning, housing and regeneration departments can steer the development of land-use and housing mix in specific high crime areas. Health authorities

The Role of Central Government

can tackle problems associated with substance misuse, and are also well place to take action against some forms of violent crime, such as domestic abuse. Local education authorities and youth services and leisure departments have an obvious role to play in preventing youth crime, through their policies for handling misbehaviour in schools and truancy, for example. The Crime and Disorder Act requires CDRPs to pursue a cyclical triennial process involving: the auditing of problems of crime and disorder; the validation of the results through consultation; and the construction and implementation of a strategy for tackling the problems.

Many, including myself, felt that the introduction of CDRPs would turn out to be a landmark in crime reduction policy. It promised to bring substantial new resources and energy to crime control. Seven years on, there is a widespread sense that CDRPs have failed to live up to their promise[2]. This paper includes some evidence in support of this pessimistic view, but essentially I have offered a judgement on the issue. Others will have reached different judgements – though the government itself was reviewing the provisions of the 1998 Crime and Disorder Act at the time of writing. Those who feel that I have sold CDRPs short will find little of value in the rest of the paper. Its main purpose is not to document CDRPs' underperformance, but to offer an explanation for it, and some may feel that there is no underperformance to explain.

The paper is written from the viewpoint of someone who has spent several years offering encouragement and support from the sidelines to central and local government efforts to reduce crime through partnership working. I was involved in the preparation of government guidance for

CDRPs (Hough & Tilley, 1998), and in the training of CDRP staff when the measure was introduced. I was a member of an inner London CDRP for several years and currently provide research-based advice to one of the ten regional government teams responsible for 'performance managing' CDRPs. With colleagues, I have evaluated many crime reduction projects that were initiated by CDRPs. I offer these biographical details not just to establish my credentials, but to indicate that I really wanted the initiative to work, and have tried, where I can, to make it work. In other words, I have reached somewhat pessimistic conclusions about the achievements of CDRPs from a starting point of prejudice in favour of them.

There is a growing literature on partnership working, both within the field of crime reduction and elsewhere (e.g. Pearson *et al.*, 1992; Tilley, 1992; Gilling, 1994, 1997; Liddle & Gelsthorpe, 1994a, 1994b; Crawford & Jones, 1995; Hughes, 1996; Crawford, 1997; Bowling, 1998). There is a consensus that it is hard to do well. Obstacles include:

- Mismatches between partner organisations' values and working cultures;
- The resultant mutual suspicion and distrust;
- Difficulties in persuading people within one organisation to undertake work whose short-term benefits accrue only to their partner organisations;
- The greater priority given to organisations' core functions over partnership work;
- The competing demands of other partnerships[3];
- Rapid staff turnover at senior management level;
- Limited capacity in analysing problems effectively and identifying solutions;
- Lack of project management skills.

The Role of Central Government

All of these factors have affected Crime Reduction Partnerships, and I do not wish to underplay their importance. What I want to do in this paper is to highlight a further factor which to date has attracted insufficient attention. This relates to the way in which current approaches to public sector reform in Britain tend to oversimplify crime reduction issues, with two important consequences:

- Crime reduction issues are cast in terms which privilege a narrow range of tactical solutions, whilst ignoring various crucial strategic approaches;

- This narrowing of potential solutions discourages the engagement of those agencies that lie beyond the perimeter of the criminal justice system.

The argument that I propose to develop is not intended to be an exhaustive explanation of CDRPs' underperformance. It is intended as an additional explanation to those listed above. However, it is of particular importance right now because, as I shall discuss at the end of the paper, the response to date of central government to CDRPs' underperformance has been to increase the intensity of focus on their performance management systems, which I would argue are part of the problem, and not the solution.

The lessons that can be learnt from the English and Welsh experience with CDRPs will be more appropriate for some countries than for others. Despite its three tiers of government, there is a relatively centralised political system. The *central* tier is by far the most important. Although there is a *regional* tier of government in England, this largely serves as the delivery arm of central government policy. It lacks political representation, and has little autonomy[4]. Historically, the lower tier of *local* government has been important, with political representation and the power to raise taxes. Over time, however, local government has becoming increasingly dependent on central government grants, and this financial dependence has progressively eroded the importance of the local tier. Those countries with federal systems may find it hard to recognise the 'new governance' that characterises British political administration, with centralised performance management. On the other hand, the broader lessons about the risks of target-setting by higher tiers of government on lower ones may have general applicability.

CDRPs' Performance – A Balance Sheet

Any assessment of CDRPs needs to take a long view, and in particular needs to remember the almost total breakdown of relationships that had occurred in the 1980s in Britain between many urban local authorities and local police[5]. There have been considerable improvements since 1998. New structures are in place, and new relationships have been built between the police, probation and local authority departments. An optimist would – probably wrongly – also point to the significant falls in crime that have occurred since then, and attribute them to new partnership work.

On the other hand, gloomier commentators would draw attention to the widespread implementation failure in partnership work, the pervasive experience of CDRPs as 'talking shops' (coupled with the suspicion that the real

The Role of Central Government

decisions were made elsewhere), the limited analytic purchase displayed in crime audits, and the way in which crime reduction strategies tend to dress up pre-existing programmes of single agency work as partnership work. There have also been some consistent absences from the partnership table: the most notable absentees are health authorities; staff from local authority planning departments; regeneration departments; and even local education authorities. Probation staff have played a significant part in some CDRPs and a marginal part in others. Experience in involving the voluntary sector, businesses and local residents has also been patchy.

These weaknesses in partnership structures are part of the explanation for the high rate of implementation failure amongst CDRP-led projects. There is no shortage of examples. By way of illustration, I shall present some findings from an evaluation my unit undertook of 20 burglary projects in the South of England between 1999 and 2002. Table 1 overleaf describes how well the 20 CDRPs in five different police forces implemented the burglary reduction programme for which each of them had been funded. Each programme had several elements, often led by different agencies within the partnership. The table shows the number of elements planned for each project, and the number actually implemented.

It can be seen that well under half of the total number of programme components were fully implemented as part of the 20 programmes. Bearing in mind that these were highly visible 'flagship' projects exposed to scrutiny through a national evaluation, the level of implementation failure is striking. The reasons for this are discussed in detail elsewhere (Hough *et al.*, 2005). For our purposes,

Community Safety: Innovation and Evaluation

Table 1. Levels of Implementation in 20 Burglary Projects in Southern England and Wales (source: Hough et al., 2005).

SDP	No. of elements planned	Elements fully completed	Elements partially completed	Elements not attempted
Project 1	5	1	1	3
Project 2	5	2	2	1
Project 3	9	3	6	0
Project 4	8	3	0	5
Project 5	6	1	2	3
Project 6	7	3	4	0
Project 7	5	4	1	0
Force A	**45**	**17**	**16**	**12**
Project 8	6	3	3	0
Project 9	7	4	1	2
Force B	**13**	**7**	**4**	**2**
Project 10	12	2	4	6
Project 11	7	7	0	0
Project 12	1	1	0	0
Project 13	5	2	1	2
Project 14	4	4	0	0
Project 15	1	0	1	0
Project 16	9	2	3	4
Project 17	10	4	6	0
Force C	**49**	**22**	**15**	**12**
Project 18	5	4	1	0
Project 19	3	2	1	0
Force D	**8**	**6**	**2**	**0**

The Role of Central Government

however, the table illustrates that CDRPs clearly find it difficult to deliver on some projects.

I do not propose to document further the extent of CDRPs' underperformance. Clearly there are hard questions to be asked. Were expectations over-inflated? Did people underestimate the time needed for new structures to bed in? But I hope that I have said enough to establish that there *has been* a degree of underperformance, and that this needs explaining. I now propose to trace the way in which the 'modernisation' agenda has contributed to this underperformance.

Modernisation

Over the last 25 years, Conservative and Labour governments in Britain have shared a 'modernisation' agenda for public services. From 1979 onward, the Conservative government aimed to get better 'value for money' out of the public sector, through a mixture of 'modern' management methods and downward pressure on budgets. The favoured solutions included budgetary cuts, applying private sector management methods to the public sector, the introduction of purchaser/provider splits (or quasi-markets) within bureaucracies and the introduction of new providers, usually from the private sector, to compete with existing ones.

Many aspects of this approach were retained – indeed developed and extended – by New Labour from 1997 onward. Reform of public services is now a key Government priority, as reflected by the establishment of the Prime Minister's Delivery Unit and the Office of Public Services Reform. As with the previous Conservative administration, their basic approach has been to secure greater accountability through performance management regimes that rely on quantitative performance indicators and target-setting. The concept of competition as a lever on performance has been retained, though the language of privatisation and 'market testing' has now been replaced by that of 'contestability'[6].

This new form of public sector governance – 'New Public Management' – emerged in the late 20th century in many developed countries (see McLaughlin *et al.*, 2001, for an account of its development within criminal justice in Britain). Under some administrations, there was a strong ideological commitment to paring down the public sector, which can be traced to neo-liberal political philosophies about the virtues of small government (see, for example, Wilson, 1989). Others have judged pragmatically that the best way to drive up public sector performance is for central government to set broad objectives and for local agencies to have the freedom to choose how best they should set about achieving the nationally set objectives. In other words, there is tight central control over the *ends* to be pursued by public services, but local control over the *means* by which the ends are to be achieved. One of the defining metaphors of modernisation was introduced by the management theorists Osborne & Gaebler (1992), who are associated with the emergence of New Public Management in the United States. They suggested that the job of government is not to *row* but to *steer*. In other words, government should ensure that public services are provided, but should not necessarily aim to provide these services directly themselves. The metaphor was taken up with enthusiasm by central government politicians and administrators in Britain – but appreciated less by their local government counterparts – who were usually cast in

The Role of Central Government

the role of rowers. This model of governance is often supported by reference to private sector organisations whose success is built on radically decentralised decision-making to local managers, within a central framework of simple performance targets[7].

Stated in these terms, the new governance has plenty to capture the imaginations, not only of central government, but also those entrepreneurial local providers to whom 'earned autonomy' is attractive.[8] As I shall argue, however, in politically sensitive policy areas such as law and order, central government finds it hard in practice to set coherent targets[9]. It also finds it hard to risk loosening its control over local delivery. The promise of localism in principle tends to be negated by forms of centralised micro-management in practice: the centre not only 'steers' policy, but succumbs to the temptation of 'rowing', in the hope of speeding things on a little, and securing some visible and electorally important successes. There are obvious tensions between a centralised system of target setting and the 'local problem solving' model that is embedded in the statutory requirements on CDRPs to audit their local crime problems and to tailor their responses accordingly – a point to which I shall return.

The new governance emerged, not by accident, but in response to real problems in conventional post-war public administration. As the size of both the central and local state grew in the second half of the 20th century, monolithic public service bureaucracies in many industrialised countries grew into powerful, slow-moving, self-serving bodies that could define the terms of their own success. Not surprisingly, some developed inflexibilities both in their management and their workforces, and the rigidities of public bureaucracies became increasingly obvious when they were unable to respond to the increasingly rapid rate of social change. The limitations of public bureaucracies began to emerge at the same time as new technologies which promised to solve them: the new style of governance was made possible by considerable advances in information technology, without which quantitative performance management from 'the centre' would be impossible, even as an aspiration.

If the key feature of the modernisation agenda is the centralised definition of ends and the decentralisation of decisions about means, various further features emerge as a consequence. The linking of funding to performance is an important one, providing the incentive to agencies to achieve targets – or a disincentive to miss them. A corollary of this is the splitting of monolithic bureaucracies into purchasers and providers, to allow greater 'incentivisation' within the agency. This simplifies the introduction of competition or 'contestability', both between public, voluntary and private sectors and within sectors, through competitive bidding for 'challenge funds'.

These features of modernisation relate to the nature of funding. Modernisation's logic also points inevitably to a particular emphasis on processes of *prioritisation*. It is hard to quarrel with the basic principle that organisations should identify their key priorities and focus their energies on them. The risk is that systematic and focused action against *misidentified* or *poorly identified* priorities can have worse consequences than poorly marshalled and ineptly implemented action against well-specified priorities.

To anticipate arguments that I shall develop later in the paper, there are features of 'law and order' politics that tend to produce over-simplified or mis-specified priorities.

The Role of Central Government

The factors that lead people to treat each other badly are complex; political and media debate cannot handle this complexity, and thus uses an oversimplified discourse about crime. The modernisation agenda feeds on this simplified discourse to develop and impose inappropriate targets on the public services that it seeks to improve. Senior managers at local level understand their organisations well, and are well aware of this reductionist process. Of particular importance in explaining the lack of engagement of key CDRP partners from outside the criminal justice system, crime problems (and solutions) become framed in ways that are largely irrelevant for all except the police.

Reductionist Knowledge Management

Those pursuing the modernisation agenda tend towards scepticism about the capacity of local agencies to do their jobs properly. Poor local performance is thought to be a consequence more of incompetence than of resource shortages[10]. The solution is for the 'steerers' to point the 'rowers' in the right direction, tell them where to focus their efforts, and give them the right tools (or right oars?) to do the job. (The tool-kit metaphor is pervasive in the crime-reduction world, and indicative of a systematic misjudgement about the complexity of the enterprise: plumbers have tool-kits; social engineers do not.) In the case of crime reduction, the task of identifying 'what works' and filling appropriate tool-kits with this knowledge has fallen to Home Office research teams.

Just as it is hard to argue with the overarching principles of priority-setting, it would be hard to take issue with the principle that implementation of any form of social policy should be firmly grounded on evidence about effectiveness. There are important questions about the admissibility of different sorts of evidence, however, and some approaches to knowledge management risk skewing social policy. I shall argue that criminal policy is currently exposed to exactly this risk.

Over the last five years, however, there has been increasing enthusiasm within government in Britain, including the Home Office, for forms of systematic research reviews associated with the Cochrane Collaboration in the field of health care, and with the Campbell Collaboration in criminal policy[11]. These systematic reviews exclude all studies that fail to reach a level of methodological quality – the threshold being set individually for each review. For example, the Maryland Scale of Scientific Methods is often used as a filtering device[12]. One of the most influential international reviews of effective practice in criminal justice, conducted by Sherman *et al.* (1997), adopted systematic review principles, identifying:

- What is known to work;
- What is promising;
- What does not work;
- What is not known.

For the purposes of the review, "known to work" meant "established as effective by at least two high quality evaluations"[13]. In fields of study which lend themselves readily to evaluation through randomised controlled trials (RCTs) or to other forms of tightly designed quantitative evaluation, the Campbell/Cochrane approach is clearly appropriate. We can reasonably expect our doctors to base their prescribing decisions on evidence that is filtered to

The Role of Central Government

remove all studies of poor quality. This is because pharmaceutical evaluations are relatively straightforward: there is usually little implementation failure – in that people in drug trials tend to take their medicine as required – and clearly measurable outcomes. Also important is the fact that pharmaceutical interventions are not usually dependent for their effectiveness on the social meaning that the recipients attach to them (though there are obviously placebo effects). Evaluating strategies for crime reduction usually tends to be more complex, and it is especially challenging when it is addressing various forms of 'social crime prevention'.

As a general rule, simple interventions that target large numbers of people or neighbourhoods in the pursuit of a single, easily measured, objective can be readily evaluated to a high standard. More complex interventions with multiple objectives are much harder to evaluate. The more aggressively that modernizers pursue the Campbell/Cochrane approach, the less they will encourage these more complex forms of crime reduction. To put this another way, the 'tool-kits' offered by central government to CDRPs will be filled piecemeal with pieces of tactical knowledge, but will have little to offer by way of strategic knowledge.

Strategic and tactical knowledge are obviously concepts that need to be defined in relation to one another, as tactics are by definition sub-components of strategies. Tactical knowledge in this field can be exemplified by the answers to questions such as:

- Is investment in CCTV a better way of reducing vehicle crime than investment in DNA analysis?

- Are 'boot camps' effective in deterring or rehabilitating young offenders?
- Does methadone prescribing reduce drug related crime?

Examples of what I mean by strategic knowledge are to be found in answers to questions such as:

- What principles should be followed in securing the legitimacy of local agencies in the eyes of their publics?
- What are effective principles for reducing social exclusion and promoting civil renewal?
- What principles should one follow in dividing resources between primary and secondary prevention?

Strategic knowledge thus comprises high level principles about crime control and order maintenance, whilst tactical knowledge comprises the answers to much more specific and detailed questions. Empirical or evaluative research tends to answer – with greater or lesser precision – tactical questions fairly directly. Research can also provide answers to strategic questions, but this is rarely done exclusively or even largely though tightly controlled evaluations. It makes more sense to think in terms of research *cumulatively* constructing and testing strategic *principles* – or middle range theories – about crime reduction. One of the weaknesses of the UK government's current approach to providing 'toolkits' is that too much attention is paid to identifying tactics that 'work', and too little attention is paid to discussion of principles of crime control[14].

The Role of Central Government

The Unintended Consequences of the Modernization Agenda

Let us now turn to an examination of some of the unintended consequences of the modernization agenda on the operation of CDRPs and the way in which a deficient approach to knowledge management has compounded these consequences. In essence the argument is that:

- Order maintenance is a highly complex process;
- But the populist nature of debate about crime precludes recognition of this complexity;
- And results in a performance management system based on 'common-sense' notions of crime control;
- These 'common-sense' notions are reinforced by the central government's approach to knowledge management, which offers tools consistent with this common sense understanding of crime control;
- And precisely those priorities and preventive options that CDRPs could effectively champion are relegated to the sidelines;
- So that key partners fail to engage with, or disengage from, CDRPs.

Complexity

Systems of crime control and order maintenance have some important institutional characteristics. Two sorts of institutional feature are worth emphasising. First, such systems work well only when they can command institutional legitimacy. For the institutions of justice, the building blocks of legitimacy are:

- Fair procedures (or procedural justice);
- Fair outcomes (or outcome justice);
- Helpfulness and concern for victims and offenders;
- Civil and even-handed treatment.

The factors that corrode legitimacy are, of course, the obverse of these: lack of respect for those passing through the system; arbitrariness; unfairness; high-handedness; rudeness; and corruption. Whilst the importance of institutional legitimacy is obvious in relation to formal policing, I would argue that the policing functions discharged by the broader local state – often through CDRPs – are also likely to work best when the agencies involved have the respect and confidence of the population.

The second institutional feature worth emphasising is the way in which systems of crime control have the capacity to communicate social meaning – to symbolise characteristics of the state and the level and nature of security that it offers (cf. Manning, 1977; Loader & Walker, 2001). Precisely what is symbolised, and how this is done, will vary from country to country, and over different historical periods. It is clear that the police – or 'the Law', as they are often called in the UK – do indeed symbolise the criminal law. The police are the most central and most visible component of our formal systems of social control, but the capacity of a private security company or a local authority body to control citizens' behaviour will depend in part on public attitudes towards those bodies. Any analysis of social control that ignores this symbolic function will be a very partial one. Any theory about order maintenance that takes a narrowly instrumental view about controlling criminal behaviour will mislead.

The Role of Central Government

The modernisation project is ill-equipped to handle complexity of this sort. It is not that any competent politician or civil servant would deny that the system displays these forms of complexity. It is just that they are on the one hand locked into the pressures of the 'here-and-now' to get *some* form of performance management system in place[15], and on the other hand, they are progressively locked into a simplified and populist discourse about law and order, to which we shall now turn.

Pressures to Populism

The increasingly populist nature of law-and-order politics (cf. Beckett, 1977; Roberts & Hough, 2002; Roberts *et al.*, 2003) is the second feature that subverts scientific rationalism when it is applied to policing. There are several possible renditions of this process[16]. The first is that, in an era of mass-media communication, the electoral system serves to select politicians whose understanding of complex social issues is about as subtle as the coverage of these issues in tabloid newspapers. This can and does occur[17], but to date, it remains the exception rather than the rule in British politics. The second is that politicians exploit the possibilities offered by the mass media to frame policy issues in ways that suit their political agenda (cf. Beckett, 1977). In other words, politicians lead the mass media to present policy issues in particular ways[18]. The third is that the media exert such power in the politics of late-modern societies that politicians have little alternative except to engage publicly with complex social issues in media-defined terms.

In a complex world, all three of these interpretations of populist processes carry some force. In particular, politicians can exercise a degree of control over the way that the mass media present events and issues – and *vice versa*. The end product is that – whether by design or constraint – politicians simplify the policy issues with which they grapple, both in their public statements and – as a consequence – in the performance management systems that they construct.

Performance Management Based on Common-Sense Notions of Crime Control

The upshot of these pressures is that the performance management systems to which the criminal justice system is exposed are based on simple – and I would argue simplistic – notions of crime control. Those responsible for the system may recognise the over-simplification, and regard it as representing a provisional 'holding position' which may be improved in the passage of time, but this does not alter the fact that complexity is being ignored. The present system of performance management has tended to:

- Over-emphasise crime control as a primary police function in contrast to order maintenance[19];
- Over-emphasise deterrent threat as the main lever for securing compliance with the law;
- Over-claim on central government capacity to exercise control over crime;
- Over-promise on crime control targets;
- Over-claim on target achievements.

Criminal justice elites – chief constables, senior judges and other senior staff in the criminal justice system – are in a position to challenge political representations of crime and disorder problems, but rarely do so. At one level, this is because they are expected and sometimes required not to stray too far, in their public pronouncements, into

The Role of Central Government

politically sensitive territory. But at the same time, they often tend to judge it to be in their organisational interests to acquiesce to the political rhetoric about crime fighting. Politicians control purse-strings and can exercise powerful patronage. Leaving this aside, statements by senior CJS figures about the complexity of their task will appear self-serving and will resonate less well with the public than ones which stress the urgency and importance of tackling crime.

Another feature of the CJS performance management systems is that they focus on crime *events* rather than on *perpetrators*[20]. This is partly a reflection of the available statistics: we know how many burglaries are recorded by the police in the country, or in a police force, or in any BCU, for example, but it is much harder to say how many active burglars are known to the authorities. But it is also likely in practice that targets requiring CDRPs to reduce the number of crime events will impel CDRPs to crime-specific approaches that ignore options such as long-term offender-based prevention, which are not offence-specific. This has important consequences for engaging in CDRP work those agencies such as education and health authorities, whose orientation is towards the processing of *people* rather than *events*.

The Government Approach to Knowledge Management

These pressures on CDRPs to pursue a particular range of offence-specific tactics are amplified by the nature of the tool-kits provided for them by central government. I suggested above that some forms of prevention are more amenable to evaluation than others, and that our knowledge is soundest about some types of offender-based secondary prevention (such as cognitive behavioural programmes for offenders) and some types of place-based primary prevention (such as crime-specific situational prevention measures). It is hard to *demonstrate* that the content of the Home Office tool-kits artificially narrows the range of preventive options considered by CDRPs. However the likelihood is that it does so.

Marginalized Preventive Options

The upshot of the combined impact of the modernization agenda and the government's approach to knowledge management is a narrowing of the range of preventive options considered by CDRPs. Crime reduction issues are cast in terms which favour subsets of tactical preventive options associated with specific categories of crime, whilst ignoring various broader strategic approaches that, on the one hand, are unlikely to contribute to target-hitting in the short term, and on the other hand are very difficult to evaluate.

This process of marginalisation reveals itself in the absence of discussion in CDRPs, or in the regional government departments with a watching brief over them, of various key issues:

- Issues of broad policing *style* are totally ignored[21];
- *Sensitive* issues such as the use of police stop-and-search tactics are avoided;
- Issues about *confidence* in local agencies and the *legitimacy* of local agencies are ignored;
- Issues to do with primary prevention (e.g. Sure Start programmes) are considered in other local arenas;
- Local authority plans for *regeneration* and economic *redevelopment* are rarely scrutinised for their

The Role of Central Government

criminogenic or preventive capacity;
- This is especially true of plans to stimulate the *late-night economy* in large cities.

Disengaging Partners

This artificial narrowing of preventive options discourages the engagement of agencies in CDRP business. Senior managers in health and education authorities or in regeneration or planning departments will, of course, notice that the government modernization agenda has had the effect of oversimplifying crime problems and solutions, and of framing them in a way that minimizes any role for their own agency.

It also seems likely that these partners will disengage from CDRPs if the key strategic issues for their colleagues in criminal justice agencies are ruled 'out of bounds'. One might expect a local partnership that was genuinely committed to maximizing compliance with the law to assess collectively, as a matter of priority, how 'the Law' in their area was perceived by its citizenry. If issues about police legitimacy and confidence in the police are sidestepped by CDRPs, the other partners will realise – with greater or lesser clarity – that the real issues in crime control are being avoided.

A further important factor behind partners' disengagement is to be found not in the *content* of targets, but in the *control* of the process. It will be remembered that CDRPs are statutorily bound to a triennial problem-solving process, where they audit crime problems, identify priority problems and develop a strategy to address these problems. This presupposes that they control the targets for local crime control. The reality now is that the content of their performance management systems has been increasingly determined by central government. This process of centralisation removes much of the rationale of the CDRPs' statutory obligations.

The Government's Solution to Underperforming CDRPS

The government solution to CDRPs' perceived underperformance has been to construct a performance management system that runs in parallel to the system to which the police are exposed. Crime reduction targets have been negotiated between CDRP members and regional government officials, within a framework set by central government. The aim is that, in aggregate, CDRPs' targets will sum to the 15% reduction in recorded crime to which the Home Office is committed over the coming three years.

The strategy would be a high-risk one – if it were not for the fact that the underlying trend in crime as measured by the BCS is still a downward one[22]. The regional government officials have no statutory powers to impose targets on CDRPs, and no powers to impose sanctions on 'failing' CDRPs. Neither CDRPs nor regional officials really have any idea of what is driving crime trends downward, and what level of investment in what activities is needed to guarantee that targets are met. Nor is there any clarity about the division of responsibility between CDRPs and local police BCUs for hitting the targets that they broadly share[23]. Many participants within the system recognise its frailties. Some regard the declaratory value of setting aspirational or 'stretch' targets as offsetting any problems inherent in the system[24]; others regard it as an elaborate form of shadow-boxing with which they must engage if they are to secure their survival within the organisation. The most likely consequences of the system are that:

The Role of Central Government

- CDRPs will continue to be constrained by an over-simple model of order maintenance;
- Formal strategies will remain focused on achieving crime-specific targets;
- Issues of real strategic importance will be ignored;
- Cynicism within CDRPs will grow, as will distrust of regional and central government officials;
- Disengagement of 'peripheral' partners will grow.

Alternative Approaches

As it settles into its third term of office, it seems unlikely that the UK government will turn its back on its preferred means of public sector reform. The safest prediction is that it will retain or extend its system of accountability to central government through centrally or regionally set targets. There are signs that central government is beginning to withdraw from the role of tight performance management. At the time of writing, a system of Local Area Agreements was being piloted, whereby previously fragmented government grants for neighbourhood development in deprived local authorities were being aggregated into a single 'pot' of money; local authorities were given great autonomy over priority setting, and were exposed to a simpler form of performance management[25]. However, in parallel with this development, the Home Office was continuing to develop what local authorities were experiencing as a more aggressive form of performance management over CDRPs.

There are things that could be done to improve the coherence of the system as it impacts on CDRPs. Perhaps the first step is to ensure that the system has some legislative coherence. There is no point in pretending that CDRPs are somehow accountable to regional and central government, and that the latter have powers to set targets for the former when in statute they do not.

The precise shape of this legislative accountability depends on the extent to which a centralised system is favoured. There is a strong argument for more decentralised performance management systems, which abandon centrally-set targets that specify a given percentage reduction in crime. National crime reduction targets have little integrity, partly because recorded crime statistics are an unreliable measure of crime, and partly because we have very little knowledge about the means of driving local crime down, or of the resources needed to do this. The difficulties in relying on a target that uses recorded crime figures (the PSA1 target to reduce crime by 15% over three years) are likely to become clear if and when the recorded crime trend is shown to be at odds with the BCS trend[26].

The government's recent strategy on prolific and priority offenders might present an opportunity to take a new approach to performance targets that could at the same time engage – or re-engage – missing CDRP partners[27]. This strategy is premised on the assumptions that a small minority of offenders account for a large amount of crime; and that these offenders typically come from problem families living in areas of intense social deprivation. They and their families are likely to be known not only to the police, but to all the partner agencies – the probation service, social services, health services, education welfare officers, and so on. Partnership work using 'people-based' strategies is the obvious way of

The Role of Central Government

tackling this particularly difficult and disadvantaged group.

The more that central and local government share a vision of CDRPs as partnerships designed to tackle the small number of persistent offenders coming from very troubled families, the more likely it is that the 'people-processing' agencies that are currently reluctant to engage in CDRP work might see the logic in doing so[28]. Targets relating to work with these groups could be designed in such a way that they complemented, rather than competed with, the targets set for these agencies by *other* government departments.

A More Radical Option

By way of conclusion, it is worth sketching a more radical decentralising option – though I recognise that there are obvious risks to any government in loosening its control over a policy area that is highly politicised.

In some areas of policy, particularly health and education, there is a groundswell of opinion that the unintended consequences of the modernisation strategy are outweighing the gains. To flog the metaphor to death, the central government 'steerers' have overestimated their navigational capacity, and keep on directing their 'rowers' on to unforeseen rocks. There are calls from the two main opposition parties to abandon national targets altogether, which are actually consistent with New Labour's ambitions for localism and civil renewal. As discussed above, the government is itself experimenting with a simpler and more decentralised form of dispensing grants and managing performance, through the Local Area Agreement system.

One can envisage a system of performance management for CDRPs in which they were required by statute, not only to prepare three-year strategies, but to set explicit targets for themselves within their strategy. In other words, central government would establish a performance management framework for CDRPs, whose precise targets would be populated at local level. Central and regional government might have a responsibility to ensure that CDRPs complied with this process, and would need reserve powers to intervene where partnerships were demonstrably failing. But normally, CDRPs would be accountable for their performance to local politicians rather than national ones.

The advantages of such a system would become clearer with the passage of time. If responsibility for crime control were seen to be a genuinely local responsibility, we might on the one hand avoid the perversity of penal populism that dogs our current justice system; and on the other, we might begin to see some truly innovative solutions that were properly tailored to local problems.

Acknowledgements

I would like to thank Gloria Laycock, Mike Maguire and Layla Skinns for comments on earlier drafts.

References and Other Publications

Audit Commission. (2002). *Community Safety Partnerships*. London: Audit Commission.

Beckett, K. (1997). *Making crime pay: Law and order in contemporary American politics.* New York: Oxford University Press.

Bowling, B. (1998). *Violent Racism.* Oxford: Clarendon Press.

Crawford, A. (1997). *The Local Governance of Crime: Appeals to Community and Partnerships.* Oxford: Oxford University Press.

Crawford, A., & Jones, M. (1995). Inter-agency co-operation and community based crime prevention. *British Journal of Criminology,* 35 (1), 17-33.

Garland, D. (2001). *The Culture of Control: crime and social order in contemporary society.* Oxford: Oxford University Press.

Gilling, D. (1994). Multi-agency crime prevention: some barriers to collaboration. *The Howard Journal,* 33 (3), 246-257.

Gilling, D. (1997). *Crime Prevention: Theory, Policy and Politics,* London: UCL Press.

Home Office. (2003). *Managing Offenders, Reducing Crime – A New Approach: Correctional Services Review,* by Patrick Carter. London: Prime Minister's Strategy Unit.

Hough, M., Hedderman, C., & Hamilton-Smith, N. (2005). The design and the development of the Reducing Burglary Initiative. In N. Hamilton-Smith (ed.), *The Reducing Burglary Initiative: design, development and delivery.* Home Office Research Study. London: Home Office.

Hough, M., & Tilley, N. (1998). *Auditing Crime and Disorder: Guidance for Local Partnerships.* No. 91. London: Home Office PRG

Hughes, G. (1996). Strategies of multi-agency crime prevention and community safety in contemporary Britain. *Studies on Crime and Crime Prevention,* 5 (2), 221-244.

Hughes, G., & Gilling, D. (2004). Mission Impossible?: The Habitus of the Community Safety Manager and the New Expertise in the Local Partnership Governance of Crime and Safety. *Criminal Justice, 4* (2), 129-149.

Liddle, M., & Gelsthorpe, L. (1994a). *Inter-Agency Crime Prevention: Organising Local Delivery.* Crime Prevention Unit Paper 52, London: Home Office.

Liddle, M., & Gelsthorpe, L. (1994b). *Crime Prevention and Inter-Agency Co-operation.* Crime Prevention Unit Paper 53, London: Home Office.

Loader, I., & N. Walker (2001). Policing as a Public Good: Reconstituting the Connections Between Policing and the State, *Theoretical Criminology,* 5(1), 9–35.

Manning, P. (1977). *Police Work: The Social Organization of Policing.* Cambridge, MA: MIT Press.

McLaughlin, E., Muncie, J., & Hughes, G. (2001). The Permanent Revolution: New Labour, New Public Management and the Modernisation of Criminal Justice. *Criminal Justice,* 1 (3), 301-317.

Osborne, D., & Gaebler, T. (1992). *Reinventing Government: How the Entrepreneurial Spirit is Transforming the Public Sector.* Reading, Massachusetts: Addison-Wesley.

Pearson, G., Blagg, H., Smith, D., Sampson, A., & Stubbs, P. (1992). Crime, community and conflict: the multi-agency approach. In D. Downes (ed.), *Unravelling Criminal Justice,* London: Macmillan.

Roberts, J., & Hough, M. (eds) (2002). *Changing Attitudes to Punishment: Public Opinion, Crime and Justice.* Cullompton: Willan Publishing.

Roberts, J.V., Stalans, L.S., Indermaur, D., & Hough, M. (2003). *Penal Populism and Public Opinion. Findings from Five Countries.* New York: Oxford University Press.

Sherman, L., Gottfredson, D., MacKenzie, D., Eck, J, Reuter, P., & Bushway, S. (1997). *Preventing Crime: What Works, What Doesn't, What's Promising: a Report to the United States Congress.* Retrieved from: http://www.ncjrs.org/works/

Tilley, N. (1992). *Safer Cities and Community Safety Strategies.* Crime Prevention Unit Paper 38, London: Home Office.

Wilson, J.Q. (1989). *Bureaucracy: What Government Agencies Do and Why they Do It.* New York: Basic Books.

Young, J. (1999). *The Exclusive Society: social exclusions, crime and difference in late modernity.* London: Sage.

Endnotes

[1]. Usually at district or borough level – an administrative unit whose population is rarely under 100,000, and rarely larger than 500,000.

[2]. This view was already emerging in 2002. The Audit Commission (2002) concluded that CDRPs had yet to demonstrate any significant impact.

[3]. Senior managers in local agencies are now required to engage in a wide range of partnerships: the overarching Local Strategic Partnership; the CDRP; the Drug Action Team; partnerships concerned with child welfare; those concerned with mental health issues; etc.

[4]. The equivalent of the regional tier in Wales is provided by the Welsh Assembly, which is a much more significant body.

[5]. For example, many local authorities in London boroughs set up Police Monitoring Units which pursued an aggressively oppositional approach to police reform.

[6]. See, for example, the Carter Review of the correctional services (Home Office, 2003).

[7]. For example, some companies let local managers have extensive freedom over their operations – provided that they meet a single target specified in terms of growth of profits.

8. The idea of earned autonomy is best exemplified in the system whereby hospitals can achieve foundation status if they achieve a given level of performance.

9. 'Law and order' is not the only politically sensitive policy area, of course. Health and education can be political mine-fields, and target-setting for these highly complex systems can have demonstrably perverse effects. However, the criminal justice system exemplifies public sector work at its most complex, reflecting the interleaving of moral and legal systems of social control.

10. This is not surprising, given the perfectly proper concern with securing better value for money. Though under-investment can be a major source of financial waste, the mind-set of modernisers is that public services generally fail to make good enough use of the resources they already have.

11. For details of the Cochrane Collaboration, see: http://www.cochrane.org ;
and for details of the Campbell Collaboration, see: http://www.aic.gov.au/campbellcj

12. The Maryland Scale assigns evaluative studies into one of five categories, according to the form of experimental control that is used to help to attribute causality. The highest score is reserved for studies that use randomised controlled trial methods. Systematic reviews usually exclude all studies that fall into the lowest two categories, and some include only the top, or the top two, categories.

13. Sherman *et al.* (1997) define programmes that work as follows: "These are programs that we are reasonably

certain of preventing crime or reducing risk factors for crime in the kinds of social contexts in which they have been evaluated, and for which the findings should be *generalizable* to similar settings in other places and times. Programs coded as 'working' by this definition must have at least two level 3 evaluations with statistical significance tests showing effectiveness *and* the preponderance of all available evidence supporting the same conclusion."

[14]. The US Department of Justice's COPS Guides (Problem-Oriented Guides for Police) pay rather more attention to issues of principle, and to the factors that underlie success or failure.

[15]. An important process here is the triennial Comprehensive Spending Review, in which the Treasury requires spending departments to offer evidence in support of their plans, and quantitative performance indicators by which to judge success. The pressure on Home Office ministers to sign up to a "dumbed down" set of targets in exchange for budgets is overwhelming.

[16]. A full explanation of the pressures to populism are well beyond the scope of this paper; but it would need to take account of the shrinking capacity of the sovereign state in late-modern industrialised societies, and that paradoxical response to this process that involves reaffirmation by the state of its crime control capabilities (cf. Garland, 2001; Young, 1999).

[17]. The 'One Nation' party in Australia under Pauline Hanson's leadership is a possible example.

[18]. Beckett's thesis is that the US political rhetoric about criminals as outsiders was politically led, and served to support a separate neo-conservative policy agenda of paring down public expenditure on social security and welfare programmes.

[19]. A complicating factor in this analysis is the British government's recent rediscovery of anti-social behaviour as a policy issue. One 'reading' of the emergence of the current anti-social behaviour strategy is that it is a necessary corrective – both politically and substantively – to a decade of over-focusing on crime control. Another is that its origins are in government thinking about civil renewal, and that it has been only superficially integrated in crime control policy.

[20]. Currently, the key target for local police areas and for their CDRPs (PSA 1) is to reduce the number of crimes in a specified group of crime categories by at least 15% over the coming three years. Some agencies, notably the prison and probation services, are subject to a range of offender-related targets, of course.

[21]. Of course, it might be argued, especially by the police, that policing style is an *operational* issue for the police to grapple with by themselves. Alternatively, it might be argued that policing style is a *political* issue, to be dealt with by the Home Secretary, or else by the local police authority. But if CDRPs are serious about controlling crime and disorder, they need to articulate the principles that inform their strategies, and they need to ensure that these are consistent with the policing principles of their police partners.

22. The British Crime Survey shows that most categories of crime in England and Wales have been falling since the mid-1990s.

23. In London, CDRPs and the corresponding police command units share the same crime reduction targets. Elsewhere targets are similar, but not necessarily the same.

24 Stretch targets are those that the workforce would generally regard as unattainable, or at least very hard to attain. They probably make some sense for organisations that have gone stale, and whose performance is some way behind the 'market leaders'.

25. http://www.odpm.gov.uk/stellent/groups/odpm_localgov/documents/page/odpm_locgov_029989.hcsp

26. The 15% reduction is only for those categories of recorded crime that can also be measured by the British Crime Survey.

27. The Home Office launched a Prolific and Other Priority Offenders Strategy in July 2004 (see http://www.crimereduction.gov.uk/ppo).

28. This is not to dismiss the difficult and complex issues about the sharing by different agencies of confidential information about these families.

COMMUNITY INTELLIGENCE IN THE POLICING OF COMMUNITY SAFETY

Martin Innes and Colin Roberts

Introduction

Information is an important prerequisite in the delivery of community safety. For it is information and the analysis of this data that enables the contours of the risks and threats to which a community is exposed to be calibrated, and the ways of effectively and efficiently targeting the causes and consequences of these risks and threats to be identified. In the absence of a sufficient quantity of high quality information it becomes more likely that the wrong problems will be targeted, their causes misdiagnosed or inappropriate solutions implemented. In this chapter, we are going to concern ourselves with thinking about the police role in community safety efforts and the approaches that the police use to collect information that feeds into defining which problems they should focus resources on. In so doing, our aim is to develop the emerging concept of 'community intelligence', propose a community intelligence methodology applicable for agencies involved in community safety work, and to use some empirical data to show some of the intriguing findings resulting from the application of this methodology.

Terms of Engagement

Prior to examining the notion of community intelligence in more detail it is first appropriate to clarify a few key issues that relate to and establish a context for the ensuing discussion. Firstly, the notion of community safety is a necessarily nebulous concept encompassing a wide range of diverse activities. The levels of safety perceived and experienced by any individual community are dependent upon a wide variety of factors that can be divided into direct and indirect kinds. Factors directly affecting experiences and perceptions of safety include crime, disorder, and traffic management. But any such experiences and perceptions can be amplified or attenuated by broader processes of social change, including changes in neighbourhood demography, economic change or inter-community tensions, that have more of an indirect effect. Perhaps even more problematic is the very notion of community itself. Much has been written and said about the problematic notion of community, debates that we do not intend to reheat here, except to say that in any practical programme of interventions it is vital to define clearly and demarcate precisely what community is having its safety interests addressed. Whether it be a geographic community, a faith community or a community of interest, it is imperative to establish whose risks and threats are the focus.

In terms of the delivery of community safety, it has been widely recorded that a range of agencies and organizations are now routinely involved in efforts to promote and manufacture improvements in safety in communities (Crawford, 1997; Garland, 2001). Whilst recognizing this to be the case, in this chapter we are focused particularly upon aspects of the police role. Delimiting the focus of our enquiry in this way can be explained on two grounds. Firstly, given the particular interest of this chapter in the informational base of community safety efforts, police probably remain the most influential institutional actor in terms of supplying the

Community Intelligence in Policing

crime and incident data upon which such efforts are founded. As Ericson & Haggerty (1997) show, police are increasingly cast as 'information brokers', supplying data to a range of other private and public sector agencies. In spite of the widespread recognition that the data that police supply is a manufactured artefact of their organizational policies and practices, rather than any real reflection of the nature and extent of the safety problems that exist across different communities, the information that they have available remains probably the most important source of material. A second justification for focusing upon police information in community safety is that, because they have a long history of seeking to manage and apply information to community problems, they have comparatively well defined processes and systems. This enables the uniqueness of the emerging community intelligence methodologies that are the main focus of the chapter to be illuminated. The hope is that in illuminating the nature of these differences, all those agencies involved in community safety activities will be able to see how the concept of community intelligence and the methodologies that are starting to emerge in relation to it can help them to think in a more structured and defined way about what they are doing.

In terms of police involvement in community safety efforts, we can differentiate between two key types of information that they routinely make use of. Intelligence is prospective information in that, when subject to some form of analysis, it is information that gives a sense of how to act at some point in the future, under certain conditions, in order to achieve particular objectives. In contrast to which evaluative data is retrospective, in that through analysis it allows an assessment to be reached in terms of how successful some set of past actions have been in achieving a defined objective. Differentiating between intelligence and evaluation in this way is important because to date, with notable exceptions, the social research community has probably been more engaged with concepts and processes of evaluation rather than thinking about how the tools and techniques they are familiar with can be applied to intelligence generation. Indeed, going further, we would argue that a lot of the time there is a basic confusion present with what is essentially evaluative data being used as intelligence to plan future activities; when, as we will show in due course, constructing the key task as strictly one of generating intelligence produces some important new insights.

The definition of intelligence provided above deliberately seeks to strip away a lot of the perjorative connotations associated with the concept of intelligence in the policing sector. Thanks to its history, intelligence as a concept routinely connotes notions of covert, secretive and politicized social control. Because of the ways in which it has been used and abused, it has come to be seen as part of the dirty work of democratic policing (Innes, 2006). If we look at other organizational settings though, intelligence has less perjorative associations. Many organizations use intelligence as a form of prospective information, providing foresight about how to act effectively and efficiently in the future, given certain conditions. In this respect intelligence can be contrasted with evaluation. Evaluative data is retrospective – concerned with the *ex post facto* calibration of the impact of some intervention that has already happened.

Community Intelligence in Policing

Community Intelligence and Laminated Intelligence Methodologies

The notion of community intelligence (commtel) is one that has been around in policing circles for several years now, although it has been employed in a variety of different ways. This non-specific quality results largely as a result of commtel being defined in terms of what it is not. That is, in terms of its current discursive deployment, it is used as a generic term to account for a range of intelligence data that does not fit the traditional types of intelligence that police have accessed. So whereas more traditional types of intelligence tend to be gleaned from covert sources, where access restrictions of some kind must be circumvented, community intelligence tends to be open source material.

In two recent studies a greater sense of conceptual precision to the notion of commtel has been sought. Innes et al. (2005a) differentiate four key master-types of intelligence: crime intelligence; criminal intelligence; community intelligence; and contextual intelligence. Developing this approach, Innes et al. (2005b) conducted interviews with a range of police staff to capture their understandings of what does and does not warrant being classified as community intelligence. They provide a synthetic analysis of these accounts to arrive at the following definition:

> Community intelligence is information acquired either directly or indirectly from a community, that when analysed can be used to inform policing interventions. The information can come from a variety of sources, but it will inform police about the views, needs and expectations of a community and the risks and threats posed to it or by it, either in terms of internal or external issues. (Innes et al.,

2005b: 2)

The significance of this definition is that it clearly differentiates commtel from other kinds of intelligence. Particularly important in this respect is the introduction of a notion of the 'direction of risk'. That is, community intelligence will provide, albeit maybe in very imprecise terms, some indication of who is constituting a risk to whom. This may be on the basis of inter-community or intra-community tensions.

Under this framework care is taken to differentiate commtel from criminal intelligence and crime intelligence, where the former is data on the law-breaking activities of particular actors and the latter is focused upon particular incidents or series of incidents.

Distinguishing between commtel and contextual intelligence is especially important in order that commtel as a concept retains some sense of definition and is not used as a short-hand phrase to cover all sorts of data that do not fit under the extant crime and criminal classifications. Contextual intelligence is that data which provides insight into the situation or contextual conditions which contribute to the make-up of a place or its people. This approach differentiates commtel from other kinds of intelligence data police use and casts it as an additional stream of data that police can draw upon in planning their interventions to enhance community safety.

Traditional approaches to crime and criminal intelligence have tended to be based upon the use of Covert Human Intelligence Sources (CHISs). Typically the information that such individuals provide to police gains its value from the proximity that they have to criminal activity. Police typically have to engage in some form of trading relationship to obtain the information (cf. Innes, 1999; Innes & Sheptycki, 2004; Dunnighan & Norris, 1999).

More recently though, police have started to innovate and adopt different methods for accessing different kinds of intelligence. These changes need to be related to structural reconfigurations in the constitution of society which have been summarized as the emergence of an 'information age' (Castells, 2000). In essence, in relation to the impact that this has had upon agencies involved in policing and community safety work, a shift has occurred that can be characterized as a move from 'information deficit' to 'information surplus'. Particularly consequential in this respect has been the development of the internet and the diversification of mass media. So whereas previously the key policing problematic was to be able to gain access to restricted data, this has now been supplemented by a need to be able to search through the vast amounts of data that are publicly available – what in police discourse is referred to as 'open source' intelligence.

As part of their response to this and other social trends police have started to rethink their approaches to intelligence. One methodology that they have increasingly adopted for accessing and processing community intelligence data, particularly in their relations with minority and vulnerable communities, is based upon developing 'strategic contacts' with community leaders and opinion formers (Innes, 2006). This strategic contact methodology is a way of engaging with communities and obtaining information from them where historically relations may have been difficult. If the CHIS methodology through which they have traditionally accessed crime and criminal intelligence works by establishing intelligence as a commodity possessed of an exchange value, the strategic contact method is based upon developing a small number of 'strong ties' with key individuals across particularly important community groups.

Whilst acknowledging the benefits that can be accrued from generating strategic contacts, Innes (2006) identifies a number of limitations of any such approach based upon the logic of Granovetter's (1982) work on 'the strength of weak ties.' Granovetter proposed his approach as a solution to what can be termed the 'diffusion of information' problem. That is, how is it best to access different bits of information that are distributed over a wide social space. He found, through empirical testing, that individuals able to activate a network of loosely coupled contacts in their information search were more effective than those reliant on a smaller number of 'deeper' contacts. A permutation of this diffusion of information problem seems to be one encountered relatively frequently in the policing of community safety. That is, how do you bring together information held by a number of individuals to map the risks and threats posed to or by a community, which is the basis of community intelligence as defined previously? For whilst the strategic contact methodology can produce such intelligence, based as it is upon developing a limited number of 'strong ties', it may not be the most appropriate way of organizing to perform this function.

Set against this approach we are now going to outline the key features of a community intelligence methodology. It is an approach to intelligence that seeks to establish the degree of collective or shared knowledge located in a community, based upon systematic scanning of a community to try and detect what different individuals

Community Intelligence in Policing

know about criminal, disorderly and problematic behaviour.

Seeking to develop a network of weak ties for the purposes of garnering intelligence provides a radically different approach to the problem of how police should acquire information about the problematic issues that they should focus their resources upon. Indeed, it runs counter to many of the expectations and culturally embedded assumptions of police culture and its expectations about who knows about criminal behaviour. That a small number of people commit the majority of crime is now well established and following on from that is the assumption that only a comparatively small number of individuals will have detailed knowledge of crime and its conduct. The mistake here though is to draw the inference that 'ordinary people' will not be aware of a range of behavioural and environmental cues that rouse their suspicions. This needs to be set against a backdrop where we are increasingly aware of the fact that community safety is not corroded by crime alone, but that anti-social behaviour and physical disorder can function as potent signals of risk (Innes, 2004). So in terms of being able to focus efforts on the things that matter to communities, this approach seems to have a particular contribution to make.

In proposing this community intelligence methodology, our argument is not that it should supplant the other two methodologies already in use (CHIS and Strategic Contacts); rather it should supplement them. Each of the three methodologies discussed is effective in accessing different types of data that are more or less suited for a range of different purposes. On this basis it might be helpful to think in terms of developing a 'laminated intelligence methodologies' (LIM) approach. By

LIM we mean that each of the three different approaches to gaining intelligence can be understood as making a unique and individual contribution to the police's efforts to construct a picture of the range of different risks, threats and hazards that different communities and individuals are subject to. In everyday usage, the concept of 'lamination' implies greater resilience than any one component of a system would have individually; lamination is a process of strengthening what would otherwise be comparatively weak materials. This is precisely what an organization employing all of these intelligence methodologies could expect - a stronger and more robust intelligence system. Because each of the respective methodologies has particular strengths in terms of the issues that police might have an interest in, by integrating them a more coherent and more detailed picture can be assembled.

Community Intelligence Capture

The community intelligence methodology outlined above was originally designed as part of the National Reassurance Policing Project. Established by the Association of Chief Police Officers and the Home Office, the NRPP was tasked to design and test a policing style that would reduce public fear of crime and increase trust and confidence in the police. A recently published Home Office impact evaluation of what happened across the 16 trial sites records that significant impacts were achieved across a number of indicators (Tuffin *et al.*, 2006). The theoretical engine for Reassurance Policing was to focus upon tackling signal crimes and disorders, as these are the incidents that have most impact in generating fear (cf. Innes, 2004). In order to do this though, the police needed a systematic methodology enabling them to identify what kinds of incidents were functioning to signal risk to individual communities.

In order to address this issue, the community intelligence model and two key data capture tools were designed by the authors of this chapter. Drawing upon a variety of principles derived from the social science methodology literature, these tools were designed to encourage police to capture community intelligence in a systematic and structured manner. The first tool was a simple notion of having a 'conversation with a purpose'. The object of this tool was to ensure that whenever police staff interacted with a member of the public who was not a victim, witness or suspect to some other incident, they saw it as an opportunity to check on any concerns that the citizen might have and if there were any, to collect intelligence upon it. In so doing, the aim was to ensure that police do not treat such encounters as unimportant or irrelevant, but as a mechanism to improve their knowledge about an area and its problems. Having a conversation with a purpose (or CWAPing – as it was described to police) with a member of the public encouraged officers to seek information about:

- *WHAT* problems are driving insecurity (including all crime, physical and social disorder types) and what other issues they are connected to;
- *WHERE* these problems are located;
- *WHEN* these problems occur;
- *WHY* they are having an impact upon the individual or community, in terms of causing fear, anger or changes in behaviour;
- *WHO* is known to be involved in causing these problems;

- HOW effective police and their partners are perceived to be in acting against these problems.

CWAP is a basic tool to improve the community intelligence feed into police systems that does not require any special equipment and very limited training. Subsequently a more sophisticated software package was written to provide a more advanced data capture and analysis tool. This was labeled the 'intelligence based Neighbourhood Security Interview' (i-NSI). Running on tablet PCs, i-NSI provides a structured interview tool that encourages people to identify the key problems in their neighbourhoods, similar in principle to other Computer Assisted Personal Interviewing packages. The i-NSI process starts by defining a territory where intelligence is required. The area is then subdivided into equally sized cells, a step that provides what equates to a sampling frame for collecting intelligence. Individuals are then selected for interview and these interactions are conducted by local police staff (either constables or PCSOs).

The data from across all the interviews conducted in an area is then analysed to establish the problems and locations where multiple interviewees are describing the same sorts of problems as occurring. This mode of analysis works by effecting a form of data triangulation that establishes how much confidence should be assigned to the data. In effect, the more people that identify a problem as occurring at a particular location, then the greater the degree of confidence we can have that this is a 'real' and significant issue.

A particular feature of the i-NSI methodology is that, informed by the research on signal crimes and disorders, it seeks to collect experiential data and knowledge, rather

Community Intelligence in Policing

than the attitudinal data that is the focus of more traditional fear of crime surveys. The questions and script of i-NSI is specifically designed to try and elicit from people information about problems in their neighbourhoods (or further afield) that they have either encountered themselves or been told about by others.

In order to give a sense of i-NSI and how it operates in terms of collecting and analysing community intelligence, some extracts from a report on Burnley in Lancashire are provided below. The report concerned was based upon 30 interviews with members of the public living in Trinity Ward.

In Figure 1, a basic screenshot from the software is provided. As can be seen, this is a fairly high resolution map. Superimposed on this is a pink line marking the ward boundary and a series of blue cells that are used for sampling purposes to ensure full intelligence coverage is achieved. Each cell must be populated by a certain number of i-NSI interviews with sources drawn from whatever the target population is in order to generate sufficient levels of intelligence and ensure coverage across the area. The sample of respondents across these cells is used to identify systematically community intelligence sources, whether it be the community as a whole, a faith community or demographic sub-group.

Figure 2 illustrates one analytic product that can be derived from operationalising the methodology. It shows how people living in this part of Burnley understand the different geographic communities present in the area. As can be seen, rather than focusing upon the political boundaries of a ward, they see the composition of the area as being far more complex, comprised of a number of

Community Safety: Innovation and Evaluation

Figure 1. Trinity Ward in Burnley.

Community Intelligence in Policing

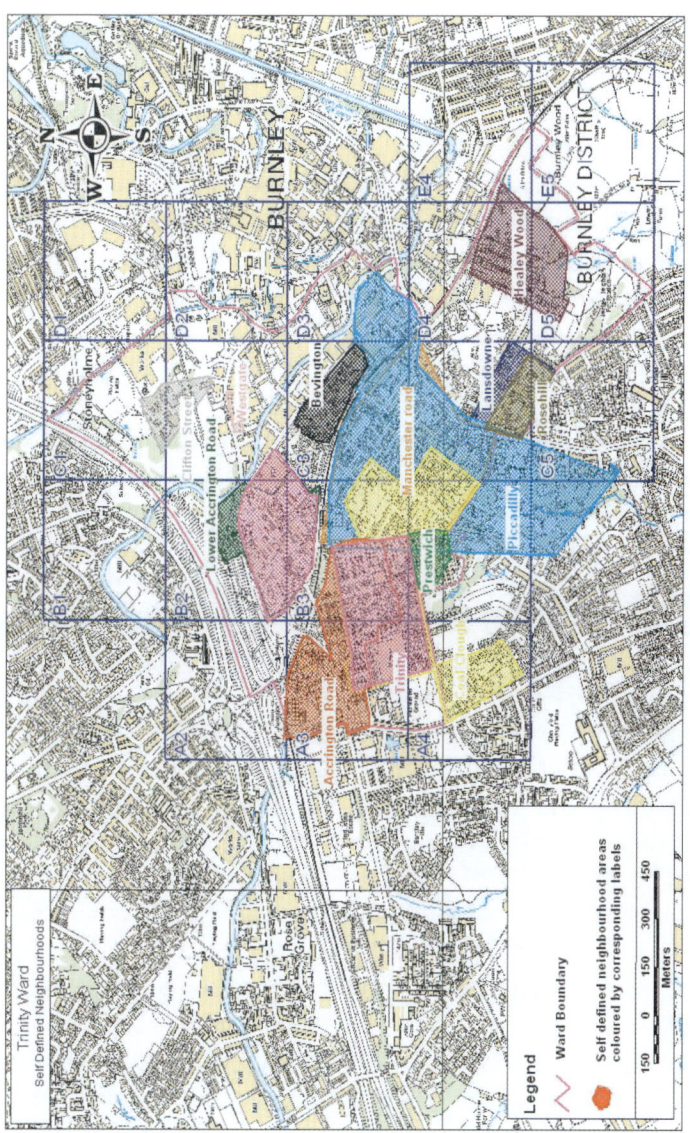

Figure 2. Symbolic Communities in Trinity Ward.

distinct communities of identity. The boundaries of these 'symbolic communities' (Hunter, 1974) are calculated by a software algorithm that takes data from the different interviews and looks for where individual respondents have marked similar boundary lines on the maps they are presented with. A potential use for such analysis is in informing engagement strategies or simply understanding which groups inhabit an area and how they relate to one another. The importance of understanding the make-up of communities is often overlooked in efforts to improve public security. It is important in terms of providing insight into establishing precisely what the problem to be addressed is. For example, for a programme designed to reduce insecurity, better understanding the make-up of local communities may assist in identifying whether the objective of any intervention should be to reduce fear of crime a little across a large number of people, or whether what is actually required is a large reduction in fear for a minority of the population. Defining the problem with a greater degree of precision such as this identifies how different types of intervention may be necessitated.

Figure 3 moves the focus of analysis away from respondent self-identification of communities, to plot all the data on the problems they are concerned about from the interviews that were conducted. The data is plotted in three forms: 'points' (for specific problems at specific locations); 'lines' (where a problem occurs along a road); and 'areas' (where problems take place across a location, i.e. a park). Of particular importance are where the larger red dots are plotted. The larger dots represent multiple respondents identifying a problem at a location. As can be seen from this mode of representation, the incidents of crime, social disorder and physical disorder around which

Community Intelligence in Policing

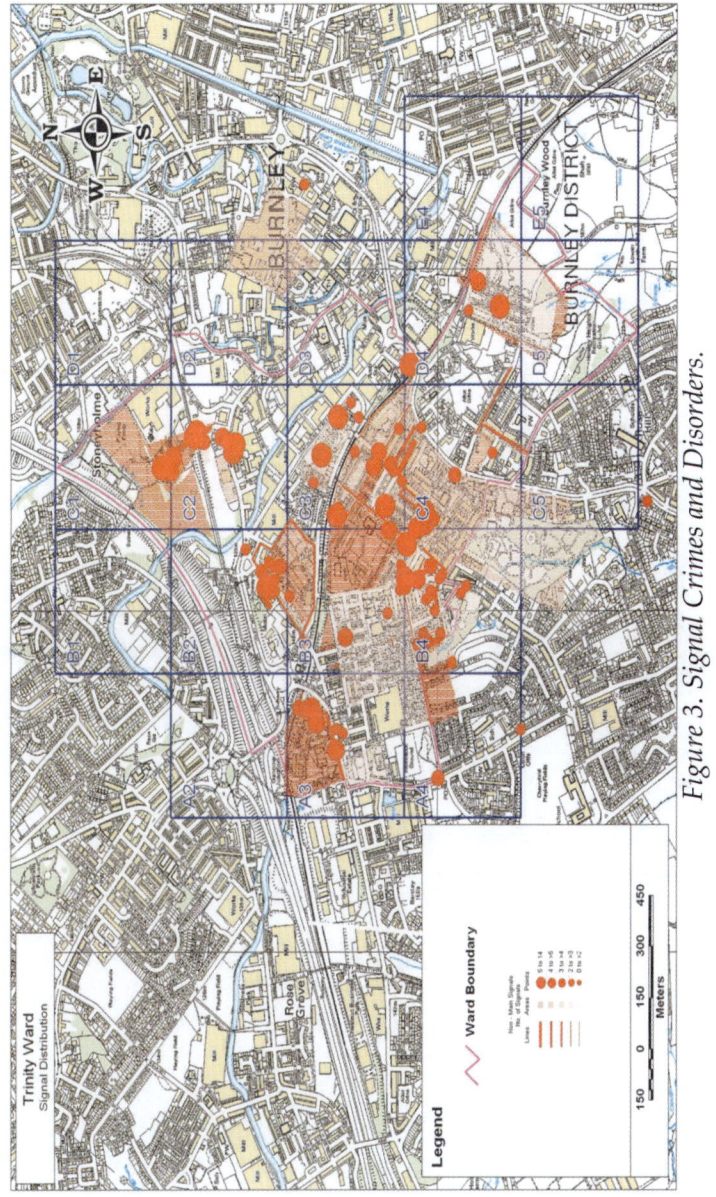

Figure 3. Signal Crimes and Disorders.

Community Safety: Innovation and Evaluation

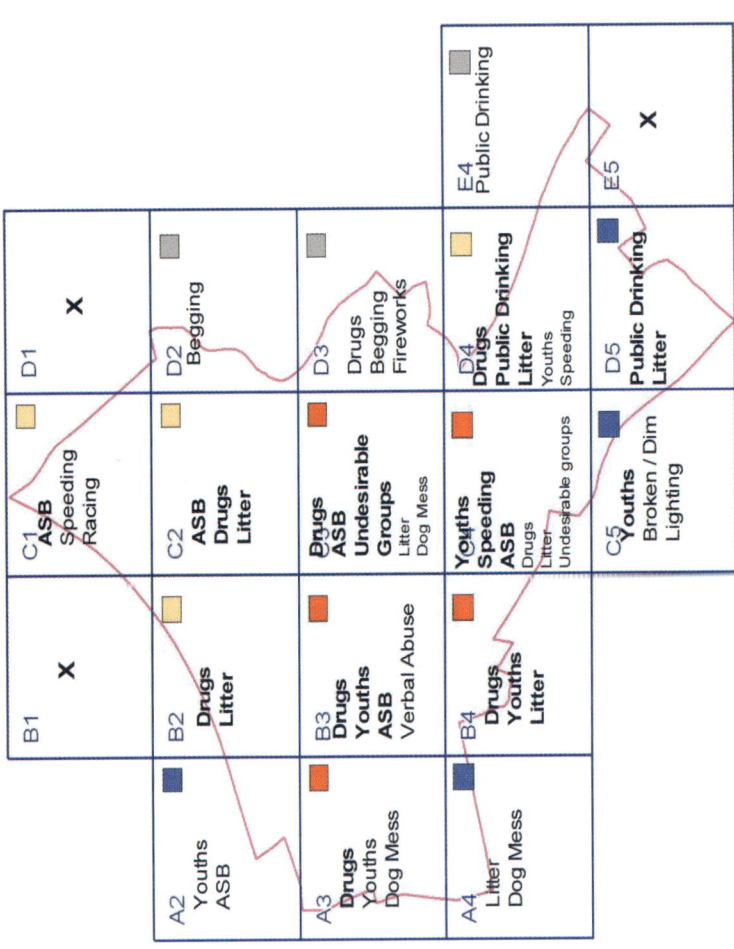

Figure 4 'Hot Cells' Analysis.

concern gravitated in this area are not evenly distributed, but tend to cluster in particular locations.

The interesting thing about this analysis is just how many of these larger dots there are, suggesting that actually perceptions of risk and threat in an area do have a collective dimension to them. There is a fairly strong degree of coherence in terms of local people identifying particular locations and incidents as problematic.

Figure 4 provides an analytic representation of what the top signal crimes and signal disorders are for each of the cells in this territory, together with the problems that are, according to the members of the public interviewed, directly connected to them.

In the corner of each of the cells is a coloured marker denoting the respective levels of signal strength and coherency in each cell. The notion of signal coherency is used as a measure of the number of people affected by a particular signal event. The greater the number of people affected by a problem, the more 'coherent' the signal is said to be. This is different from the strength of a signal which is concerned with the impact that an event has upon an individual's perceptions of vulnerability. Thus, in Figure 4, those cells where the marker is red denote the micro-locations in the ward where the signals are comparatively intense and concentrated, and often the signal radiates out from these locations to drive insecurity across a much wider geographic area. As can be seen, there are strongly coherent signal crimes and disorders present in cells: A3; B3; C3; B4 and C4. These are the micro-locations in the ward that community safety efforts should be targeted towards in order to achieve maximum impact upon levels of public security.

In each of the cells are listed the signal types that are functioning as key drivers of insecurity in that particular micro-location. Problems in emboldened capitals are the principal signals, whilst those in ordinary typeface are ancillary problems, identified by the interviews as being in some way connected to the main signals. Importantly, it can be seen that the key drivers of insecurity differ across the cells, although drug related crime and disorder feature especially prominently. So, in the micro-location correlating with cell A3, drugs and crime and disorder involving young people constitute the main signals present; whereas, for example, in cell C4 public insecurity gravitates more around youth-related disorder, anti-social behaviour and traffic management issues relating to the prevalence of young people racing, using cars and motorbikes.

The particular significance of this analysis is in how it can be contrasted with more orthodox techniques employed in the community safety field. Standard survey instruments might be used to identify top level issues at a ward level, but ordinarily would not provide the level of granularity to differentiate the problem locations and the signal events located therein with such precision. This enhanced precision and problem definition is significant, though, in as far as it enables resources to be targeted to those problems and locations that are really impacting upon levels of neighbourhood security.

Conclusion

This chapter has sought to do three things. Firstly, it has introduced the concept of community intelligence, illuminating how thinking in terms of commtel can encourage police and other agencies involved in community safety efforts to think carefully and precisely about the data and information they make use of in the planning and conducting of their interventions. An important distinction has been drawn between forms of intelligence as prospective data and more retrospective forms of evaluative data. Secondly, developing this argument, a concept of 'laminated intelligence methodologies' has been developed in an effort to stimulate thinking about how different sorts of intelligence data can be related to each other. Three distinct methodologies for accessing different forms of intelligence have been identified and it has been suggested that these make different contributions to understanding the range of risks and threats that individuals and communities are subject to. By using all three different methodologies, agencies involved in trying to make communities safer are better placed to build up an accurate picture of the problems affecting places and their people. The strength derived from adopting a laminated approach is that findings derived from one mode of intelligence can be cross-referenced with intelligence data from the other two methodologies to check its reliability and validity.

To date, it is community intelligence that is the least developed form of intelligence data in terms of its integration within contemporary community safety practices. Consequently, in the latter parts of this chapter a fairly detailed description of a new commtel methodology was provided. The approach outlined is based upon a systematic scan of a community or territory to establish the degree of knowledge about problems and their impact across an area or population. So whereas the CHIS and strategic contact methodologies are structured by the demand or supply of intelligence, the community intelligence methodology outlined herein simply takes a sweep of a community at fixed points in time, in order to establish what are the risks and threats currently posed by or to a defined group of people.

The emphasis in this chapter has been upon the role of the police in community safety efforts, but the intention has been that the sorts of issues and considerations discussed should be relevant to all agencies involved in community safety work. A good quantity of high quality intelligence is a vital precursor for all those involved in the provision of community safety if their efforts are to be efficient and effective.

References

Castells, M. (2000). *The Rise of the Network Society*. Oxford: Blackwells.

Crawford, A. (1997). *The Local Governance of Crime*. Oxford: Clarendon Press.

Dunnighan, C., & Norris, C. (1999). The detective, the snout and the Audit Commission: The real costs in using informants. *The Howard Journal*, 38: 67-86.

Ericson, R., & Haggerty, K. (1997). *Policing the Risk Society*. Oxford: Clarendon Press.

Garland, D. (2001). *The Culture of Control*. Oxford: Oxford University Press.

Granovetter, M. (1982). The strength of weak ties: a network theory revisited. *Sociological Theory*, 1: 201-33.

Hunter, A. (1974). *Symbolic Communities*. Chicago: University of Chicago Press.

Innes, M. (1999). Professionalising the Police Informant: the British experience. *Policing and Society*, 9/1: 357-383.

Innes, M. (2004). Signal crimes and signal disorders: notes on deviance as communicative action. *British Journal of Sociology*, 55/3: 335-55.

Innes, M. (2006). Policing uncertainty: countering terror through community intelligence and democratic policing, *Annals of the American Academy of Political and Social Science*, 605, 222-41.

Innes, M., & Sheptycki, J. (2004). From detection to disruption: some consequences of intelligence-led crime control in the UK. *International Criminal Justice Review*, 14: 1-14.

Innes, M., Fielding, N., & Cope, N. (2005a). The appliance of science: the theory and practice of crime intelligence analysis. *British Journal of Criminology*, 45/1: 39-57.

Innes, M., Roberts, C., & Maltby, S. (2005b). *Community Intelligence: a Report to the National Community Tensions Team*. (unpublished)

Tuffin, R., Morris, J., & Poole, A. (2006). *An Evaluation of the Impact of the National Reassurance Policing Programme*. London: Home Office.

CRIME AND DISORDER AUDITS AND THE PROBLEMS OF BECOMING TOO LOCALISED

R.I. Mawby

Introduction

The introduction of Crime and Disorder Partnerships may be viewed as a victory for localism (Loveday, 2001). In the face of an ever more centralised state and a Home Office that, under David Blunkett, appeared to be circulating more and more advice to local agencies, the 1998 Crime and Disorder Act in England and Wales offered a degree of local independence. The establishment of local multi-agency crime and disorder groups, Crime and Disorder Reduction Partnerships (CDRPs), with the expectation that they would produce regular audits of crime and disorder and use these to inform strategy, and the creation of CDRP family groupings (Home Office, 2000; Povey *et al.*, 2001), suggested that CDRPs would be able to assess their crime and disorder problems compared with other similar areas and introduce policies at the local level that were in response to these and thus not necessarily the same as the policies implemented by other CDRPs.

Subsequently, however, the practical limitations to local autonomy have been spelt out. Central government has proffered increasing amounts of 'advice' to partnerships (Garland, 2002) that has had the effect of setting their agendas. At the same time, increased central directions to the police, the most powerful agency within the partnership structure (Crawford, 1998; Hughes, 1998; Gilling, 2000) have severely restricted partnerships' attempts to set their own agendas.

What has seldom been confronted, however, is the uncomfortable possibility that in certain respects localism may have been taken too far, and that there are inherent disadvantages to small, localised audits and strategy developments. One aspect of this is the differing research strategies and methodologies deployed by CDRPs in carrying out audits, such that, despite the creation of family groupings (Hall et al., 2003),[1] and more recently 'closest relatives', very little data exists that allows CDRPs to draw direct comparisons with similar areas. Here, however, on the basis of our work on the 2001 and 2004 audits in one rural county of England, I want to develop this theme and consider the limitations of audits that are restricted by geographical boundaries. Essentially I shall argue that assessing the crime and disorder problems of individual CDRPs and responding with appropriate policies is sometimes made more difficult because the public, including victims and offenders, are not constrained by CDRP borders. To illustrate this, I shall take three practical examples:

- Victims who move: the problem when being attacked leads victims to leave the CDRP area;
- Citizens as commuters: when members of the public, including offenders, cross CDRP boundaries on a temporary basis;
- Visitors as a disenfranchised community: the problem of identifying the separate problems encountered or caused by tourists.

Before that, however, the following sections briefly describe the auditing process in which I was involved and the CDRP areas included.

---

[1] See also www.homeoffice.gov.uk/rds/pdfs2/hosb703sup1.pdf

The Auditing Process

CDRPs were created following the 1998 Crime and Disorder Act, building on the earlier Morgan (1991) Report. The Act required local authorities, the police, health authorities, police authorities and probation to work together to address crime and disorder problems in their area. Specifically, the Act placed a statutory duty on CDRPs, on a three yearly basis, to:

- Produce an audit of crime and disorder for each district, borough and unitary local authority in England and Wales;
- Publish a crime and disorder strategy based on the audit and consultation process.

These requirements were renewed in the 2002 Police Reform Act.

The first phase of audits was produced in 1998/99. This was followed by a second round of audits in 2001 and a third in 2004. This paper is based on audits of people in Cornwall carried out in 2001 (see especially Mawby, 2003) and 2004 (for some preliminary findings, see Mawby, 2005). The six Crime and Disorder Reduction Partnership areas (CDRPs) on mainland Cornwall[2] worked in partnership with the present author in collating data for the audits.

The audits concentrated in each year on six research strategies:

---

[2] The seventh CDRP in Cornwall covers the Isles of Scilly and is excluded from this discussion.

- Analysis of police data;
- Collation of other secondary data;
- The Cornwall Crime Survey (CCS), a survey of a random sample of electors from each CDRP area;
- The Cornwall Business Crime Survey (CBCS), a survey of local businesses across the county;
- Surveys of local politicians and local government officers (2001 only);
- The Cornwall Youth Crime Survey (CYCS), a survey of youths in local schools (2004 only);
- Canvassing the views of key players in the area.

Cornwall

The county is comprised of six districts: Caradon, Carrick, Kerrier, North Cornwall, Penwith and Restormel, each with between 18 and 23 wards. For policing purposes, it forms one of four Police Command Units (PCUs) within the Devon and Cornwall Police Force Area. It has an overall population of about 497,000. Cornwall is known to most people as a tourist base, but is also a rural county with high levels of poverty and deprivation.

Cornwall is clearly a rural county. As Table 1 indicates, only nine towns in Cornwall have populations in excess of 10,000 and three districts have only one such town. The only sizeable city in the vicinity is Plymouth (with a population of a quarter of a million) in neighbouring Devon. Table 1 also charts the population density in each district. This is 0.1381248 people per 1,000 hectares in the county as a whole, being highest in Restormel and Penwith and lowest in North Cornwall.

Community Safety: Innovation and Evaluation

Table 1. Towns in Cornwall with Populations in Excess of 10,000 and Population Density.

	Main towns		Pop. per 1000 ha
Caradon	Saltash		0.1166326
Carrick	Truro	Falmouth	0.1859823
Kerrier	Camborne	Redruth	0.1931181
North Cornwall	Bodmin		0.0665267
Penwith	Penzance		0.2026019
Restormel	Newquay	St Austell	0.2087405

However, Cornwall is also an impoverished county (Cemlyn *et al.*, 2002; Williams, 2003), as illustrated through its accreditation with government Objective One status, signifying that, as one of the poorest areas of the country, it is eligible for significant European Union funding [3]

It is often difficult to quantify poverty in rural areas, where the criteria used in urban settings may be inappropriate. For example, the proportion of rented housing is lower, and high rise blocks commonly associated with deprivation are less evident, and where rural transport systems are inadequate a car may be even more of a necessity than a luxury. Socio-economic data for Cornwall illustrate these points. The proportion of car owners, for example, at 79.5% is above the average for England and Wales (73.2%), as is the proportion of owner-occupiers (72.3% compared with 68.9%). On the other

---

[3] When EU structural funds were last reviewed, Cornwall was one of only three parts of the UK to be awarded Objective One status, due to its exceptionally low GDP per head of population, which the EU takes as the best single measure of poverty.

hand, the standard of housing, as measured by homes without central heating, is low, 18.3% compared with 8.5% in England and Wales, and unemployment levels also exceed the national average.

Tourism is also a crucial feature of the local economy. While the juxtaposition of deprivation and tourism may seem surprising, and indeed tourism may be crucial for the local economy, the seasonal nature of the tourist industry contributes to high rates of unemployment in the close season.

The 2001 census indicates that in each district the numbers employed in hotels and catering alone exceeded the combined total in agriculture and fishing, the two traditional employment sectors. At the peak of the season there are over 270,000 visitors to the county, which adds more than 50% to the all year population. London and Devon are the only areas in the UK that attract more visitors. Tourism accounts for at least 30,000 jobs, with many more at the peak of the season. It consequently attracts a sizeable number of seasonal workers.

The CCS and CBCS confirm the importance of tourism to the county. No less than 76.9% of residents felt that tourism was important to the town they most often visited and 65.3% felt it was an important industry in the area where they lived. In the business survey, 56.6% felt that the tourist industry was important in the area where their business was located and 26.8% said their business was dependent on tourism.

Table 2. Indicators of the Extent and Impact of Tourism in the Different Districts of Cornwall.

	Jobs related to tourism spending	Percentage employment supported by tourism	Spend by staying visitors (£m)	Spend by day visitors (£m)	Percentage housing second homes
Caradon	6,822	18	£114.172	£ 68.611	3.8
Carrick	10,203	30	£155.768	£115.771	3.5
Kerrier	6,410	16	£ 98.277	£ 62.524	2.8
N. Cornwall	11,465	33	£226.838	£110.036	8.2
Penwith	8,077	34	£160.913	£ 70.032	7.1
Restormel	12,043	28	£253.019	£ 87.645	2.7

However, the districts of Cornwall are not uniform in their popularity amongst visitors and Table 2 illustrates the impact of tourism on each of the districts, using official sources. Overall, the data suggests that tourism is especially important to Carrick, North Cornwall, Penwith and Restormel, less so to Caradon and Kerrier, although the pattern for second home ownership is somewhat different.

Tourist Board statistics indicate that the five most visited locations in the county are St Ives (visited by 29.2% of tourists), Penzance (19.0%), Newquay (17.3%), Truro (15.9%) and Land's End (15.6%). The places visitors are most likely to stay in are Newquay (12.4%), St Ives (9.7%), Penzance (7.5%), Falmouth (6.0%) and St Austell (6.0%). On a town level, seven towns in the county were considered by respondents to the CCS as especially tourism-oriented:[1] Bude, Falmouth, Looe, Newquay, Penzance, St Ives and Wadebridge. Notably, only three of these (Falmouth, Newquay and Penzance) had resident populations exceeding 10,000.

It is also important to stress that the nature of the tourism industry varies in different parts of the county. Restormel, and Newquay in particular, is the only area characterised by mass tourism, with young singles comprising a significant section of the market, partly but not exclusively through the appeal of surfing and special events like the annual *Run to the Sun*.

Cornwall can thus be described as a predominantly rural county, dependent upon tourism, but with high

---

[1] i.e. over 90% of those who frequented it said that tourism was important there.

levels of deprivation. The first two of these are particularly important in the context of the issues raised in the remainder of this paper.

Victims Who Move: the Problem When Being Attacked Leads Victims to Leave the CDRP Area

There is some evidence that for a minority of victims their experiences may be such as to lead them to move home (Dugan, 1999), although there is no indication of how far they move, or in the present context, whether they move outside their CDRP area. Although police data will include reported offences against victims before they move, survey data will omit this group, with perhaps the most negative views of crime and disorder and policies in the area.

One example where this is of particular relevance concerns victims of domestic violence, where victims may move considerable distances to escape from abusive partners, especially in rural areas where anonymity is often difficult. In Cornwall in 2001 the CDRPs were particularly concerned to measure the extent and concentration of domestic violence and match need to service provision, and we were encouraged to use police statistics as well as data from the two refuges in the county (in Penzance and Truro) to assess the need for an additional refuge in the east of Cornwall (Mawby, 2003). However, while police figures indicated that domestic violence was a problem across the county, data for both referrals and admissions to the two refuges indicated a skewed pattern. First, as Table 3 indicates, a considerable number of referrals – 54.0% to Penzance and 39.6% to Truro - came from outside the county, indicating a policy of moving women considerable distances to maximise their safety. Second, a much higher proportion of local referrals were drawn from the west of the county, where the refuges were sited, rather than from eastern CDRP areas such as Caradon.

Table 3. Referrals of Women Residing in Cornwall to Women's Refuges in Penzance and Truro, 2000-2001, According to Area of Residence.

	Penzance		Truro		Total		
	n	%	n	%	n	%	%
Caradon	2	1.9	9	4.2	11	3.4	16.3
Carrick	27	26.0	77	35.8	104	32.6	17.7
Kerrier	36	34.6	48	22.3	84	26.3	18.6
North Cornwall	7	6.7	28	13.0	35	11.0	16.5
Penwith	23	22.1	24	11.2	47	14.7	12.2
Restormel	9	8.7	29	13.5	38	11.9	18.7
Out of county	122		141		263		
Total	226		256		582		

On one level, these findings support the argument for a refuge in the eastern part of the county. However, they tell us little about the precise requirements of abused women from these areas. For example, one or more of the following scenarios might apply:

- Women who are attacked by their partners may be deterred from leaving home by the lack of local facilities and thus remain in abusive relationships;
- They may leave but find other accommodation;
- They may react to the lack of local facilities by moving into refuges elsewhere;
- They may choose to move to refuges outside the local area, irrespective of what is available locally.

While we were able to use our local contacts to demonstrate that few women from Cornwall were admitted to the Plymouth refuge, clearly it is important to build up a picture of the (mis)match between needs and services by being able to chart which refuges, nationwide, women from Cornwall are admitted to, a task that is clearly beyond the resources of the CDRPs. But that is only the starting point. To assess fully the need for local services, it would be necessary to interview those admitted to other refuges, and ideally women who chose not to enter any refuge.

Citizens as Commuters: Where Members of the Public Cross CDRP Boundaries on a Temporary Basis

CDRP areas are, by their very nature, geographically discrete: citizens, by their very nature, cross their boundaries on a regular basis. Some of these commit offences, some are victimised, and others adjust their views of crime and safety according to their experiences elsewhere.

Population surveys generally focus on local residents. They may include questions on offending by locals, but more commonly cover the experiences of locals as victims and their perceptions of crime and disorder. However, although it is commonly assumed that these perceptions and experiences relate to their local area, they may not.

In Cornwall, for example, we included in the questionnaire a list of 30 towns or cities in or close to Cornwall, and respondents were asked which one they most often frequented. We subsequently asked series of questions about both the area around where they lived and their 'most used' town. The most common towns that people went to were Truro (14.1%), Penzance (10.8%) and St Austell (8.7%). Most respondents named a 'most used town' within their own district. However, Truro was cited by a number of those from outside Carrick, notably with 11.3% of Restormel residents saying it was their 'most used' town. Plymouth, in Devon, was also mentioned by 2.8%, who were almost entirely residents of neighbouring Caradon district (14.8% of whom cited Plymouth). For these respondents, then, experiences and perceptions of crime may well be formed outside the CDRP boundaries. Concern about crime and anti-social behaviour among Caradon residents was demonstrably increased by the higher levels evidenced by those frequenting Plymouth. Conversely, concerns among Restormel residents were reduced by the replies of those who frequented Truro, generally considered a safer town than Newquay or St Austell.

While police statistics relate to victimisation within the boundaries of a CDRP area, they are more suspect when it comes to offenders' addresses. In Cornwall, and many other areas, there is a difficulty with using police data on offenders' addresses, since these are recorded for monitoring purposes only, and are consequently updated when offenders move. Identifying where the offender lived at the time of, or prior to, the offence therefore requires a detailed review of case files, which is generally impractical in the audit timeframe. It is time-consuming to tease out the various possible scenarios:

- Offenders living in the CDRP area who commit their offences there;
- Offenders living in the CDRP area who offend elsewhere;

- Offenders from elsewhere who travel into the CDRP area and commit crimes there.

Research on 'travel to offend' patterns suggests that most crime is committed within a relatively short distance of offenders' homes. This is particularly so for crimes like burglary. A number of researchers have noted that while in general city centres are high crime areas, if we focus on residential areas, those with high rates for burglary tend to be areas where burglars live (Forrester *et al.*, 1988). More recently, Barker's (2000) research in a small English town found that burglars operated relatively locally, but that as they gained in experience they tended to travel slightly farther afield. Maguire (1982) also suggested that high status areas in the Thames Valley were likely to attract professional burglars from outside. Wiles & Costello (2000) noted that, although burglars tend to commit their crimes farther from home than in the past, a majority are still local. They also suggest that rural areas may attract burglars from adjacent urban areas. But the relationship between where offenders live and where they commit their crimes is more complex than that. Burglars may commit crimes in other areas as the result of planning, but they may also act spontaneously and burgle properties they pass *en route* to somewhere else; for example between their home and the city centre or other leisure centres (Cromwell *et al.*, 1991; Wiles & Costello, 2000).

Since data on offenders' addresses was not available for Cornwall as a whole, a pilot survey was commissioned as part of the audit process to assess what was known about domestic burglars operating in two districts, Caradon and Kerrier, deploying an in-depth review of police files. Over the three year period covered by the audits, 162 burglars operating in Caradon and 86 operating in Kerrier were

Crime and Disorder Audits

identified. In common with earlier research, most of these were male, working on their own. All were white. Most were also relatively young. In Caradon, 29.6% were aged under 20 and 39.5% 20-29. In Kerrier even more, 50.6%, were aged under 20, with most of the rest, 32.5%, aged 20-29.

The 'travel to offend' issue is of particular relevance in Cornwall, since the local police often alleged that burglars from Plymouth commuted to Caradon to commit their offences. Given the emphasis that has been placed in recent years on target hardening in Plymouth (Mawby, 2001), it is also possible that Plymouth burglars commute to Caradon in search of easier targets. If this were the case, we might expect more burglaries in Caradon to be committed by Plymouth residents, and this to be particularly so in those parts of the district most easily reached from Plymouth. Comparison of Caradon and Kerrier burglaries supports this hypothesis.

In Kerrier, most known burglars were local, commonly either committing their offences in their 'home town' or nearby. This is well illustrated by focusing on detected burglaries in the three main towns: Redruth, Camborne and Helston:

- Burglaries in Redruth involved 30 burglar/burglary combinations: 21 (70.0%) were burglars from Redruth (six of which were from the same street); 6 were burglars from adjoining Camborne; and the remaining 3 burglars from neighbouring Carrick;
- Burglaries in Camborne involved 28 burglar/burglary combinations: 19 (67.9%) were burglars from Camborne (five of which were from the same street); 6 were burglars from adjoining Redruth; 2 burglars from

neighbouring Carrick; with the remaining one a Plymouth resident;
- Burglaries in Helston involved 19 burglar/burglary combinations: no less than 15 (78.9%) were burglars from Helston itself; 3 burglars from Redruth; and one burglar from Camborne.

The pattern is very different in Caradon, where a number of Plymouth-based offenders committed burglaries. Comparing the five main towns:

- Liskeard. Detected burglaries involved 38 burglar/burglary combinations: of these no less than 32 (84.2%) were burglars from Liskeard itself (two from the same street); two more had recorded addresses elsewhere in Caradon, one in Plymouth and three from outside Devon and Cornwall;
- Looe. Detected burglaries involved 28 burglar/burglary combinations: of these no less than 15 (53.6%) were burglars from Looe (three from the same street); one had a recorded addresses elsewhere in Caradon; two came from other districts in Cornwall; 5 had Plymouth addresses; one came from elsewhere in Devon; and four from outside Devon and Cornwall;
- Callington. Detected burglaries involved 14 burglar/burglary combinations: of these 6 were burglars from Callington itself (one from the same street); 6 had Plymouth addresses; and two came from elsewhere in Devon;
- Torpoint. Detected burglaries involved 39 burglar/burglary combinations: of these 17 were burglars from Torpoint itself (two from the same street); one had a recorded address elsewhere in Caradon; no less than 20 (51.3%) had Plymouth addresses; and one came from elsewhere in Devon;

- Saltash. Detected burglaries involved 35[2] burglar/burglary combinations: of these only 6 were burglars from Saltash itself (three from the same street); one had a recorded address elsewhere in Caradon; no less than 27 (77.1%) had Plymouth addresses; and one came from outside Devon and Cornwall.

Clearly there is not only a marked difference between Kerrier and Caradon, but notable differences within Caradon itself. In Liskeard, and to a lesser extent Looe, burglary appears – as in Kerrier - to be a local enterprise. In Callington, burglaries were split between locals and Plymouth-based offenders. Torpoint burglaries involved a slight majority of Plymouth 'commuters'. At the extreme, Saltash burglaries were overwhelmingly committed by Plymouth-based offenders.

The fact that the pattern is most distinctive in Saltash and Torpoint, the two main access points to Cornwall from Plymouth,[3] is not surprising. However, this does not result in a high rate of burglary in either these towns or Caradon overall. Indeed, police data suggest that Caradon has a below average rate of domestic burglary and, although Torpoint East has the highest rate of burglary in Caradon, Saltash wards do not have particularly high rates.

Finally, of course, we should be wary of generalising from this to other offences. A brief review of patterns for 'non-domestic' violent crime in Caradon suggested that:

- 'Travel to offend' patterns were quite different;

---

[2] Excluding one of unknown address.
[3] Via the Tamar Bridge and Torpoint Ferry, respectively.

- Violent crime hotspots were less pronounced, possibly because Caradon youths 'cross the bridge' into Plymouth for nightlife and commit offences there.

The policy implications of this are intriguing. With regard to burglary, the findings suggest that, in Caradon, the CDRP might adopt target hardening approaches to burglary reduction in order to reduce its attraction to both local and commuting burglars, but that social crime prevention measures would be less effective, unless aimed at Plymouth offenders and potential offenders! In Kerrier, in contrast, a mix of social and situational measures might be more appropriate. Conversely, it is unlikely that Caradon CDRP would be persuaded to commit funds to social measures aimed at reducing violence and disorderly behaviour if its residents create problems outside the area in neighbouring Plymouth!

Visitors as a Disenfranchised Community: the Problem of Identifying the Separate Problems Encountered/Caused by Tourists

Similar issues arise where those involved in crime and disorder are temporary residents in the CDRP area. In a tourist area like Cornwall, this applies to both tourists and seasonal workers employed in hotels and the leisure industry. Police data incorporate crimes committed by or against both tourists and seasonal workers, but are unlikely to discriminate between these and more permanent residents. In the case of seasonal workers, it is highly unlikely that anything other than a current address will be recorded. For tourists, the police may record either home or temporary addresses but, again, do not flag up cases involving tourists. It is likely that where the probation service is involved in writing reports on

Crime and Disorder Audits

suspects, tourist/migrant status will be noted, but to unearth this level of data would require more detailed analysis. Population surveys are even less likely to cover tourists or temporary workers.

This raises a number of problems:

- We are unable to assess how far crime is committed against tourists or local residents;

- Support services (such as Victim Support) may be unable to respond to crimes against tourists;

- The extent to which tourists may be deterred from returning to the county due to their experiences of crime and disorder is unknown.;[4]

- The extent to which crime and disorder is a by-product of tourism is unknown.

However, in an area like Cornwall, the impact of seasonal workers and tourists on levels of crime and disorder is likely to be extensive. This is particularly so in Newquay, which caters for the youth tourism market and puts on special events like *Run to the Sun* that are associated with anti-social behaviour (Barton & James, 2003); and Newquay has developed a national reputation as Britain's answer to Faliraki (Hattersley, 2004). Certainly there is evidence that similarly marketed resorts abroad attract high levels of anti-social behaviour and crime (Homel *et al.*, 1997), but conventional crime is also high in

---

[4] For more general literature on the impact of crime on tourists' decision making, see Brayshaw (1995) and George (2003).

areas marketing mass tourism (Albuquerque & McElroy, 1999; Fujii & Mak, 1980; Kelly, 1993; Prideaux, 1996; Walmsley *et al.*, 1983).

Crime and disorder may be committed by tourists or seasonal workers, perhaps attracted to the area by this reputation (Prideaux, 1996). Research elsewhere also suggests that tourists themselves experience relatively high risk of victimisation (Chesney-Lind & Lind, 1986; Mawby, Brunt & Hambly, 1999; Michalko, 2004; Stangeland, 1998).

We have no evidence either way for Cornwall, although we did ask residents for their views. The findings indicated that, while in Cornwall generally there was seen to be a close association between crime and disorder and tourism, this varied markedly between different parts of the county. To illustrate this, data are included herein for Newquay and Penzance. These two towns appear to have greater problems with crime and anti-social behaviour than other parts of the county (according to both police data and the CCS), and, as already noted, each is a tourist centre. However, data from official statistics and the CCS show that Penzance is a much more disadvantaged town than Newquay (Mawby, 2005).

Table 4 indicates that, within Cornwall as a whole, crime and, to a greater extent, anti-social behaviour were clearly seen to have increased as a result of tourism. However, those residents who described Newquay as their 'most used' town saw tourism as having a greater negative impact on local life, including its impact on crime and disorder, than did those frequenting Penzance.

Crime and Disorder Audits

Table 4. Impact of Tourism on the Following, where a Positive Response is Scored 1, a Negative Response –1 and 'No Difference 0.

	Newquay	Penzance	Total
Income and standard of living	0.65	0.73	0.70
Employment opportunities	0.65	0.74	0.65
Area's overall prosperity	0.63	0.72	0.63
Availability of leisure facilities	0.29	0.43	0.39
Quality of life in general	-1.1	0.21	0.16
Noise	-0.87	-0.50	-0.51
Violent crime	-0.56	-0.16	-0.23
Property crime	-0.58	-0.21	-0.25
Litter, vandalism, etc.	-0.80	-0.56	-0.25
Disturbances/public disorder	-0.79	-0.32	-0.35
Alcohol abuse	-0.82	-0.33	-0.39
Drug abuse	-0.71	-0.21	-0.29
Amount of affordable housing	-0.55	-0.62	-0.59
Traffic congestion	-0.82	-0.78	-0.76

In Tables 5 to 7, the views of residents throughout the county have been compared with those who said their most used town was Newquay or Penzance in terms of their perceptions of who committed crime and anti-social

Table 5. *Percentage of those Frequenting Newquay and Penzance who Attributed 'Burglaries or Thefts from the Person ... Experienced by Local People' to the Following, Compared with Cornwall Totals.*

	Newquay (n=78)	Penzance (n=205)	Total (n=1848)
Local residents	38.5	67.3	58.9
Tourists	29.5	5.4	11.3
Local casual labour	25.6	24.9	23.9
Outside casual labour	65.4	39.5	43.1

Table 6. *Percentage of those Frequenting Newquay and Penzance who Attributed 'Violence or Threats ... Experienced by Local People' to the Following, Compared with Cornwall Totals.*

	Newquay (n=78)	Penzance (n=192)	Total (n=1757)
Local residents	38.5	71.9	64.5
Tourists	42.3	6.8	14.5
Local casual labour	23.1	21.9	18.8
Outside casual labour	59.0	35.4	35.6

behaviour. Two points are evident here. First, respondents generally saw crime as committed by local people, but they were also inclined to blame seasonal workers for property crime and violence and tourists for drunk and disorderly behaviour. Second, in Newquay – but not Penzance – they were most likely to consider seasonal workers to be responsible for property crime and violence and tourists for drunk and disorderly behaviour, and to a lesser extent violence.

Table 7. *Percentage of those Frequenting Newquay and Penzance who Attributed 'Drunken Behaviour or Other Disorderly Conduct ... Experienced by Local People' to the Following, Compared with Cornwall Totals.*

	Newquay (n=81)	Penzance (n=206)	Total (n=1842)
Local residents	44.4	79.1	77.2
Tourists	76.5	25.7	32.8
Local casual labour	17.3	20.4	15.3
Outside casual labour	39.5	24.8	20.2

Finally, we asked local residents about a series of problems that might be evident in their 'most used' town. One of these referred to tourists/visitors causing a nuisance, another to tourists/visitors being victimised or picked on. In Cornwall as a whole, residents were more likely to see tourists as instigators (13.5%) than victims (6.9%) of problems. However, while those frequenting both Newquay (18.8%) and Penzance (15.1%) were particularly likely to feel that visitors to the town experienced harassment, those frequenting Newquay (84.0%) were far more likely than those frequenting Penzance (14.3%) to see tourists as the instigators. This response from Newquay stands out, being *four times* that of any other town in Cornwall.

On the basis of the data available, we would therefore suggest that the underlying causes of crime and anti-social behaviour in Penzance and Newquay are rather different. The crime and disorder problem in Penzance appears to stem from a cocktail of tourism and disadvantage. Seasonal work results in large numbers of unemployed workers through the close season, while the disparity between relatively impoverished local people and more affluent day visitors generates property crime – notably tourists are relatively more likely to be seen as victims than the cause of the problem. Local drug agencies have long seen the drug problem in the county as concentrated on Penzance, and local people concurred, and this – along with other social and physical cues of disorder – generates a feeling of insecurity in the town. However, locals did not blame tourists and tourism for Penzance's crime and disorder. Rather, tourists were as likely to be seen to suffer from crime as cause it. In this sense, tourism was a 'generator' of crime and disorder in Penzance in so far as it brought a surplus of potential victims to an area where economic hardship operated as a 'community related generator' (Tilley *et al.*, 1999).

In contrast, it seems to be tourism, particularly the specific nature of the local tourist industry, that explains much of Newquay's crime and disorder problem. As already noted, Newquay is the major tourist destination in Cornwall and is distinctive in marketing young single tourists. It has been associated both by academics (Barton & James, 2003) and the national press (Hattersley, 2004) with high levels of anti-social behaviour. While respondents frequenting Newquay identified some 'conventional' crime problems, like burglary, with the town, the main crime and disorder problems in Newquay were unequivocally related to tourism. Respondents correspondingly focused on street crime, violence and anti-social behaviour, particularly associated with alcohol misuse, as endemic to the town. Notably, a staggering 97.5% felt there was a problem with public drunkenness, while 84.0% felt that tourists/visitors caused a nuisance. In comparison, far fewer (18.8%) - albeit more than in any other town - considered tourists to be victimised. Tourism

Crime and Disorder Audits

was thus seen as a 'generator' of crime and disorder in so far as it attracted a surplus of potential offenders (Tilley *et al.*, 1999).

This poses a number of questions for local CDRPs in the county. However, the audit findings also raise a series of questions regarding the need for further analysis of the tourism/crime connection. For example:

- Are local residents correct in their assumptions about who is responsible for crime and anti-social behaviour and who is victimised?
- How do tourists' perceptions of crime and disorder (in Cornwall, Newquay and Penzance) compare with those of local residents?
- Do different tourist subgroups differ in their views?
- Do tourists' perceptions of crime and anti-social behaviour influence their decisions on future holidays?

Summary and Discussion

While the introduction of Crime and Disorder audits provided local areas with some opportunities to focus on local issues, I have argued that in some respects this emphasis can be misleading. Crime and disorder are spatially located, but those who create problems, those who are victimised, and those who pass judgement on community safety regularly cross borders from one CDRP to another. Thus, residents of a CDRP area may have relevant views and experiences of crime outside the area, and outsiders may have relevant views and experiences related to crime and anti-social behaviour within the area. Here, using personal experience of carrying out audits in the six districts of mainland Cornwall, I have discussed three sets of issues that transgress local boundaries:

- Victims who move: the problem when being attacked leads victims to leave the CDRP area;
- Citizens as commuters: when members of the public, including offenders, cross CDRP boundaries on a temporary basis;
- Visitors as a disenfranchised community: the problem of identifying the separate problems identified, encountered or caused by tourists.

I have argued that a comprehensive audit of crime and disorder, as the basis for developing local policies, needs to address these issues. However, the way audits are conceived and carried out makes this at best difficult, at worst impossible.

In the case of victims who move, the example of victims of domestic violence illustrates the difficulties of gleaning data from agencies in other CDRP areas. In developing policies to meet need, it would be useful to know how many women from Cornwall moved to refuges elsewhere in the country and whether this was due to the lack of local options. However, this would depend on access to the records of other refuges and on a willingness to engage in national evaluation, both of which fall outside the capabilities of individual CDRPs.

In the case of commuters or visitors as victims, the difficulties are more manageable but vary according to whether we are referring to recorded data or population surveys, and according to whether or not offences are committed locally and offenders are locals or outsiders.

Police data refer to all offences committed within the district, and data for the force area are easily accessed. This will cover offences committed in the area, by or against locals or outsiders, but it is unlikely that temporary residents such as seasonal workers will be distinguished, and visitors who are victimised may be listed under their home or temporary address. However, instructing officers to flag up the residential status of offenders and victims would solve these problems. This would allow CDRPs to identify the extent to which crimes in the district were caused by or committed against outsiders, and thus adopt crime and disorder and harm reduction strategies that are most appropriate. Police data on offences committed by or against residents that occur outside the district/force area are more problematic and would require cross-district/force protocols relating to specific circumstances where this is considered a relevant issue. In the present context, offences committed in Plymouth by residents of Cornwall are a case in point.

Population surveys almost exclusively target local people. Asking them about their perceptions and experiences outside the district is unproblematic. However, asking commuters or visitors about the district is more difficult, if only because of the lack of a sampling frame. In the case of visitors this might be overcome by drawing samples from different types of holiday accommodation (hotels, caravan sites, etc.), but again this requires detailed planning. Nevertheless, in areas that depend on tourism it is crucial. Tourist areas need to respond to the concerns of both local people and visitors: if the latter perceive security to be a problem, they may react by holidaying elsewhere in the future, depriving the local economy in places like Cornwall of necessary income.

The emphasis upon local issues that has emerged since the 1998 Crime and Disorder Act is to be applauded.

Nevertheless, CDRP areas have found it increasingly difficult to fund and manage the audits. The fact that crime and disorder in one district inevitably impinges on the situation in neighbouring districts, which often fall within different police force areas, magnifies the difficulties. As a result, there is a danger of audits becoming too localised. This creates problems when victims move out of the area, or potential victims and offenders commute across CDRP boundaries In the latter case, these are exacerbated in areas that attract large numbers of tourists, who are – effectively – disenfranchised from the audit process.

References

Albuquerque, K. de, & McElroy, J. (1999). Tourism and crime in the Caribbean. *Annals of Tourism Research, 26.4,* 968-984.

Barker, M. (2000). The criminal range of small-town burglars. In Canter, D. and Alison, L. (eds), *Profiling Property Crimes,* pp. 57-73. Aldershot: Ashgate/ Dartmouth.

Barton, A., & James, Z. (2003). Run to the sun: policing contested perceptions of risk. *Policing and Society, 13.3,* 259 - 270.

Brayshaw, D. (1995). Negative publicity about tourism destinations: a Florida case study. *Travel and Tourism Analyst, 5,* 62-71.

Cemlyn, S. *et al.,* (2002). *Poverty and Neighbourhood Renewal in West Cornwall: Final Report.* Bristol: University of Bristol (Townsend Centre for International Poverty Research).

Chesney-Lind, M., & Lind, I.Y. (1986). Visitors as victims: crimes against tourists in Hawaii. *Annals of Tourism Research, 13,* 167-191.

Crawford, A. (1998). *Crime Prevention and Community Safety: Politics, Policies and Practices.* Harlow: Addison Wesley Longman.

Cromwell, P.F., Olson, J.N., & Avary, D'A. W. (1991). *Breaking and Entering.* Newbury Park, California: Sage.

Dugan, L. (1999). The effect of criminal victimization on a household's moving decision. *Criminology 37.4,* 903-928.

Forrester, D., Chatterton, M., & Pease, K. (1988). *The Kirkholt Burglary Prevention Project, Rochdale.* London: HMSO (Crime Prevention Unit Paper no.13).

Fujii, E.T., & Mak, J. (1980). Tourism and crime: implications for regional development policy. *Regional Studies, 14,* 27-36.

Garland, J. (2002). Surfing the crime net: conducting Crime and Disorder Audits. *Crime Prevention and Community Safety: an international journal, 4.2,* 55-60.

George, R. (2003). Tourists' fear of crime while on holiday in Cape Town. *Crime Prevention and Community Safety: an international journal, 5.1,* 13-25.

Gilling, D. (2000). Policing, crime prevention and partnerships. In Leishman, F., Loveday, B. and Savage, S. (eds), *Core Issues in Policing,* pp. 124-139. Harlow: Pearson Education Ltd.

Hall, R., Vakalopoulou, V., Brunsdon, C., Charlton, M., & Alvanides, S. (2003), *Maintaining Basic Command Unit and Crime and Disorder Partnership families for comparative purposes: 1 April 2003 results.* Home Office Online Report 40/03. Retrieved from:
www.homeoffice.gov.uk/rds/pdfs2/rdsolr4003.pdf

Hattersley, G. (2004). Welcome to Sin on Sea. *Sunday Times, 18 July (News Review),* 1-2.

Home Office. (2000). *Consultation on the Development of Families of Similar Basic Command Units (BCUs) and Crime and Disorder Reduction Partnerships (CDRPs).* London: Home Office.

Homel, R. et al. (1997). Preventing drunkenness and violence around nightclubs in a tourist resort. In Clarke, R.V. (ed.), *Situational Crime Prevention: Successful Case Studies (second edition),* pp. 263-282. Guilderland, New York: Harrow and Heston.

Hughes, G. (1998). *Understanding Crime Prevention: Social Control, Risk And Late Modernity.* Buckingham: Open University Press.

Kelly, I. (1993). Tourist destination crime rates: an examination of Cairns and the Gold Coast, Australia. *Journal of Tourism Studies,* 4.2, 2-11.

Loveday, B. (2001). Police accountability in the provinces: the changing role of the police authority. *Crime Prevention and Community Safety: An International Journal,* 3.2, 49-63.

Maguire, M. (1982). *Burglary in a Dwelling.* London: Heinemann.

Mawby, R.I. (2001). *Burglary*. Cullompton: Willan Press.

Mawby, R.I. (2003). Conducting crime audits in a rural county of England: processes and outputs. *International Journal of Police Science and Management, 5.3,* 161-179.

Mawby, R.I. (2005). Crime, place and explaining rural hotspots. Paper to British Criminology Conference, July, 2005, Leeds.

Mawby, R.I., Brunt, P., & Hambly, Z. (1999). Victimisation on holiday: a British survey. *International Review of Victimology, 6,* 201-211.

Michalko, G. (2004). Tourism eclipsed by crime: the vulnerability of foreign tourists in Hungary. *Journal of Travel and Tourism Marketing, 15.2-3,* 159-172.

Morgan, J. (1991). *Safer Communities: The Local Delivery Of Crime Prevention Through The Partnership Approach.* London: Home Office (Standing Conference on Crime Prevention).

Povey, D. et al. (2001). *Recorded Crime: England and Wales, 12 months to March 2001.* London: Home Office (12/01).

Prideaux, B. (1996). The tourism crime cycle: a beach destination case study. In Pizam, A. and Mansfield, Y. (eds), *Tourism, Crime and International Security Issues,* pp 59-76. Chichester: Wiley.

Stangeland, P. (1998). Other targets or other locations? An analysts of opportunity structures. *British Journal of Criminology, 38.1,* 61-77.

Tilley, N., Pease, K., Hough, M., & Brown, R. (1999).

Burglary Prevention: Early Lessons From The Crime Reduction Programme. London: Home Office (Crime Reduction Research Series Paper no.1).

Walmsley, D.J., Boskovic, R.M., & Pigram, J.J. (1983). Tourism and crime: an Australian perspective. *Journal of Leisure Research, 15.2,* 136-155.

Wiles, P., & Costello, A. (2000). *The 'Road To Nowhere': The Evidence For Travelling Criminals.* London: Home Office (HO Research Study no. 207).

Williams, M. (2003). Why is Cornwall poor? Poverty and in-migration since the 1960s. *Contemporary British History, 17.3,* 55-70.

PARTNERSHIPS – LOOKING TO THE FUTURE

Judith Million

'Partnership', like 'community engagement', has become something of a buzz word in recent years, but there is actually nothing new about the concept. As far back as 1984, a landmark Home Office circular signalled central government's support for a partnership approach to crime prevention and highlighted the potential of a multi-agency approach involving the police and other local service providers in the fight against crime (Home Office Circular 8/84). Government sponsored Five Towns and Safer Cities partnership demonstration projects followed. Then, in 1990, the inter-department circular *Crime Prevention: The Success of the Partnership Approach* was published, endorsed by the Permanent Secretaries of 10 government departments and accompanied by examples of partnership practice from across the country (Liddle & Gelsthorpe, 1994). Of course, the most enlightened public sector agencies have always recognised that they will only achieve their community safety goals if they work closely with their partners. However, not all local partners have been eager to work with the police, for a variety of reasons, and sometimes the police have been keener to lead than to learn from others.

In 1991, a Home Office working group was established under the chairmanship of Sir James Morgan "to monitor the progress made in the local delivery of crime prevention through the multi-agency or partnership approach" (Home Office, 1991). Morgan found that much of the early work to promote crime prevention at local level had a community development focus, with initiatives developed by the voluntary sector and, crucially, involving local residents.

Approaches emphasised the need to deal with crime as just one of many problems encountered by people living in disadvantaged areas. The aim was to promote a co-ordinated response to these multiple problems which would improve the physical environment, develop neighbourhood facilities and services and engender a greater sense of community spirit through the involvement of local people in a range of initiatives to reduce crime.

The seminal Morgan Report recognised the opportunities and challenges that existed for agencies wanting to work together in this way, but clearly affirmed partnership as the way forward. In Morgan's words: "a successful multi-agency approach to community safety requires the formulation of an overall crime reduction strategy and structure within which agencies can co-operate as well as deliver their own particular contribution" (Home Office, 1991).

The twin concepts of partnership and community engagement have since become key tenets of community safety at all levels, from the very local to the national.

Both found voice in one of the early pieces of legislation introduced by the New Labour Government - the 1998 Crime and Disorder Act. The Act enshrined the principle of multi-agency co-operation in statute by placing a duty on the police and local authorities to work together to develop and implement a strategy for tackling local crime problems. Although not formally named as such until the Police Reform Act of 2002, this is essentially when Crime and Disorder Reduction Partnerships, or CDRPs as they are more commonly known, were born. Significantly, the 1998 Act placed emphasis on partnerships working with communities and the voluntary sector to achieve a

Partnerships

citizen-focused approach to tackling crime and disorder, on the basis that local people know their own neighbourhoods and probably understand their own problems better even than local agencies. It enshrined in legislation the requirement on partnerships to consult local people about the findings from their triennial crime and disorder audits to determine local priorities for action. In 1998, the key agency partnership was seen as between the police and local authorities, but it soon became clear that others had a major role to play too. So the 2002 Police Reform Act identified Police Authorities, Fire Authorities and Primary Care Trusts as responsible authorities with a statutory role to play in CDRPs and recognised the clear link between drugs and crime, encouraging Drug Action Teams and CDRPs to work closely together. It also provided for the merger of CDRPs.

Many CDRPs work well, implementing robust community safety strategies shaped by the needs of local people leading to tangible benefits for local communities. Some have regular and systematic dialogues with the communities they serve and respond innovatively and effectively to local concerns. They increasingly employ the principles and processes of the police National Intelligence Model in the partnership setting. Drawing together and analysing a wide range of intelligence, they identify those local issues most in need of attention and, through multi-agency tasking and co-ordination, deploy resources to drive a more focused assault on the drivers of crime, anti-social behaviour and substance misuse. Many involve communities in partnership initiatives and some directly involve local people in partnership decision-making. There are a number of benefits to this. Local people can be very creative with ideas for tackling crime and disorder, quick to report when initiatives are working well, and equally quick to report when they are not. Solutions to local problems are more likely to be sustained with the direct involvement of communities. Consultation and engagement increases partnership and single agency visibility. This, of course, links directly with local accountability.

Crime and Disorder Reduction Partnerships do appear to have made a difference. A National Audit Office Report published in December 2004 concluded they had contributed to reductions in crime reported through the British Crime Survey over the last few years, although it was impossible to quantify how much (National Audit Office, 2004). Although no figures were included in that report, it is encouraging that 73% of CDRPs showed decreases in British Crime Survey comparator crime in 2004/5, when compared with 2003/4.

However, more needs to be done. A significant number of partnerships struggle to maintain a full contribution from key agencies and even the successful ones are not as sufficiently visible, nor accountable, to the public as they should be. Some smaller CDRPs lack the capacity to get the analysis right, to turn neighbourhoods round and to make a difference to the lives of individuals. In recognition of this, the Police Reform White Paper, *Building Communities: Beating Crime*, published in November 2004, trailed the Government's concern to see partnerships improve their ability to deliver on neighbourhood level priorities, agreed with communities, through a better understanding of the needs and concerns of local people, greater clarity about their roles and responsibilities, increased visibility and clearer lines of accountability – including to the local citizen. All formed part of a review of the partnerships of

Partnerships

the Crime and Disorder Act, carried out from November 2004 to January 2005 (Home Office, 2004).

Many are keen to hear the outcome of this review. The issues are complex and it is a measure of the importance of getting it right that they have been discussed extensively at the highest levels in the Home Office since the review was concluded. Ministers are keen that the result should be more effective partnership working and hope to demonstrate just that. Meanwhile, the White Paper also sets out plans to introduce a specific mechanism to trigger action on the part of community safety agencies to acute or persistent problems of crime and anti-social behaviour when local communities have been unable to secure an effective response. ODPM proposed a wider local government trigger in their 'neighbourhoods' paper, published in 2005 (ODPM, 2005a). The Home Office is currently working with ODPM and other key stakeholders to develop detailed proposals for the implementation of the trigger mechanism. In so doing, it is clear that local councillors will need to play a central role in any dialogue between local agencies and local people. As leaders of, and advocates for, their communities, local councillors are ideally placed to act as a conduit at neighbourhood level for relaying local issues to community safety partner agencies. The trigger is really the new duty on local councillors to take action in response to community concerns. Once the trigger has been pulled, the councillor then has a variety of formal and informal methods of resolving the issue. These might range from discussions with CDRP chairs and BCU commanders, amongst others, to referral to a council scrutiny committee.

This development is fully consistent with the Government's wider 10-year vision for local government

(ODPM, 2004). The main thrust of the Government's reforms involves passing power from the political centre to local people and communities to create new democratic accountabilities and scrutiny at local level. Police reform and local government reform have a shared aim – the creation of sustainable communities. Sustainable communities are safe communities. Indeed, one of the proposals frequently made in the CDA Review was that CDRPs should be renamed 'Community Safety Partnerships' – as in Wales – to reflect that what is happening on the ground extends beyond mere crime reduction and prevention.

Since the creation of CDRPs, partnership working has increasingly been seen as the key to achieving progress in other areas of Government business. For example, the 2000 Local Government Act introduced a requirement on local authorities to work in partnership with local communities and agencies to produce a Community Strategy – now known as the Sustainable Community Strategy – to which crime reduction and prevention have an obvious contribution to make. The Strategies are delivered through Local Strategic Partnerships which involve a wider range of partners than CDRPs and Drug and Alcohol Action Teams, extending, crucially, to the local business sector. Many of these additional partners have something to bring to the crime reduction and community safety agenda too. Also, in 2003, Local Criminal Justice Boards were set up to bring criminal justice agencies together in partnership to deliver the national priorities of improving confidence in the criminal justice system and bringing more offences to justice.

However, one result of this very laudable decision to increase partnership working and to seek the views of the

Partnerships

local citizen is that we have a multiplicity of partnerships with different, but overlapping membership, sometimes at unitary and district council level and sometimes at county level, but sometimes aligned with neither. The delivery landscape looks *very* complex. It is therefore imperative that we join up these agendas at local level, maintaining a focus on delivering real and sustained improvements that local people will recognise as such and which chime with the neighbourhood level priorities which CDRPs have agreed with their communities. There are already encouragements to do just this.

From this financial year, the funding for much of what the ODPM and Home Office want to achieve in relation to the safety of local communities is being brought together. The Safer and Stronger Communities Fund brings together ODPM and Home Office funding streams aimed at tackling crime, anti-social behaviour and drugs, empowering communities, and improving the condition of streets and public spaces: in particular, for disadvantaged neighbourhoods where these issues often require more attention. These programmes have a very similar impact on the ground and it makes no sense to those outside central government to see the funding streams delivered separately. So they have been merged into the Safe and Stronger Communities Fund (SSCF), strengthening partners' ability to target resources where they are most needed and making public services more responsive to local needs, empowering local communities to influence their delivery, while also meeting national priorities and standards through a framework of high level outcomes. If central government can join up in this way, it makes even more sense to join up locally and the SSCF is only the start.

Also in 2005, 20 areas across the country drew up Local Area Agreements (LAAs): a new approach to improve the way Government works with local authorities and their delivery partners. LAAs bring together even more funding streams and government departments than the SSCF covers and, in return for clearly specified outcomes, such as percentage reductions in crime, will grant more freedom and flexibility in the way that funding can be used. The result is fewer funding streams, greater flexibility, reduced bureaucracy and a focus on outcomes, delivering *local* priorities within a broad framework set by the Government. It is also producing what so many seek increasingly: a single conversation between central government and local partners. It is strengthening partnership working too.

LAAs operate at top tier local authority level, with the LSP acting as the "partnership of partnerships". Those CDRPs that operate at district level have often found it difficult to engage those county council services responsible for delivering community safety objectives. LAAs are overcoming this by ensuring counties and districts *do* talk to each other across a wide range of subjects. Another 67 areas will develop LAAs from 2006-07 and by 2007-08 the whole country will be covered, building on the initial steps taken by the SSCF.

There are a number of national initiatives where partnership working has been key and which are likely to influence the way agencies work together locally in the future. First, through the Tackling Violent Crime Programme, the Government is working closely with partnerships in a small number of local areas with high levels of violent crime. In particular, the focus is on

Partnerships

alcohol-related crime and domestic violence. The first tranche of the programme began in November 2004, with 12 areas involved. A further seven areas joined the programme in the second tranche which began in May last year. Areas have been given some funding with which to take forward specific local initiatives and practitioners from all the areas are also being brought together to share experiences and ideas on good practice. It is still early days, but the initial analysis of results and outcomes is promising, with indications of reductions, particularly in more serious violence. Evidence suggests the value of intelligence-led activity, enabling resources to be targeted effectively. Areas reporting success stress the importance of partnership working.

Secondly, the Prolific and Other Priority Offenders Initiative, where key professionals, such as the police, probation and prisons, are working through CDRPs and LCJBs to identify those prolific offenders causing most harm to their communities and delivering a premium service to them across the criminal justice system; by ensuring, for example, that the Prison Service gives the police advance warning of release dates or through Youth Offending Teams working with other services to identify and focus on those on the cusp of offending. The PPO strategy has provided a powerful catalyst for smaller CDRPs, particularly in two-tier areas, to work much more closely together to create the critical mass to manage effectively the delivery of this targeted programme. Three such CDRPs in South Worcestershire became the first to be formally approved for merger by the Home Secretary in August 2005. The indications are that about 30 further mergers are in the pipeline.

Thirdly, tackling anti-social behaviour where the Government's TOGETHER Campaign, by its very title, demonstrates the importance of partnership; encouraging the community to come forward – to report anti-social behaviour and take a stand – then local services taking action in response to those concerns and finally, and critically, for those local services to communicate their actions back to the community. The maxim is the same for tackling anti-social behaviour as it is for delivering on neighbourhood policing: tell people what you are going to do, do it, and tell them you have done it, over and over again.

The Government sees neighbourhood policing as the key to ensuring that mainstream policing services are driven by neighbourhood and community needs (Home Office, March 2005). It envisages communities served by a mixed economy of partnership delivery teams involving police officers, community support officers and special constables working effectively alongside local authority wardens, housing officers, anti-social behaviour co-ordinators, youth workers and environmental services to make a significant difference to the quality of public services locally. The benefits for all are considerable. The importance of visibility and responsiveness and the value of detailed community intelligence were so amply demonstrated after the tragic events of July 7, with integrated partnership teams working with all sections of the community to promote cohesion. The benefits go beyond reductions in crime and disorder. They can extend to helping young people in need and providing links to the relevant services for support and intervention. They can lead to health gains through improved physical environments, reassurance and a corresponding reduction in the fear of crime. There are challenges too, especially in

Partnerships

securing commitment and a corporate response from all local delivery partners and embedding neighbourhood delivery arrangements into local democratic processes.

Making a difference locally is what matters most. The Government is committed to providing a framework for local action within which partnerships can flourish. Community safety matters enormously to the people of this country, and is thus something which the Government also has a duty to take very seriously. Crime is falling, but it is still too high. A step change is required. That is why the first National Community Safety Plan was published in November 2005 (Home Office, 2005). The Plan places the citizen at the centre of public services and requires all institutions at central and local level to work together to tackle local problems effectively.

The Plan not only brings together all that central government does in this area, but what local partners are seeking to achieve too. It provides a clear view of the Government's community safety priorities. It joins up work across central government departments, involving as it does contributions from 11 government departments on these priorities. It provides a more holistic response aimed at supporting better local delivery and building a new relationship between public services and the communities they serve, which encourages accountability, trust and co-operation.

The Government's priorities from 2006 to 2009 are built around five themes:
- Making communities stronger and more effective;
- Further reducing crime and anti-social behaviour;
- Creating safer environments;
- Protecting the public and building confidence; and

- Improving people's lives so they are less likely to commit offences or re-offend.

The Government's intention is not to impose new burdens or responsibilities on local organisations. Rather the National Community Safety Plan "defines the Government's minimum expectations of key partners" in clear and unambiguous terms and "draws together the contributions each can make, emphasising the broadly based nature of successful community safety" (Home Office, 2005). The Government regards the direct involvement of local people in helping to define and tackle local problems as integral to effective local delivery and pivotal to the step change the Plan is designed to generate. It is premised on the belief that effective partnership is the only way to ensure the safety of our communities.

References and Other Publications

Home Office. (1984). *Interdepartmental Circular 8/84.* London: HMSO.

Home Office. (1991). *Safer Communities: The Local Delivery of Crime Prevention.* London: Home Office.

Home Office (1997). *Getting to Grips with Crime: A New Framework for Local Action Through the Partnership Approach (the Morgan Report).* London: Home Office.

Home Office. (2004). *Building Communities, Beating Crime: A better police service for the 21st century.* London: HMSO.

Home Office. (2005). *Neighbourhood Policing, your police; your community; our Home Office (2005).* National Community Safety Plan. London: HMSO.

Liddle, M., & Geslthorpe, L. (1994). *Inter-Agency Crime Prevention: Organising Local Delivery. Crime Prevention Unit, Series paper 52.* London, Home Office.

National Audit Office. (2004). *Reducing Crime: the Home Office working with crime and Disorder Reduction Partnerships.* London: HMSO.

ODPM (Office of the Deputy Prime Minister). (2004). *The Future of Local Government - Developing a 10 year Vision.* London: HMSO.

ODPM (Office of the Deputy Prime Minister). (2005a). *Citizen Engagement and Public Services: Why Neighbourhoods Matter.* London: HMSO.

ODPM (Office of the Deputy Prime Minister). (2005b). *Vibrant Local leadership.* London: HMSO.

NO PAIN, NO GAIN: THE SAFER DERBYSHIRE RESEARCH AND INFORMATION TEAM STORY

Kevin Pellatt

"Exchanging information is just a pain. And that, in a nutshell, is the bottom line."

Introduction

'Safer Derbyshire' is the banner under which many Community Safety stakeholders operate. Many are co-located in offices at the County Council. They are:
- County Council Community Safety Unit;
- Youth Offending Service;
- Drugs Alcohol Action Team;
- Representatives from: The Police (a police inspector and crime prevention by design advisors); Social Services; Fire Service.

The Safer Derbyshire Research and Information Team that occupies an office within the suite supports them.

Problem

Availability, Quality and Timeliness of Data

> "What we want and what we actually get are two very, very different things ..."

The eight Community Safety partnerships in Derbyshire had high expectations of the analyst during their formative stages. The reality was that there were too few staff, mainly on short term temporary government funding, remotely located, with little management afforded them.

With the formal information system failing to deliver the expected level of service, practitioners would attempt to gather the information through informal sources. This led to inconsistent and inaccurate data being used by Partnerships with little understanding and no quality checking of the information.

Lack of project evaluation

> "There is little evidence of effective evaluation."

> "There is little evidence of sharing best practice."

A joint, cross-cutting, multi-agency Best Value Review of community safety services in Derbyshire indicated there was little time for problem solving work and the evaluation that underwrites this process. It suggested there were few trained in evaluation techniques. It made the point that agencies within the partnerships accorded higher priority to new work rather than re-visiting projects on their completion. In short, it was difficult to ascertain what worked, where and why, thus preventing the transfer of good practice between partnerships.

Root Causes

Formalisation

> "As the Partnerships became more formal, in some respects the information exchange facilities became more difficult."

In formalising the information-sharing process, the trust that existed between two people was lost to a bureaucratic process that highlighted all the dangers of sharing data, leaving some individuals unsure. Sharing data left them exposed to sanctions, but they needed to share data to achieve personal and partnership aims. This may explain the evidence of informal, almost clandestine, local links formed to maintain Community Safety Partnership business.

If these links delivered what the partnerships needed, then a formalised system may be considered a low priority. It was clear that a solution had to be found that allowed information to flow legally, accountably and with the ease of the informal systems.

Conflicting Priorities

> "They have all got their own jobs from their organisation ... the trick of the group is to try and fit our agenda with theirs or make theirs fit ours."

Data sharing was adversely affected by a lack of common goals and difficulty was experienced in aligning the different agency priorities. There was an acknowledgment that, whilst they tended to think outside their agency 'silos', there was still an element of self-seeking by partners. This had a twofold effect on partnership information sharing.

Firstly, data could be withheld by partners to avoid resources being directed towards a project of no benefit to them.

Secondly, to deploy a central, independent information and research team would drain resources from their own individual targets.

For this reason, there may have been a lack of desire to implement a formal cross-agency data sharing system.

Partnership Development

> "I think people like xxxxxx, they share information with the police all the time and there's not a problem; whereas we can't manage that for crime and disorder. I think this is because crime and disorder is new."

The formative development of a Community Safety Partnership also impacted on the ability to share data. Matters such as understanding the purpose of Community Safety Partnerships and the format and development of databases and systems were noted as reasons for difficulty in delivering data. It appeared that staff within the agencies and departments needed time to build trust and confidence in each other. Technical difficulties revolved around the lack of computer networking capacity, internet access and an uninformed choice of software. In short, partnerships needed a degree of structure and a clear understanding of each partner's role before the detailed information could flow formally.

Individuals

> "I would say at this moment in time 90 something percent is down to individuals. If individuals don't get on board it doesn't happen."

The importance of individuals could not be overestimated. It can be argued that it is between and through individuals, rather than agencies, that information is processed. Individuals are the valves that direct and control the flow of information around a network; they can make or break the system. The importance of goodwill and partnership-oriented people was cited by many people around the county as essential in sharing data.

The wide range of skills and abilities across the county meant that some were able to handle quite complex data, others had the skills but the systems were so complex they abandoned them, and some saw data in certain formats and just ignored it. Clearly all three skill levels needed to be considered when designing a formal system.

Legislation

> "A lot of people are worried about data protection...there's a lack of awareness of how much can be shared ..."

The Data Protection Act was commonly cited as a reason for failing to share data. However, under Section 115 of the Crime and Disorder Act, it is permissible to do so. It was established that an understanding of the protocols of data protection was lacking, leaving people unclear as to what could be shared. One partnership acknowledged that they had protocols, but they had not been fully adopted.

It was considered that some agencies maintained a confidentiality culture that expressed itself in a 'risk averse' attitude to information sharing. In order to share data as those drafting Section 115 envisaged would not just need a better understanding of Data Protection legislation, but a cultural change within the agencies.

The Safer Derbyshire Research and Information Team Story

Solutions

Joint Funding of Partnership Analysts

The Safer Derbyshire Research and Information Team funding is on 'a third, a third and a third' basis. The Police contribute a third, the County Council likewise, the eight Local Councils combine to provide the final third. Integral to the joint funding is the existence of a Service Level Agreement. The critical element is that it outlines what and when stakeholders will receive reports and products. An annual review is built into the agreement.

Centrally Locating Analysts

A key element of a coherent information sharing process was to have a central hub where data flow could be managed to ensure quality, safe storage and timely dissemination to key people. The vision was to have Partnership Analysts sitting alongside the Youth Offending Service, Drugs and Alcohol Action Team and County Council Analysts. This has been achieved. The team has a wide range of skills and expertise:

- Mapping;
- Census;
- Local Government;
- Marketing;
- Statistical Modelling;
- Police systems;
- Youth offending databases;
- County Council Systems;
- Crime Recording rules.

Co-location allows analysts to discuss suitability and availability of data to inform their various projects, gain an understanding of other partners' information sources and information needs, and work jointly on mutually beneficial tasks without leaving the office or having to make an appointment.

Information Sharing Protocols

There is a broad 'umbrella' agreement that outlines the legal basis and necessity to share data to individual level between the partners. Underneath this agreement lie 'thematic' agreements, for example about Anti-Social Behaviour. Where the thematic agreement is too broad, a specific agreement can be drawn up between individuals about quite specific data. This approach does provide a common framework in which quite specific agreements can be detailed.

Performing

Objectives
These objectives are described in the Safer Derbyshire Research and Information Team Business Plan.
- Service to Community Safety Partnerships:
  To engage effectively with County, City and District-based Community Safety Partnerships to deliver information, analysis and evaluation to assist those partnerships to reduce crime and disorder identified as priorities in their strategies;
- Service to Safer Derbyshire:
  To engage effectively with Safer Derbyshire partners and by prior arrangement deliver information, analysis

and evaluation in order to assist in the delivery of key strategies, priorities and section 17 responsibilities;
- Marketing:
  To brand and raise the profile of the Safer Derbyshire Research and Information Team successfully. to encourage involvement of key partners in the sharing, provision and use of data;
- Risk assessment:
  To promote a risk management approach to crime reduction across the county, in which the focus is on anticipating and preventing problems;
- Team development:
  To review constantly customer requirements and develop Safer Derbyshire Research and Information Team capabilities to deliver an effective top quality service.

Products

The team uses problem-solving methodology to produce regularly documents that identify problems and monitor performance. Some *ad hoc* evaluation of projects has taken place. The inventory is outlined below:
- Statutory Crime and Disorder Audits;
- Partnership community consultation co-ordination, through the existing Citizen Panels, to assess people's experience, perception and fear of crime and disorder;
- Annual and Quarterly Strategy Reports to:
    Eight Community Safety Partnerships;
    Derbyshire Partnership Forum;
- Monthly Crime Figures report on count and cost by Partnership area. Published to the Safer Derbyshire Website;
- Specific Research Projects;

- Project Evaluation;
- Newsletter.

Evaluation

The co-location of the Safer Derbyshire Research and Information Team provides a number of benefits:
- It facilitates the development of a corporate evaluation model;
- It allows discussion between staff across agency boundaries on the meaning of each other's data, giving a greater understanding of a situation;
- There are shorter communication channels along which to share good practice;
- The team is a central contact point for operational staff looking for good practice.

The team's aim to be objective and independent, enabling a realistic critical evaluation of any project.

Customer Comments

> "Thanks – this looks really good, and is exactly what we wanted. Can we distribute this information to our eight District managers for them to put in their District Unit Profiles for the Ofsted inspection?" (Education)

> "Thank you for the assistance and expertise you have afforded the Fire and Rescue Service. Without your help we would have had difficulty to gather and display certain information to demonstrate that we effectively target our resources to areas of greatest need." (Fire Service)

The Safer Derbyshire Research and Information Team Story

"That's really good, exactly what we were after and shows we have had good results there, and made real progress. Thanks very much." (Partnership Community Safety Officer)

"We have always found the reports that your team produce very useful and are an excellent tool for us in our dialogue re performance with the 8 CSPs." (GOEM)

Conclusion

In the space of three years the research and information facility in Derbyshire has gone from being little known, little used and little understood to a centrally located corporate team, delivering to a wide range of partners through existing mainstream systems. It would appear from the customer comments that information sharing is no longer "just a pain".

DEFINING DEVIANT LIFESTYLES: UNDERSTANDING ANTI-SOCIAL BEHAVIOUR AND PROBLEM DRUG USE THROUGH CRITICAL METHODOLOGIES

Craig Paterson and Allyson MacVean

Introduction

In recent years, politicians across the United Kingdom have become increasingly preoccupied with the social management of anti-social individuals and groups. Translating governmental strategies and policies into action at street level requires an understanding of the mechanics of deviant lifestyles and the ways in which lifestyle choices increase the amount of contact that individuals have with the police and other crime control agencies. The subjective nature of terms such as 'anti-social behaviour' (ASB), 'problem drug use' and 'deviant lifestyles' makes it particularly difficult to generate valid data concerning their prevalence or otherwise and presents challenges for methodological approaches. In part, this is due to the governmental drive to regulate and control groups of generally young people without a clear evidence base for these actions. This political strategy bypasses the complexities inherent in understanding ASB and, more broadly, what are perceived to be deviant lifestyles.

In order to make sense of the extent of ASB, it is essential to create a critical understanding of how different groups of people define both anti- and pro-social behaviour. In particular, these include the different perspectives of victims of crime, offenders, people who live in different communities and those who have different life

Defining Deviant Lifestyles

experiences. It would also take account of gender, generational and class differences.

Through police case file analysis and interviews, it has been possible to investigate how different categories of people who come into contact with the criminal justice system understand ASB and deviant lifestyles, particularly in relation to offenders and victims. By using methodology in a more creative way, it is possible to develop a greater understanding of what ASB means to different groups of people. These methodological approaches highlight the fluid nature of victim and offender groups and the importance of subjectivity in understanding terms such as 'anti-social behaviour', 'problem drug use' and 'deviant lifestyles'.

Questions still remain concerning what acts constitute ASB and, because of this, this chapter asks whether there are any similarities between ASB discourse and previous debates about deviance. These debates are illuminated by two recent research studies concerning the policing of ASB and an evaluation of drug lifestyles, both conducted in the Chiltern Vale police area. These examples provide a critical appreciation of two distinct forms of deviant lifestyle that are often misunderstood in the public arena. A bottom-up focus moves the emphasis of the study away from official statistics and instead provides a more holistic vision of community safety issues that emphasises the lived reality of deviant lifestyles. These findings have direct implications for national initiatives concerning the use of ASB legislation and the development of effective harm reduction strategies for drug users. Finally, key questions are raised concerning the problematic role played by political actors in the development of policy and practice and the potentially harmful consequences that this presents for local communities.

The Policing of Anti-Social Behaviour

Public anxiety about crime and individual security is increasingly being accompanied by localised concerns with ASB. Indeed, it has been argued that ASB often has a greater impact than crime upon citizens' day-to-day life, especially on those in vulnerable groups (MacVean, 2001). Though the term ASB is a modern one, a precise definition remains elusive. ASB has been defined as a range of problems – from rowdy behaviour on the streets to littering and abandoned vehicles. The behaviour ranges from criminal activity to that causing lifestyle clashes and is clearly a subjective rather than a prescriptive term.

The Crime and Disorder Act 1998 defines ASB as acting:

> ... in a manner that caused or was likely to cause harassment, alarm or distress to one or more persons not of the same household as the offender.

With such an all-encompassing definition, it can be argued that most citizens will encounter or be engaged in some form of ASB from time to time. For some, it will be an occasional irritant. For others, it is more intrusive. However, it is important to note that behaviour that is regarded as acceptable by some may be completely unacceptable to others. What is acceptable behaviour to young people or people in one community may be difficult for older generations or different communities to tolerate.

Defining Deviant Lifestyles

Although the fear of disorder and ASB has increased significantly, there is little reliable data available on the prevalence of such behaviours. In part, this may be due to the lack of a precise definition of ASB and the fact that data collection is often made problematic by under reporting and non-recording of complaints. On Wednesday 10th September 2003, the ASB Unit undertook the first national day count of reports of ASB in England and Wales. More than 1,500 organisations recorded incidents of ASB over a 24 hour period. During this time, 66,107 reports of ASB were collected. Despite collecting data on the amount of ASB, the one-day initiative did not make any distinction between victims and offenders or their circumstances nor did it provide any analysis of causal factors or harm incurred.

The purpose of the ASB research undertaken in the Chiltern Vale area (MacVean, 2001, 2004) was to evaluate the impact of mental health problems, plus drug and alcohol abuse, upon ASB within a specific region. In order to understand fully ASB (and the fear of it), it is necessary to examine, and gain a greater understanding of, the extent of victimisation, as well as victims' experiences and perceptions. Information on the characteristics of ASB victims is not extensive. Despite this, there is some evidence to suggest that certain groups of people, more than others, are liable to become the victims of ASB (Home Office, 2001). These groups include:

- the poorest individuals and families who are least able to move away from the problem or bear the cost of such behaviour;
- those who are already discriminated against and who have fewer support networks;

- young people who may be susceptible to negative peer pressure or are vulnerable because they are outside traditional support structures, such as school or work;
- other vulnerable groups such as women, children and disabled or elderly people.

Previous research has implied that individuals with a mental illness may be particularly vulnerable to becoming involved in ASB cases. In Leeds, for example, it has been estimated that 30% of ASB cases involve someone with a mental health problem (Bright, 1997). In MacVean's (2004) study, one in seven ASB offenders were recorded as having mental health problems. Indeed, it has been argued elsewhere that ASB sometimes needs to be understood as a symptom of mental illness (Flood-Page, 1999).

In addition, there exists evidence to indicate that certain people and places suffer *repeated* incidents of crime. The British Crime Survey 2000 has estimated that 4% of victims account for between 38% and 44% of all crime reported to the survey (Kershaw *et al.*, 2000) and, according to Pease's (1998) research on repeat victimisation, high crime areas have such high levels of crime because they have more heavily victimised victims, *not* because they have a greater number of victims. The relationship between victimisation, crime and ASB remains unclear. While 4% of victims were recorded as being involved in criminal activity, this was a relatively low figure when compared to the 28% of offenders who were involved in criminal activity in addition to being ASB offenders.

In many cases of ASB, defining who is the victim and who is the offender remains problematic, as people shift in and out of these different roles. Because of this, victims and

Defining Deviant Lifestyles

offenders can perceive themselves to be victimised by the circumstances in which the ASB manifests itself. MacVean's (2001) research has indicated clear patterns in cases of ASB that support these findings:

1. 39% of victims of ASB were the immediate next-door neighbours of the offender;

2. 38% of ASB cases involved several neighbours as victims;

3. 12% of ASB cases involved a dispute within the family.

Demographically, clear links can also be made between housing and ASB. 80% of victims of ASB lived in social housing. In contrast, only 8% of victims of ASB lived in private housing. The remaining 12% of victims had no available details recorded. Similarly, 70% of ASB offenders lived in social housing, whilst only 6% of ASB offenders lived in private housing. 24% of ASB offenders did not have their full details recorded. The following case study highlights the complexities inherent in understanding ASB in its local context.

Chiltern Vale Case Study

A married couple (Mr and Mrs P) have lived in the same property for 22 years. The housing estate that they lived on was originally council owned, but following the government's right-to-buy initiative over 10 years ago they purchased their property. The housing estate was therefore a mix of privately, Council and Housing Association owned properties. This case starts to illustrate the complexity between defining who are the victims and who are the offenders of ASB and, more importantly, how each of them perceives their role. Whereas the couple that were interviewed perceived themselves as victims, there were instances when their behaviour could clearly be defined as anti-social and/or criminal.

The issue of ASB was brought to the attention of the district council over six years ago, when Mr and Mrs P complained about a single parent family living opposite. The nature of the complaint concerned drug dealing and the type of people visiting the property. Mr and Mrs P thought that the housing department did not deal with their complaint effectively and decided to tackle the single parent family directly. This direct contact was aggressive and created further conflict. As a result, Mr and Mrs P saw a further deterioration in the behaviour. They claimed that the family and their visitors were urinating in the hedges and creating disorder, particularly at night. At this stage, Mr and Mrs P contacted the police.

During the next two and half years, the police and housing department of the district council dealt continually with complaints from Mr and Mrs P, at a considerable cost to each agency. Mr P would telephone both the police and the council up to six times a day. Mr and Mrs P also installed CCTV for the specific surveillance of this particular neighbour:

> I installed CCTV that was directly focused on their property ... I had it set up so that you could see their front door and windows. We could even see into the rooms at night – see who was there and what they were up to. The sound quality was really good. You could even hear the people when they spoke quietly. We heard every time someone knocked on

their door. We had a TV in every room in our house that could be used as TVs or monitors to the CCTV. So we could watch what was going on day or night and hear what was being said.

Mr and Mrs P felt that most agencies took a soft view on nuisance neighbours and that they needed to be "... a lot tougher with them". In light of this view, Mr and Mrs P felt that they needed to make a stand against such behaviour and embarked on what can only be described as a crusade against anyone they felt was behaving in an anti-social manner. Mr and Mrs P's perceptions about ASB offenders were that they came from broken families and poor backgrounds. There was a lack of discipline at home and in most cases alcohol or drugs were a factor. However, it was at this point that the behaviour of Mr and Mrs P also started to change, when they threatened their neighbour with a gun:

> The neighbour's brother shouted out to my wife and used language that was foul. I felt I had to stand up to him or this problem would go on forever. So I took my shotgun over and said "... if you ever speak like that to anyone else again, I would make sure it would be the last time you do". Then I went back and called the police.

Mr and Mrs P felt that the ASB had now escalated beyond control and blamed the agencies for not taking a tougher stance:

> The kids smash bottles in the park and put the glass on the slides and swings. They (the young people) just sit and drink and do drugs all evening ... and they always hang around in large groups. It's intimidating and so no one will challenge them. I do. Last week I saw a gang of youths walking down the street. They had pulled up a road sign and was dragging

it along. I stopped my car and got out and challenged them. One of them started being mouthy to me so I grabbed him and put my arm around his neck. Then I saw one of his friends move, so I said, "...if you touch me, I'll break your friend's neck'. Anyway, I made them return the sign up the Road. If more people intervened and became involved, we wouldn't have all these problems.

At this stage, Mr and Mrs P admitted to making up to 30 calls a day to the police and district council complaining about ASB. They felt that the police did not communicate with them enough and, when the police did become involved, the young offenders of ASB knew how to "muck the police about so they don't deal with the issue properly". As a result of Mr and Mrs P's self-driven stance against ASB, the community were starting to retaliate against their behaviour. This lead to several cases of quarrels and arguments with local residents:

> People have to take responsibility for themselves. I know what reasonable force is and I'm not afraid to use it. Part of the problem is that the punishment does not fit the crime anymore and so people have formed vigilante groups. The kids know they can get away with it ... the parents don't care what they do.

This case illustrates how Mr and Mrs P were prepared to engage in criminality to pursue what they considered to be a stance against ASB. What is also notable in this case is what Mr and Mrs P defined as ASB. What was unacceptable behaviour to them was in fact acceptable to the other residents. For example, youths gathering in the local car park or just walking down a street represented a situation that they would challenge. Many of the residents had objected to the way in which Mr and Mrs P treated the young people in their community and this had created

Defining Deviant Lifestyles

problems both for them personally and for the agencies involved with the ASB.

Discussion

This is by no means a unique case. MacVean's (2004) research highlighted that ASB is not just committed by young people. Indeed, the study highlighted that some entire families are persistently engaged in ASB. There are also problems generated when intervening with ASB. In this study, the more that the authorities intervened and were seen to be intervening in local disputes, the more members of the public complained about ASB and generated increased demands on already stretched policing and local authority resources. Given this feedback mechanism and the imprecise nature of ASB, it is difficult to see how ASB can be effectively managed. Whilst some people are obsessive in their pursuit of others for what they regard to be ASB, others may be more tolerant.

The relationship between defining who are victims and who are offenders in cases of ASB is often complex and fluid. Whilst there are many cases in which victims and offenders are clearly defined, there are many in which the roles are liable to change over the course of the case. There are also indications that the longer the case is left unattended, the more the roles of victim and offender become complex. Thus, it is desirable to deal with cases of ASB as soon as possible in order to prevent an escalation of ASB.

Despite this, helping and supporting those most at risk through addressing the root causes of ASB creates a conflict between the punitive and rehabilitative models of intervention, because of the difficulties in separating offenders from victims. For example, linkages between drug and alcohol use and vulnerability were identified in this study, as drug users and alcoholics living alone were targeted by other drug users and alcoholics in a predatory fashion. This leads to a blurring of the victim and offender distinction that is traditionally maintained in criminal cases. Thus, it becomes important to develop an understanding of local lifestyles in relation to local crime and ASB issues, especially those that can be interpreted as deviant or dysfunctional.

MacVean's (2004) study highlights the need to understand anti-social or deviant behaviour within its local context and the limitations presented when trying to understand ASB through a traditional offender-victim dichotomy. Consequently, an understanding of local community safety issues and patterns of offending needs to be expanded into a broader appreciation of deviant lifestyles. This form of analysis escapes the limitations of traditional, audit-oriented counting methods and enables the construction of a bottom-up picture of local needs that is able to make sense of the, often contradictory, demands made upon crime control agencies by diverse communities.

By conducting research in the community, previous methodological limitations can be circumvented and a more holistic understanding of problems of disorder generated. In particular, it is possible to identify the causes of ASB and other types of disorder, rather than responding to their more obvious symptoms. In the second study, analysis was undertaken of drug lifestyles in the Chiltern Vale area in order to assist community safety and drug action team strategies. Once again, the aim was to avoid constructing a traditional offender-victim dichotomy and

Defining Deviant Lifestyles

to focus upon constructing a bottom-up vision of drug lifestyles and their associated problems.

Drug Use, Drug Lifestyles and Anti-Social Behaviour

Although there have been numerous research projects linking drugs and crime, there has been little research on the drug lifestyles of those who are taken into police custody and the impact that their lifestyle, drug use and offending has upon the local community. Knowledge about the range and variance of drug lifestyles within a local community, particularly from those who have come to the attention of the police through criminal activity and ASB, can assist in a more pragmatic and informed understanding of community safety problems. The point of arrest represents a potential gateway into deviant and anti-social lifestyles that are often hidden from view. Previous research has found that some arrestees are initially detained in custody for relatively long periods of time before being released without charge (Choongh, 1997), a process that permits the police to conduct body and house searches that can uncover evidence associated with drug lifestyles. Viewed in this way, regular visitors to custody quickly become viewed as 'police property', by which I mean 'permanent suspects rather than suspects for a particular offence' (McAra & McVie, 2005:7). Criminological research has assisted an understanding of the 'working rules' (Reiner, 2000:87) utilised by police officers and the ways in which they generate a broad suspect population of 'police property'. These rules include demographic factors, such as gender, age, class and ethnicity, alongside previous offences and a subjective understanding of suspiciousness (McConville et al., 1991). Analysis of this suspect population can also illuminate an understanding of ASB and deviant lifestyles. In particular, this enables an understanding of the variable ways in which the public and police officers subjectively define deviant and ASB, and as a result, the policing response to these acts. There is a clear link here with labelling theories. Hanging round with the 'wrong crowd' or in the 'wrong place' makes an individual more likely to be defined as potentially 'anti-social' or 'deviant' and subsequently to become part of the permanent suspect population highlighted above. This labelling process can contribute to additional, and often more serious, contact with the criminal justice system (McAra & McVie, 2005), as an individual or group is increasingly targeted by the crime control machinery.

Evidence from research indicates that the police are most likely to target youngsters from less affluent backgrounds as a consequence of the specific interactions that take place between these individuals and the police (McAra & McVie, 2005). The socio-historical relationship between individuals, groups and the police serves to construct a permanent deviant or suspect population, in which victims and offenders are not clearly differentiated. With enhanced police powers having been provided through ASB legislation, deviant populations find their day-to-day activity increasingly targeted. In the case of drug lifestyles, this means that individuals who have an association with drugs are more likely to encounter searches and arrest and subsequently to be detained in custody. It is clear that once an individual is defined as deviant, they become increasingly subjected to coercive legal strategies.

Police officers are required to make normalising judgements about individuals and groups during their day-to-day work, yet they do not have a monopoly on the use of subjectivity. Subjective judgements about illegal drug use exist within drug cultures and most illegal drug users have clear boundaries when considering which substances they regard as safe (Barton, 2003). This means that a similar labelling process is identifiable within drug cultures, particularly differentiating between occasional or recreational drug use and problem users of heroin and crack cocaine. Equally, this raises questions about the subjective in which occasional or recreational drug use is regarded as normal and is not associated with other offences. This has clear policy implications, particularly concerning anti-drug strategies that conflate all types of illegal drug use. The recent downgrading of cannabis to class C represents the first formal recognition that legislation and policies concerning illegal drug use have not necessarily represented a public consensus or the lived reality of drug lifestyles.

This is not to suggest that drug lifestyles do not produce associated problems. Research from the United States has shown that 'an out-of-control drug user' is likely to commit 80-100 serious property offences per year (Chaiken & Chaiken, 1990). The clear message is that these figures highlighting the relationship between 'an out-of-control drug user' and high levels of offending are closely associated with heroin and crack cocaine use and are less closely associated with other drugs. The endemic problems associated with heroin and crack cocaine use arise once drug markets are established within specific areas. These local drug markets subsequently become increasingly difficult to disrupt as a population of long-term drug users, effectively isolated from mainstream society, develops and many individuals' lifestyle become increasingly dictated by drug use. When tackling the issue of 'drugs lifestyles', it is important to be aware of the multitude of preconceptions that exist. Many people assume that drug addicts are violent criminals or moral degenerates, that they aim to convert non-users into users, and that their reason for using drugs is down to having an 'inferiority complex'. These misguided preconceptions feed into community safety strategies through attempts to manage fear of crime and everyday signs of disorder. Because of this, the governmental focus upon ASB often directly targets the day-to-day lifestyles of all illegal drug users.

The association between problem drug use and ASB has been made at the local level. Research conducted by MacVean (2001) identified that the use of illegal drugs was a contributory factor to the incidence of ASB in 9% of cases. This finding was replicated in a study undertaken by Hedge (2003), in which illegal drug use was identified as an issue in 10% of cases of ASB. A national study undertaken by the Home Office in 2002 (Campbell, 2002) also identified that drug use was put forward as an underlying problem for ASB in 18% of cases.

By expanding upon this quantitative data, it is possible to generate a deeper understanding of the relationship between drugs, ASB, crime and disorder. This can be done through studying the lifestyles of individuals who come into contact with the criminal justice system. In the study highlighted here, the point of contact was the High Wycombe custody suite and the main data source arose from interviews undertaken with arrestees who were awaiting the police's decision regarding whether to charge. In this environment, the researchers worked alongside police officers, drug referral workers and a range of other criminal justice professionals in order to generate a background picture of the lifestyles of individuals in custody.

Understanding Drug Lifestyles in the Chiltern Vale Area

Although High Wycombe's level of overall crime is considerably less than the national average, the level of drug offences is higher. The aim of this study was to develop a more detailed understanding of the lifestyles of drug users, in order to approach and manage the problems presented by drug use to the local community. The use of semi-structured interviews conducted in a police station presented an opportunity to interview a 'hard to reach' group, yet it was also recognised that this would present methodological limitations concerning the validity of data (Patton, 2005). These limitations were partially offset by the use of Police National Computer records and the cross-checking of interviewee's responses. Convenience non-probability sampling was utilised in the study, as each interview required an individual's consent and was dependent upon who was under arrest in custody during each visit. Each interview took place under slightly different circumstances as a consequence of the variable needs of police officers, offenders, solicitors and other professionals.

The research was undertaken over a period lasting from August 2004 to June 2005 and involved spending a total of 98 hours in High Wycombe custody suite. The research involved 48 semi-structured interviews with arrestees in custody, as well as numerous informal discussions with police officers, custody officers and drug referral workers about the lifestyles of drug users. The interviews varied in length from 10 minutes up to 45 minutes. All interviewees were granted anonymity, a factor that was especially important for arrestees in obtaining trust and ensuring as frank and honest a discussion as possible.

High Wycombe has a population of 92,300 and, in comparison to other areas across England and Wales, has a large proportion of the population in its central urban area aged under 30. This has clear consequences for levels of criminality and ASB in the central part of the town, with 65% of arrestees interviewed in High Wycombe being aged under 30. Accentuating this, while the overall rate of unemployment in High Wycombe was 3.5%, the overall rate of unemployment for arrestees in custody was 43%. It was also noted that 27% of all arrestees interviewed in custody came from one postcode area. Once the remit of analysis was restricted solely to arrestees who lived in the Wycombe district area, statistics showed that exactly 50% of arrestees came from this one postcode area. This demonstrates a startling concentration of arrests made within one area of a town. The overall rate of unemployment for arrestees from this area was 50%.

Closer analysis of this area revealed that the most significant local problem was acquisitive crimes, that made up 46% of all offences. Thames Valley Police have recognised the continuing problem presented by acquisitive crime in High Wycombe and its links with the entrenched drug problem. Recognition of this problem was confirmed through analysis of the relationship between drug use and arrest. The research showed that 74% of all arrestees stated that they had used drugs at some point in their lives, while 52% of arrestees stated that they currently used drugs and 58% of arrestees who currently used drugs stated that they did so on a daily basis.

Arrest referral schemes have endeavoured to encourage problem drug users to utilise available treatment services but, for a variety of reasons, the problem still remains. Although 20% of arrestees in custody claimed to have used support services, 31% said they were unwilling to use them and a further 49% said that they were unaware of the services. In part, the poor response to support services arises from a sense of mistrust of the organisations, as well as the first point of contact taking place in a police station. Accompanying this, arrestees who were registered in treatment commonly cited the role of support services as being part of the day-to-day 'game' of acquiring drugs through a variety of legal and illegal avenues. For those involved with the support services, treatment was viewed as a part of the day-to-day drug culture rather than as a separate resource. Compounding this cynicism, in some cases, arrestees saw imprisonment as the only realistic route to giving up drugs. This contextual data on drug lifestyles sheds light on the problems encountered when encouraging problem drug users to enter treatment and the areas of resistance that develop against official harm reduction strategies.

Discussion

In MacVean's (2001) ASB study, Chiltern Vale Police recorded the majority of drug offences as having been committed by individuals in the 18-25 age group. Over 70% of these drug offences involved cannabis and just over 10% involved heroin. In the 2005 study in High Wycombe, 48% of drug users stated that they smoked cannabis, whilst

15% stated that they used cocaine, 15% heroin and 11% crack cocaine. The majority of calls made to the local Crimestoppers agency concerned the use of drugs and the local papers frequently ran stories on drug use and police responses to it. This recognition of the threat to community safety was recognised by the police force's priorities; these included acquisitive crime, drug misuse and the targeting of prolific offenders. Studies of heroin users in Merseyside during the 1980s highlighted how increases in burglary rates followed on from increases in heroin use (Parker & Newcombe, 1987) and served to create endemic heroin populations that spread from the North West of England and London into new, provincial areas during the 1990s (Parker et al., 1998). Once drug markets were established within these areas, they became increasingly difficult to disrupt, as a population of long-term drug users, effectively isolated from mainstream society, developed in areas with high levels of deprivation.

This is similar, although by no means identical, to the situation in High Wycombe. High Wycombe is ranked as the fifteenth wealthiest local authority district in the UK, yet the policing of populations with drug problems has proved to be difficult. Whilst the removal of suppliers can disrupt markets in the short term, all the drug users interviewed stated that this had never stopped them from obtaining drugs. Clear data on the early commencement of drug use, plus the concentration of so many interviewees in one specific geographical area, highlights the entrenched nature and concentration of those living what we refer to as deviant lifestyles.

- 82% of arrestees were initially introduced to illegal drug use through cannabis;

Defining Deviant Lifestyles

- 38% of arrestees first used an illegal drug between the ages of 10 and 13;
- 41% of arrestees first used an illegal drug between the ages of 14 and 17;
- 15% of drug users estimated their weekly expenditure on drugs as being over £500; figures that are supported in Home Office research (National Audit Office, 2004);
- 62% of interviewees had no academic qualifications;
- 64% of arrestees had previous criminal convictions.

The intense concentration of arrestees in a specific geographical location, coupled with the high levels of unemployment experienced by those individuals, ensures that punitive strategies are only able to provide short-term social management solutions to long-term social problems. The early onset of drug use and its clear links with deviant lifestyles and ASB presents problems that cannot be wished away by political moralising and 'tough' crime control strategies. Instead, they require positive, community-oriented, problem solving strategies that are able to appreciate the nature of the causes of social exclusion rather than its associative symptoms.

Conclusion

National public and political debates about ASB, problem drug use and their associative deviant lifestyles have been dominated by assumptions derived from inner city areas and areas of high deprivation (Thames Valley Partnership, 2005), rather than provincial areas. For areas like Thames Valley, this enhances public fear of disorder and leads to the increased likelihood of punitive intervention strategies being utilised rather than low-level community-based resolutions. Understandings of social exclusion have a tendency to highlight problems such as drug use, crime and anti-social behaviour, rather than unemployment, education and housing issues (Watt & Jacobs, 2000). This is particularly relevant to High Wycombe, where a large proportion of social housing has been privatised. This has condensed local problems, such as drug misuse and the release of individuals with mental disorders into the community, into a confined area, thus enhancing the potential of social conflict (MacVean, 2001).

It is through critical analysis of the politicisation of crime control strategies that one is able to understand how rebuilding communities for the majority can reinforce the social exclusion of minorities (Young, 1999). The increasing focus upon low-level ASB, such as vandalism, graffiti, and the (visible) use of alcohol or illegal drugs, encourages strategies of social management that move already socially marginalized people from public view. This strengthens the relative socio-economic differences between housing areas and subsequently increases the risks in poor, socially excluded areas (Kempa et al., 2004). In these areas, social management strategies increasingly emphasise the regulation of problematic individuals and groups through forms of contractual compliance such as curfew orders, ASBOs and Acceptable Behaviour Contracts (ABCs).

Political scaremongering and its 'evidence-based' justifications can only be counteracted by ethnographic studies that enable an understanding of the lived reality of problems at the ground level and dispute the audit-oriented 'regimes of truth' (Foucault, 1980) produced by central government. Local problems concerning crime and anti-social behaviour vary to a great degree because of the socio-cultural context that they have developed within, and subsequently require locally tailored responses to problems of disorder (Grieve, 2004). This article presents an introduction to studies incorporating a 'bottom-up' understanding of the 'anti-social' problems generated by deviant lifestyles and provides a framework for local agencies to identify current service gaps and to target their resources within a specific area.

Despite the national drugs strategy placing considerable emphasis upon the role of communities in responding to the problems presented by drugs, this is an area that remains underdeveloped and there is still relatively little evidence of drug user or ex-drug user involvement in strategic decision-making structures (Shiner *et al.*, 2004). Equally, while the term 'ASB' initially incorporated a wide range of problematic but normally sub-criminal behaviour, the political capital subsequently placed in Anti-Social Behaviour Orders (ASBOs) led to a blurring of the boundaries between criminal and civil cases and a heightening concern about the extent and severity of ASB in local communities. Qualitative case studies produce more practical guidance on local problems of disorder and potential solutions than many national audit-oriented studies, yet this does not mean that their findings are not equally as susceptible to subsequent politicisation.

References and Other Publications

Barton, A. (2003). *Illicit Drugs: use and control*. London: Routledge.

Bright, J. (1997). *Turning the Tide*. London: Demos.

Campbell, S. (2002). *A Review of Anti-Social Behaviour Orders*. Home Office Research Series 236. London: Home Office.

Chaiken, J.M., & Chaiken, M.R. (1990). Drugs and predatory crime. In Tonry, M., and Wilson, J.Q. (eds), *Drugs and Crime*. Chicago: University of Chicago Press.

Choongh, S. (1997). *Policing as Social Discipline*. Oxford: Clarendon Press.

Flood-Page, C. (1999). *Disengaged Teenagers: Findings from the 1998/9 Youth Lifestyle Survey* (unpublished research). London: Home Office Research, Development & Statistics Directorate.

Foucault, M. (1980). Truth and Power. In C. Gordon (ed.), *Michel Foucault, Power/Knowledge: Selected Interviews and Other Writings 1972-1977*. Brighton: Harvester.

Grieve, J. (2004). Developments in UK criminal intelligence. In J. Ratcliffe (ed.), *Strategic Thinking in Criminal Intelligence*. Sydney: Federation Press.

Hedge, J. (2003). *Anti-Social Behaviour: Tackling the Problem Together*. A Report commissioned by Thames Valley Partnership.

Home Office. (2001). *Crime Reduction Toolkits: anti-social behaviour*. Retrieved 27th October 2005, from: www.crimereduction.gov.uk/toolkits

Kempa, M. Stenning, P., & Wood, J. (2004). Policing Communal Spaces: A reconfiguration of the "Mass Private

Property" Hypothesis. *British Journal of Criminology,* 44 (4), 562-81.

Kershaw, C., Budd, T., Kinshott, G., Mattison, J., Mayhew, P., & Myhill, A. (2000). *The 2000 British Crime Survey England and Wales.* Home Office Statistical Bulletin 18/00, London: Home Office.

MacVean, A. (2001). *A Report on the High Wycombe Anti-Social Behaviour Partnership.* A Report commissioned by Thames Valley Police.

MacVean, A., Watt, P., & Giles, N. (2004). *The Policing of Anti-Social Behaviour in the Chiltern Vale Police Area.* A Report commissioned by Thames Valley Police.

McAra, L., & McVie, S. (2005). The usual suspects: streetlife, young people and the police. *Criminal Justice,* 5(1), 5-36.

McConville, M., Sanders, A., & Leng, R. (1991). *The Case for the Prosecution.* London: Routledge.

National Audit Office. (2004). *The Drug Treatment and Testing Order: Early lessons.* Retrieved 7th October 2005, from: www.nao.org.uk/publications/nao_reports/0304/0304366 .pdf,.

Parker, H., Bury, C., & Egginton, R., (1998). *New Heroin Outbreaks amongst Young People in England and Wales: Crime Detection and Prevention Series – Paper 92.* London: Home Office.

Parker, H., & Newcombe, R. (1987). Heroin use and acquisitive crime in an English community. *British Journal of Sociology*, 38, 331-50.

Patton, D. (2005). An Exploration of the external validity of self-report amongst arrestees. *Surveillance and Society*, 2(4): 564-580.

Pease, K. (1998). *Repeat Victimisation: Taking Stock*. Crime Detection and Prevention Series – Paper 90. London: Home Office.

Reiner, R. (2000). *The Politics of the Police – 3rd Edition*. Oxford: Oxford University Press.

Shiner, M., Thom, B., MacGregor, S., Gordon, D., & Bayley, M. (2004). *Exploring Community Responses to Drugs*. The Joseph Rowntree Foundation: Drug and Alcohol Series.

Stenson, K. (2002). Community safety in Middle England: the local politics of crime control. In G. Hughes and A. Edwards, *Crime Control and Community*. Cullompton: Willan.

Thames Valley Partnership. (2005). *Mending Fences: The development of a problem solving and community oriented approach to anti-social behaviour*. Project Workbook June 2005.

Watt, P., & Jacob, K. (2000). Discourse of social exclusion: an analysis of Bringing Britain Together: A National Strategy for Neighbourhood Renewal. *Housing, Theory and Society*, 17, 14-26.

Young, J. (1999). *The Exclusive Society*. London: Sage.

BACK TO THE FUTURE: INNOVATION, EVALUATION AND REVERSE SURVIVAL ANALYSIS

Kate Bowers, Shane Johnson and Ken Pease

Introduction

Much ink has been spilled and many trees felled to fuel debates about evaluation strategy. In particular, the status of the Randomized Control Trial (RCT) as the *ne plus ultra* of evaluation has been extensively debated, and will not be discussed further here, beyond noting a sympathy for the approach advocated by Pawson & Tilley (1997) as scientific realism. The debate about the putative effect of lighting on crime, which will be referred to later, is sterile insofar as it simply compares one state (lit) to another (not lit). Pease (1999) argued that the thrust of the research enterprise should move towards an examination of lighting variation (by time and place) and its crime co-variates. The suggestion is in line with the Pawson & Tilley emphasis on understanding context-mechanism-outcome relationships, and is developed below as 'effect signatures'.

The starting point for this chapter is that the RCT, however desirable it may be, is not always, indeed not often, practicable for community safety evaluations, limited as they typically are by time and budget. How does one get most value out of the non-RCT evaluations which *are* practical? The key notion is of effect signatures. This concerns the pattern of results which reflect mechanism, just as signatures bespeak identity – and equally important, which fail to reflect cherished but erroneous ideas about mechanism. Attention to effect signatures has recently been increased by the popular appeal of the research of the ingenious Steve Levitt. He showed, *inter alia*, that discrimination by black people and gender is not evident (but discrimination against Hispanics and the elderly is) in voting to eliminate contestants in TV quizzes, by analysing eliminations, having taken into account question-answering ability. He uses shortfall in takings under an honour system of payment for bagels as a way of determining factors driving levels of honesty (see Levitt & Dubner, 2005). Other Levitt originals include the extent to which estate agents use expert knowledge to their clients' disadvantage, and the effects of racially specific forenames on employability. The approach is most persuasive when disparate analyses point to the same effect signature, as in Levitt's analysis of apparent corruption in Sumo wrestling.

While the Levitt portfolio of work provides much pleasure and insight, that comes from the cleverness with which he hunts effect signatures, rather than from the intrinsic novelty of the approach, which has already been deployed extensively in criminology (see, for example, Farrell & Buckley, 1999; Milgram *et al.*, 1965; Wasik & Pease, 1986), and in social science more generally (for example, Webb *et al.*, 1966). Moreover, beyond the social sciences, where the experimental manipulation of phenomena is impossible or unrealistic, the effect signature approach is commonplace, as for example in astronomy (see Vogt *et al.*, 2000) and epidemiology (see Elliott *et al.*, 2000). None the less, the Levitt work usefully sensitizes the reading public to the scope for pursuing effect signatures, as a means of hunting down or testing hypotheses about socially important mechanisms. Arguably, the optimal time for the deployment of RCT comes when effect signatures have done all they can to exclude impossible and clarify possible mechanisms. At that point an RCT sharply focused on a specific, plausible and partially tested hypothesis about the operation of a relatively well-defined mechanism may be needed.

Where to Look for Signatures

Recognizing effect signatures usually depends upon intimate knowledge of the putative mechanism involved. Demonstrating the existence of distant planetary bodies, for example, depends upon measured deviations from expected orbits of other such bodies. Because signatures will only be anticipated and recognized by the prepared mind, there can be no general 'recipe' for finding them. Arbitrating between competing hypotheses about mechanisms, however, often involves working through what the different effect signatures would be and then collecting data to determine which yields the better prediction.

What is offered below is a heuristic device to accompany any initiative where time-flagged data are available, whose use is likely (but not certain) to circumscribe the range of possible mechanisms in operation. The underpinning for what follows stemmed from consideration of the debate mentioned above concerning the effects of street lighting on crime. The stages of the debate can be followed in Marchant (2004) and Farrington & Welsh (2006), but appears now to turn on the disentangling of treatment effects from regression effects. The technique described below has this issue as a convenient starting point, and will be discussed with that in mind, but it now appears to have more general application for discerning effect signatures, and their consideration beyond the regression context is developed in the second half of the chapter. The approach is very simple, and surely must have been used somewhere before. At its present stage it is a heuristic device, but ideas about how to develop it into a formal statistical approach will be raised, albeit only fleetingly, in this chapter. The relevant work is in hand. The writers are prepared to cede originality when they encounter prior use, having been so far unable to find any in the major statistical textbooks on survival analysis or elsewhere.

Treatment Effects, Regression Effects, and Telling the Difference

Areas or people targeted for intervention because they are extreme relative to others are also likely to be extreme relative to themselves at other times. They are more likely to become less extreme over time, by the process known as regression to the mean. This is a mixed blessing. In his classic paper, 'Reforms as Experiments', Donald T. Campbell (1969) invented his 'trapped administrator' who, by acting only when things were at their worst, was rewarded by apparent success. While regression to the mean offers relief to the trapped administrator, it is the bane of evaluators' lives. Self-evidently, initiatives will be taken where they are perceived to be needed. Police crackdowns will focus on problem areas, programmes for offenders on those judged most prolific. They may thus, though lacking merit, be doomed to success as regression comes into play.

Proposed below is a variant of survival analysis, a technique well-established in medical and engineering contexts, as an approach to (*inter alia*) establishing programme effects net of regression. Survival analysis is traditionally used to establish treatment efficacy or product durability, with the crucial advantage over fixed-term follow-up periods of incorporating time-censored data. It allows trial termination at whatever point statistical reliability is achieved and is thus particularly suited to use in clinical trials. In the medical context, survival can only operate forwards in time. Possible religious exceptions aside, no-one who was dead yesterday is alive today. In engineering settings likewise, survival works in only one direction. Few non-organic things heal themselves. However, survival analysis can be applied in other contexts for any state transition. Within criminology, it was first used to look at the reconviction of offenders (Carr-Hill & Carr-Hill, 1972) and this remains its most common criminological application (see, for example, Tarling, 1993).

In most criminological contexts, survival analysis can be deployed working forwards or backwards in time. In criminal careers, the survival time to the last conviction can be calculated as readily as that to the next conviction. For crime victimization, the same applies. Johnson and Bowers (in press) have used forward survival analysis as an efficient method of evaluating a location-based crime reduction initiative. To the writers' knowledge, this has not been done before. However, regression to the mean may compromise their conclusions.

Reverse survival analysis may seem counter-intuitive, and the appropriate first step is to provide a simple example. Readers already comfortable with the notion are invited to skip to the next section.

Let us suppose that all households in an area are fitted with new locks on a given date, in the hope of preventing burglaries. Figure 1 shows forward survival rates, specifically the proportion of homes remaining unburgled a number of months later. (The rates of burglary depicted are obviously too high, but make the depiction clearer.) It

Community Safety: Innovation and Evaluation

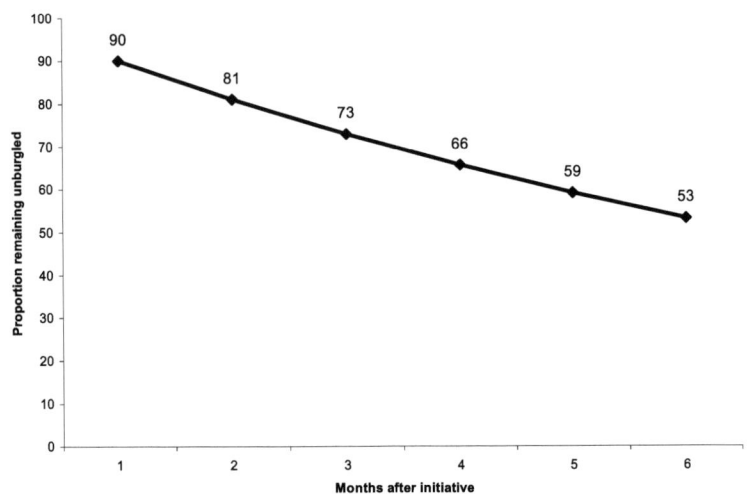

Figure 1. Simple Forward Survival.

will be seen that after one month, 90% of homes remain unburgled, falling to 53% after 6 months.

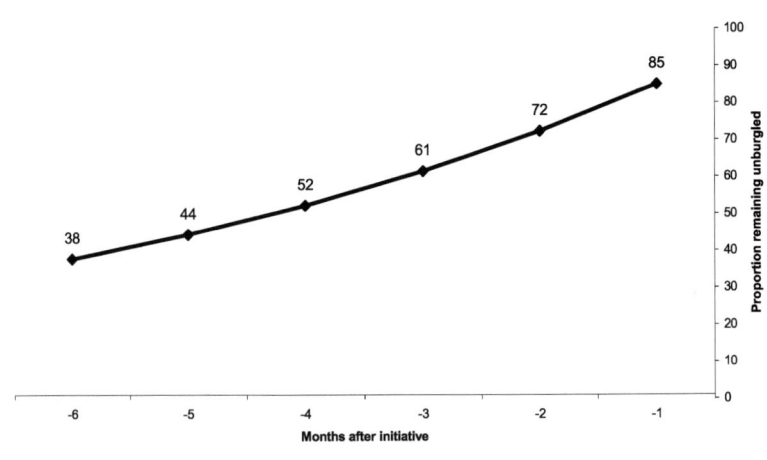

Figure 2. Simple Backward Survival.

Innovation, Evaluation and Reverse Survival Analysis

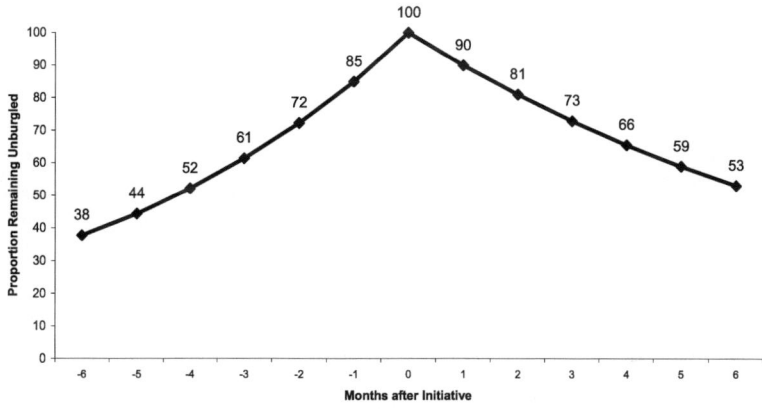

Figure 3. Survival Forwards and Backwards.

There are two ways of moving towards interpretation of the line in Figure 1: comparing survival rates over the same time in a different area or comparing survival rates within the area at different times. Working backwards in time from the implementation date might yield something like Figure 2, so that in the month before implementation, 15% of homes had been burgled (hence 85% remaining unburgled), and so on. Combining Figures 1 and 2 yield Figure 3. Scrutiny of Figure 3 makes it reasonably clear that survival rates are higher after than before the initiative. The picture becomes much clearer when Figure 3 is folded at the point when the initiative starts, so that the backward (minus) elapsed times lose their negative sign. Figure 4 shows Figure 3 folded in this way. Figure 5 presents Figure 4 as after-before odds-ratios. For example, one month after the initiative, 90% of households remain unburgled. Counting backwards from the initiative, at the one month point 85% of households remain unburgled. Thus the after-

Community Safety: Innovation and Evaluation

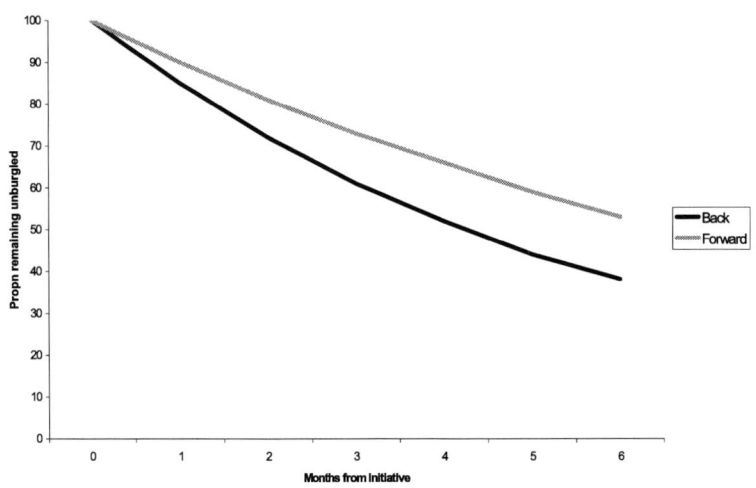

Figure 4. Survival Back and Forwards (Folded).

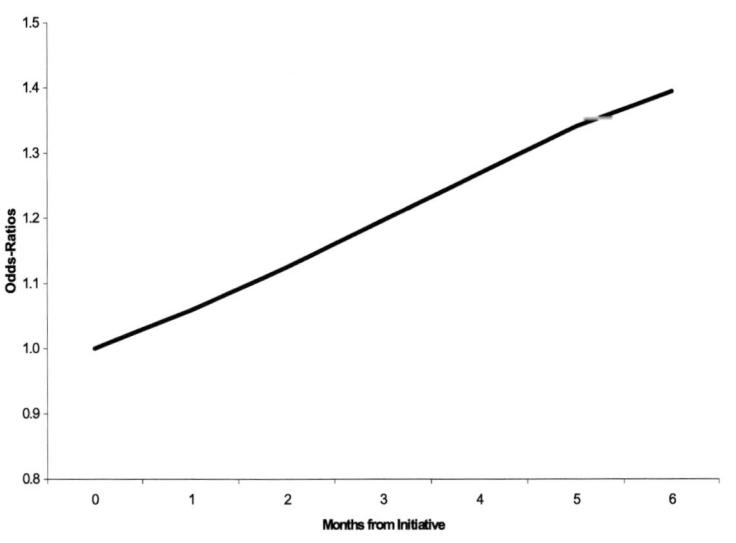

Figure 5. Forwards/Backwards Survival Odds-Ratios.

Innovation, Evaluation and Reverse Survival Analysis

before odds-ratio at this point is 0.9/0.85 = 1.06. The after-before odds-ratio, and changes in it, provide a simple way of thinking about effect signatures. [1]

It was noted earlier that effects could be assessed (imperfectly) both by examination of trends in the treatment group and by the use of a comparison group which, for everything apart from the RCT, will be imperfect. If the same steps set out above are followed for a comparison group, we end up with two lines representing after-before odds-ratios, one for the treatment group and one for the comparison group. In the interpretation of the two odds-ratio lines lies the heuristic value of the approach set out here. In what follows, survival curves rather than their derived odds-ratios are displayed, because they are more easily understood by those new to the ideas set out, but the reader should bear in mind that it is odds-ratios and their change which may form the basis of developments of this technique in later publications.

In order to illustrate the way in which having details of the survival of action and control groups both forwards and backwards in time can help in the interpretation of the outcome of an intervention, we describe and graph a number of different scenarios below. In each case, the y axis represents the point of intervention from which we track survival backwards and forwards. At each time point, the y value represents the proportion of the action and control groups that are still 'surviving', those who have not experienced a crime event between the date of

---

[1] This is a simplifaction for the purposes of exposition. If the probability of an event P is p, the odds are $p/(1-p)$ rather than $p/1$ as implied in the text. The odds-ratio in the illustration thus calculated is about 1.08.

intervention and the end of the particular time period. The x axis represents the time that has 'elapsed' (or in the case of backwards survival 'un-elapsed') since the intervention. The scale of the x axis is left unspecified. This could be days, weeks or months since intervention, according to taste.[2]

It Works!?

In the case illustrated in Figure 6, the action and control groups are perfectly matched. This is evident from their identical historic survival pattern looking back from the date of intervention (time point zero). Looking forwards following the date of implementation, the survival of the control group perfectly mirrors its own historic survival - showing that the risks to this group do not change following the intervention. In contrast, the average survival time in the action group is longer in comparison to the historic survival of the action group *and* the post-implementation survival of the control. This provides evidence that the intervention was successful in reducing levels of victimisation over the period considered. The confidence with which that conclusion can be reached depends upon further analysis of odds-ratios or the survival curves from which they were derived (see below).

Regression Rules

In Figure 7, the interpretation is of regression. The action group's survival rates more distant in time from the

---

[2] In the second and last footnote for the statistician, it should be noted that the charts do not depict the conventional cumulative hazard function.

Innovation, Evaluation and Reverse Survival Analysis

Figure 6. Treatment Effect? Black: treatment. Grey: comparison. Solid: forwards. Dashes: back.

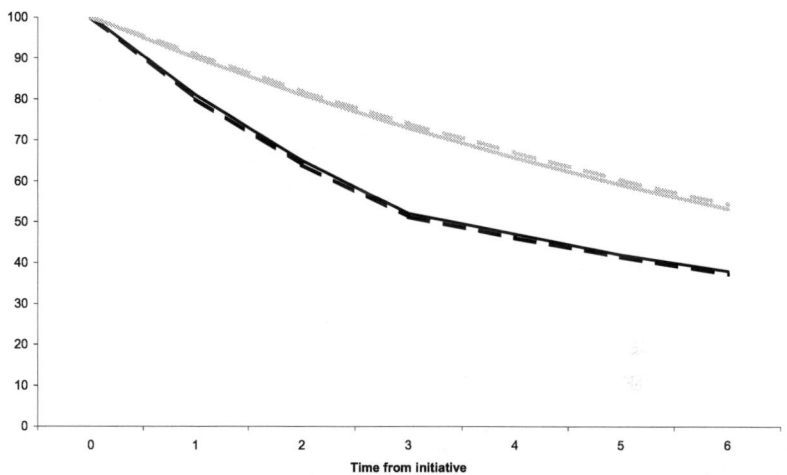

Figure 7. Regression Effect. Black: treatment. Grey: comparison. Solid: forwards. Dashes: back.

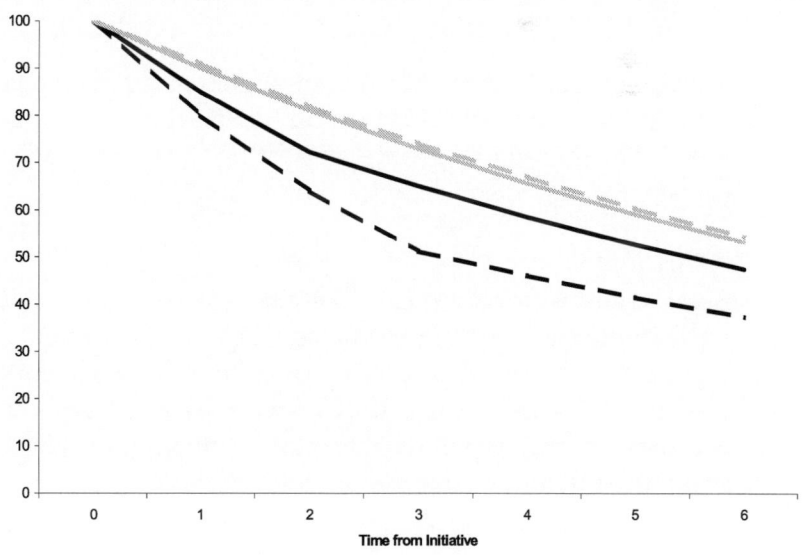

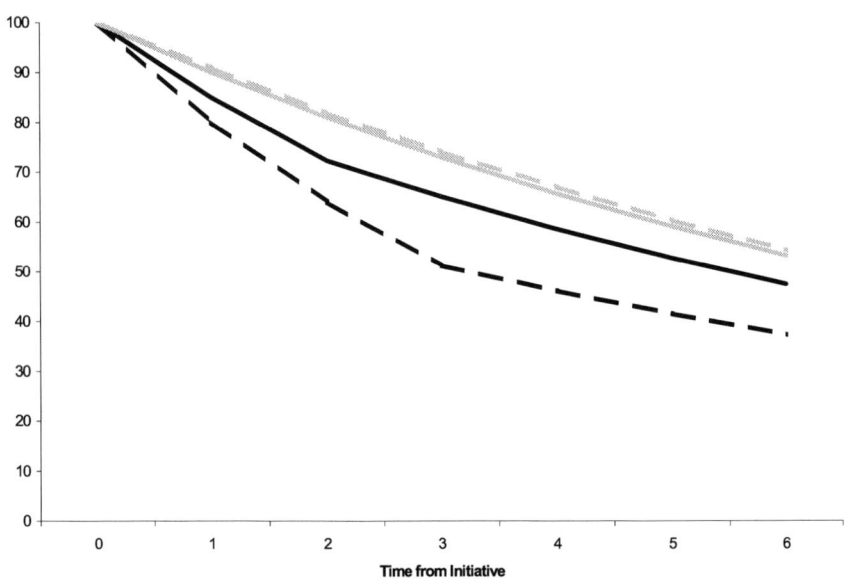

Figure 8. Treatment + Regression. Black: treatment. Grey: comparison. Solid: forwards. Dashes: back.

initiative, both forwards and backwards, are similar to each other and to those of the comparison group. However around the point of intervention the survival rates are lower for the action group, indicating that times were, transiently, bad specifically for that group.

A Mixture
Because life is not simple, a likely outcome involves both regression and treatment effects. This is illustrated in Figure 8. The position of the treatment forward curve relative to the treatment backward curve and the comparison curves yields information about the relative strength of treatment and regression effects.

Innovation, Evaluation and Reverse Survival Analysis

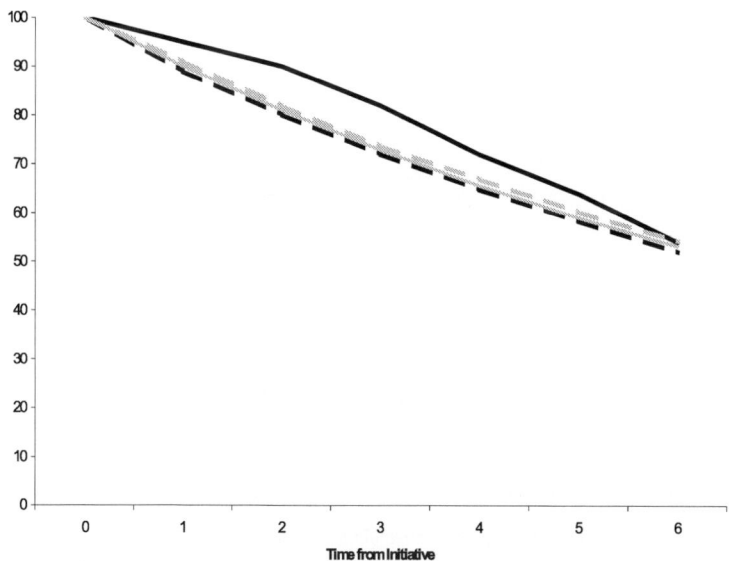

Figure 9. Transient Treatment Effect. Black: treatment. Grey: comparison. Solid: forwards. Dashes: back.

Beyond Regression

As noted earlier, backwards survival analysis has value beyond simply distinguishing treatment and regression effects. The next three figures illustrate signatures that are likely to prove common.

Figure 9 illustrates a transient treatment effect. Figure 10 shows a situation where there is no treatment effect and the comparison group was ill-matched with the treatment group. Figure 11 illustrates anticipatory diffusion of benefits, where the onset of the treatment effect comes before the date the initiative begins and which is extremely common in crime reduction initiatives (see Johnson & Bowers, 2003; Smith *et al.*, 2002).

Community Safety: Innovation and Evaluation

Assuming that the reader has now become familiar with the underlying thinking, rather than drown the chapter in figures, Table 1 sets out the putative (not definitive) implications of some of the other possible effect signatures in a crude descriptive way.

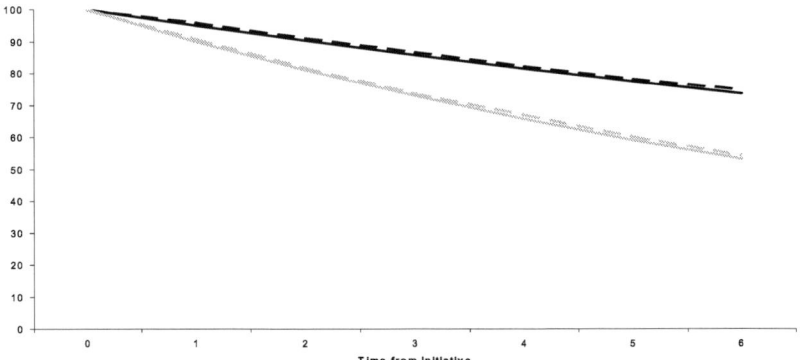

Figure 10. Ill-Matched Comparison, No Treatment Effect. Black: treatment. Grey: comparison. Solid: forwards. Dashes: back.

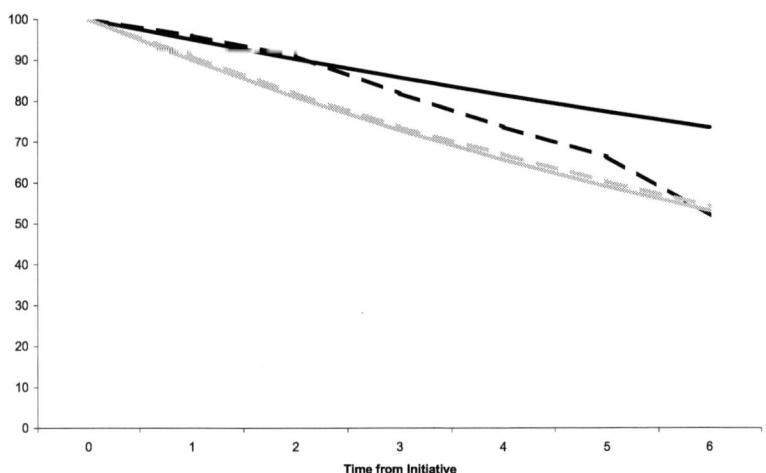

Figure 11. Anticipatory Diffusion of Benefits. Black: treatment. Grey: comparison. Solid: forwards. Dashes: back.

Table 1. Patterns and Putative Effects (NB > means higher survival hence less victimisation).

Backward	Curves	Forward	Curves	Interpretation
Treatment < Comp	Converge	Treatment < Comparison	Converge	Regression only (see Fig. 7)
Treatment = Comp	Coincide	Treatment > Comparison	Converge	Time-limited treatment effect (see Fig. 9)
Treatment = Comp	Coincide	Treatment > Comparison	Diverge	Strengthening Treatment effect
Treatment < Comp	Converge	Treatment > Comparison	Diverge	Treatment area getting better before and after
Treatment = Comp	Coincide	Treatment < Comparison	Converge	Things got transiently worse *immediately* after initiative
Treatment = Comp	Coincide	Treatment < Comparison	Diverge	Things got worse and worse after treatment
Treatment = Comp	Coincide	Treatment = Comparison	Coincide	Nothing happens
Treatment = Comp	Coincide	Treatment > Comparison	Diverge	Treatment effect
Treatment = Comp	Coincide	Treatment > Comparison	Diverge	Better and better
Treatment > Comparison	Converge	Treatment < Comparison	Converge	Regression?

Community Safety: Innovation and Evaluation

FPQ's (Frequently Pondered Questions – By Us)

We are confident that simply looking at the curves as set out will help preliminary thinking as to effects and their mechanisms, and that it will lead to further analyses of effects provisionally identified – for example, whether the transient area risk associated with a regression effect is distributed across sub-areas or victim characteristics or reflects a passing increase in rates of repeat victimization. However, we recognize that the more rigorous use of the approach depends upon assigning confidence levels to particular apparent patterns, and then applying the approach to crime reduction initiatives. Both of these tasks are in hand. In the meantime, there are some points to which enough thought has been given to mention here.

a. Crime risk and crime spates
Often an intervention is installed where the vulnerability of the 'action' group has recently increased (notably where the action household has suffered a recent victimization). In this case, due to the widely acknowledged finding that an initial offence leads to a greater likelihood of a repeat event (and nearby events, as a crime spate: see Johnson & Bowers, 2004) in the short term, it is expected that the survival time will fall in the action group anyway, and this effect will occur independent of any intervention. However, the predictive value of victimization applies whether somewhere has been designated as a comparison or a treatment area. As long as treatment-comparison matching is consistent with the mode of deployment of the treatment, the approach is not compromised. Thus, if a home receives protection from burglary immediately upon a burglary event, the start time is specific to each burgled home. The clock starts running (both forwards and

backwards!) from the time of the offence. That should apply to comparison areas also. If an initiative is area-wide, the unit of count is the area, and the clock starts for all homes in both treatment and comparison areas at the same time. The approach further provides both an indication of the precision with which a comparison area has been chosen with respect to the phenomenon of interest, and fluctuations around the point of intervention.

b. Asymmetric censoring
What effect does asymmetric censoring have? Backwards survival does not involving censoring data in the same way that forward survival does. Of course, cases that have to be censored going forward can be censored backward by matching, but it would be better to understand the principles involved, which is work in progress.

c. Building on survival modelling
Justice has not been done in this chapter to prior work on survival modelling, and it may be that some simple extension of that work will incorporate time direction, for example by incorporating it as a co-variate in a proportional hazards model (see Cox, 1972). Work in progress attempts to apply such an approach.

In Conclusion

This paper suggests that looking backwards in time at the historic survival of action and control households can help assess whether any differentiation in forwards survival might be due to real effects of intervention, or measurement bias such as regression to the mean. Studying effect signatures in this way should also give insight into other aspects of intervention outcome, such as transitory effects, delayed effects, anticipatory benefits and estimations of sustainability.

One additional advantage survival analysis as currently conceived offers over more traditional approaches such as area-level pre- and post-intervention comparisons, or time-series analyses, is that the latter approaches actually introduce measurement error. The reason we suggest this is that area-based interventions are rarely (if ever) fully implemented within a concentrated interval of time; rather implementation is usually more temporally diffuse, taking months or even years. Thus, where the impact of an intervention is modelled as starting from one particular point in time (as is usually the way), imprecision is introduced, thereby increasing measurement error. By using a survival analysis, where the starting point of intervention is measured with more acuity, being exact for every unit in receipt of treatment, this form of measurement error is minimized. Thus, the inclusion in the analysis of backwards survival times can help distinguish the variance explained by measurement error attributable to regression to the mean, and the use of the actual start dates for each unit of treatment helps reduce measurement error still further.

The initial discussion of this chapter frames the conceptual use of backwards survival, but does not venture into the issue of the measurement of the statistical significance of outcome based on such models. The reason for this is that the authors did not want the discussion to get lost in the detail. It is the signatures that are paramount. That said, our initial thoughts for inferential statistical testing favour the use of approaches such as Cox regression. Such an approach would compare differences in forwards survival, as measured by hazard rates.

Explanatory variables for hazard rate differences would include group (whether the household was action or control) and backwards survival time (time since previous victimization). Interaction terms could prove a useful way of assessing the possible influence of regression to the mean, or in disentangling subtle effects. Further analysis might examine relative changes in the odds of survival for the action and control groups over time. Backwards odds ratios should provide an indication of 'normal' variation in the absence of intervention. This could then be used to assess signatures in forward survival to identify points in time where the difference in survival between groups is especially low or high.

Acknowledgements

We are grateful to Mark Dancox and Graham Farrell for comments on this chapter.

References

Campbell, D.T. (1969). Reforms as Experiments. *American Psychologist*, 4, 409-429.

Carr-Hill, G.A., & Carr-Hill, R.A. (1972). Reconviction as a Process. *British Journal of Criminology* 12, 35-43.

Cox, D.R. (1972). Regression models and life tables. *Journal of the Royal Statistical Society, Series B*, 34, 187-220.

Elliott, P., Wakefield, J.C., Best, N.G., & Briggs, D.J. (2000). *Spatial epidemiology: methods and applications.* Oxford: Oxford University Press.

Farrell, G., & Buckley, A. (1999). Evaluation of a Police Domestic Violence Unit using Repeat Victimization as a Performance Indicator. *Howard Journal of Criminal Justice and Crime Prevention,* 38, 42-53.

Farrington, D.P., & Welsh, B. C. (2006). How Important is Regression to the Mean in Area-Based Crime Prevention Research? *Crime Prevention and Community Safety,* 8 (1), 50-60.

Johnson, S.D., & Bowers, K.J. (2003). Opportunity is in the eye of the beholder: The role of publicity in crime prevention. *Criminology and Public Policy,* 2, 201-228.

Johnson, S.D., & Bowers, K.J. (2004). The stability of space-time clusters of burglary. *British Journal of Criminology* 44, 55-65

Johnson, S., & Bowers, K. (in press) *Evaluating Crime Prevention: The Potential of Using Individual-Level Matched Control Designs.*

Levitt, S.T., & Dubner, S.J. (2005). *Freakonomics.* London: Allen Lane.

Marchant, P. (2004). A Demonstration that the Claim that Brighter Lighting Reduces Crime is Unfounded. *British Journal of Criminology,* 44, 441-447.

Milgram, S., Mann, L., & Harter, S. (1965). The Lost Letter Technique: A Tool of Social Research. *Public Opinion Quarterly,* 29, 437-438.

Pawson, R., & Tilley, N. (1997). *Realistic Evaluation.* London: Sage.

Pease, K. (1999). A Review of Street Lighting Evaluations: Crime Reduction Effects. In K.Painter and N.Tilley (eds), *Surveillance of Public Space: CCTV, Street Lighting and Crime Prevention*. Monsey NY: Criminal Justice Press.

Smith, M., Clarke, R., & Pease, K. (2002). Anticipatory Benefits in Crime Prevention. In Tilley, N. (ed.), *Analysis for Crime Prevention*. Monsey NY: Criminal Justice Press.

Tarling, R. (1993). *Analysing Offending*. London: HMSO.

Vogt, S.S., Marcy, G.W., Butler, P., & Apps, K. (2000). Six New Planets from the Keck Precision Velocity Survey. *The Astrophysical Journal*, 536, 902-914.

Wasik, M., & Pease, K. (1986). Parole and Party Politics. *Criminal Law Review*, 379-382.

Webb, E.J., Campbell, D.T., Schwartz, R.D., & Sechrest, L. (1966). *Unobtrusive Measures; nonreactive research in the social sciences*. Chicago: Rand McNally.

WHAT DO WE MEAN BY 'WHAT WORKS?'?

Nick Tilley

Evaluation has become something of a contemporary shibboleth. All policies, projects and programmes have to be weighed, measured, costed and assessed for outcome and value for money. It is through this that accountability is supposed to be achieved. By evaluating what we do, it is assumed, furthermore, that informed decisions can be made about where to allocate future resources. We are expected to learn from evaluations about how better to achieve our objectives. Whether we be in education, health, social services, criminal justice or any other part of the public service, we face the prospect of evaluation, review, inspection, audit and a welter of performance indicators. Unfortunately, those of us in public service lack the politicians' periodic encounter with their electoral paymasters to adjudicate on our performance; moreover, we miss the commercial world's bottom lines as a benchmark of our achievement. Whether we work in universities, schools, local authorities, health services or the police, we pursue diffuse, hard-to-measure objectives, with no mechanism for chickens automatically to come home to roost if we fail. A veritable evaluation industry has grown to meet the gap.

A strong argument could be made that there is rather too much evaluation. A great deal is certainly crass and misleading, with foolish questions eliciting foolish answers – we come to this in more detail in due course. Moreover, there is a danger that the foolish answers to the foolish questions will receive more attention than the sensible answers to the sensible questions. Much recent evaluation-related activity takes the form of performance indicators.

What Works

These select for attention specific functions and specific ways of capturing those functions, at the expense of wider public service aims. There is little doubt that Postman Pat, glorious as a public servant though he may have been, would be found very seriously wanting according to standardised performance measurements. (After writing this, a real example came to light with the removal of Adele Dawson from her 17 years of delivering post in Kellington, North Yorkshire, because she was too slow, as a result of her services to those, including the elderly and infirm, to whom she delivered letters – see Mark [2005].)

Evaluation in the field of crime prevention has been notoriously weak. It was my responsibility when I was seconded to the then Crime Prevention Unit in the Home Office in 1992 to see what could be squeezed from the evaluations required from the 3,500 schemes run in Phase One of the Safer Cities Programme. I'd been brought in because an earlier review of scheme-level evaluations had found them individually to be so poor. There were only a few aspects of Safer Cities work where I was able to piece together enough to say anything with much confidence – the introduction of CCTV in car parks (Tilley, 1993a), a range of efforts to prevent domestic burglary (Tilley & Webb, 1994), and various attempts to reduce crime against small businesses (Tilley, 1993b). In one Safer City, over 100 schools had been fitted with an innovative alarm system. Neither the local authority, nor the school, nor the police could provide usable data either about dates of alarm installation or about patterns of crime and disorder before and after the introduction of the alarms. This is no criticism of Safer Cities. The same is found pretty much wherever crime prevention schemes and their evaluations are at issue.

A 575-page review of all evaluations of local crime prevention efforts, led by Lawrence Sherman (and available on the internet), confirms the weakness of most evidence about the effectiveness of most crime prevention efforts. From his side of the Atlantic, he quotes conclusions from this side, where he says:

> A recent review of the crime prevention evaluation literature by two prominent English criminologists concluded the field was "dominated by ... self-serving unpublished and semi-published work that does not meet even the most elementary criteria of evaluative probity" (Ekblom & Pease, 1995:585-6). What they meant by "evaluative probity" was fairly basic to any inference of cause and effect. Measures of crime, for example, are very often missing from publicly funded crime prevention "evaluations", which simply describe how the program worked and whether it achieved its administrative objectives: services provided, activities completed. Despite the recent emphasis at reinventing government to focus on results, most crime prevention evaluations still appear to focus on efforts. (Sherman *et al.*, 1997)

Sherman advocates a much more focused approach in which, instead of a very thin veneer of fairly meaningless evaluation across a huge range of schemes, what is needed are substantial resources targeted on a much smaller number of technically adequate pieces of work.

There are several reasons for the weakness of much evaluation:

- evaluation is rather dull compared to the creative and exciting business of conceiving and launching a project;
- evaluation as such does not help anyone, and is expensive if done properly;
- evaluation is technically difficult;
- evaluation can be rather threatening for those with interests in the projects and programmes subject to it.

When the findings do not suit them, 'victims' of evaluations are apt to complain that their evaluators did not understand what they were doing, applied measurements that were too crude, or looked for effects too early.

Independent evaluators are apt to find their subjects uncooperative and defensive, unable or unwilling to keep proper records, to dig out data or to face up to failed efforts (Tilley, 2000). The following discussion does not address all these issues directly. What it raises instead is the very forms that evaluation questions may take. Different ways of framing questions clearly affect the answers that are given. We need to be careful to ask questions in sensible ways. We need equally to be careful in interpreting answers. There are better and worse ways of putting evaluation questions. A by-product of ensuring that questions are asked well is that some of the blocks to good evaluation may be dissolved.

The following discussion briefly presents sets of evaluation questions under each of the following headings:

- The opportunist questions;
- The purely historical questions;

- The constant conjunction questions;
- The prophetical questions;
- The realistic questions;
- The options questions;
- The practical questions.

Of course, some of these sets of questions are in some cases interdependent. As we go through each, I shall discuss the relationship between them.

I should add that all the variants on the 'what works?' questions examined here share a concern with the **outcomes** of initiatives, not simply their **outputs**. The distinction is an important one. Outputs refer to what is delivered by an initiative - say numbers of locks or alarms fitted, neighbourhood watches set up, or victims visited. Outcomes refer to the effects that the initiative has, including both intended and unintended ones. For example, reduction in the rate of victimisation is an intended outcome and the increase in fear of crime is generally an unwanted one. Where the relationship between output and outcome is well-established, it may be reasonable to disregard outcome questions, since they are much more complex to address, involving as they do complex matters of causality imputation which do not need to be addressed when we restrict our attention to outputs.

The cynical/opportunist questions, including:

- What can be made to seem to work?
- What can be made to seem to have only beneficial side-effects?
- What can be made to seem to be cost effective?

Unfortunately these questions are all too often those that are asked, even if only implicitly. The agenda is often flagged when those contracting an evaluation are asked why they want one undertaken. Where the answer is, as it often is, 'Because we want to prove what a good job we're doing', that normally indicates that from their point of view the conclusion of the evaluation is a foregone one. And, given the range of choices over what data to use, over the selection of before and after periods, and over which *ad hoc* comparison groups to use, it is almost always possible for someone with enough ingenuity to contrive a success story. A prize-entry project I recently reviewed selected the highest and lowest month at the start and a plausible end-point of the initiative. There was indeed a downward trend, but with a great deal of fluctuation in between, and hints at seasonal variation too, but all this was disregarded in favour of headline claims that a 90% fall had been achieved.

Advertisers and marketers, as well as competition entrants, will have an interest in weaving plausible success stories to build into their sales pitch. Ministers can be interested in good news for their speeches, and officials can tout for success stories. Community Safety steering groups will want to motivate partners with accounts of achievement. Scheme workers will want to pick out successes, since jobs and careers may depend on them. Local authorities can want to be seen to run schemes with positive outcomes, because grant applications are more persuasive if past spending can be shown to have produced a positive impact. Yet these forms of evaluation are a menace if we are really interested in improving our ability to control crime problems effectively and efficiently. It is most damaging when negative evidence is suppressed (and it sometimes is) and when schemes are talked up into widely championed successes and others are invited to emulate them.

Whilst the temptation to elicit evaluations responding to these questions may seem overwhelming in some cases, they should always be resisted. It would be naive, however, to expect those with strong vested interests in representing their activities or products as successful not to be selective in their use of evidence. Planners of schemes, though, can learn to read success claims critically. Those providing information on crime prevention activities as a public service can usefully either refuse to incorporate data on supposed impacts, or use quality controls to avoid reproducing spurious success stories.

One Safer Cities evaluation that I reviewed related to a scheme that had cost £100,000. The report was prepared by a researcher attached to the project. I read it and the data seemed to suggest that no impact had been had. The researcher's stated conclusions suggested that it had been a triumph. I asked the researcher about it. She told me that the scheme had had to be defined as a success, given the amount of money spent and given that it had been important in cementing police-local authority partnership working. The 'success' was duly publicised as a means both of celebrating what had already been achieved and of underlining what might in future be expected from further partnership activity.

The purely historical questions, including:

- What did work?
- What side-effects were produced?
- What did work effectively and efficiently?

Some very sophisticated experimental evaluations address these questions and do so painstakingly. Measurement systems are established to find out whether there really was a change associated with the introduction of the crime prevention measure or scheme. Efforts are made to check that there was nothing other than the intervention that could explain any change that has taken place. Efforts are made to find an adequate control group to compare with the experimental group to establish whether the change would have happened anyway. Ideally, there is random allocation to experimental and control conditions, to side-step selection bias. All this will deliver more or less robust evidence that the introduction of some measure or some scheme was genuinely associated with a given set of changes. It aims at 'internal validity'. It assembles strong evidence for the counterfactual - that things turned out differently from they way they would have done had the intervention not taken place.

History is most interesting, of course, for historians. Unfortunately, as we shall see, policy-makers and practitioners are more interested in the future. The purely historical question and the experimental methods used to address it can be poor guides to the future, for reasons I shall give in due course. As we shall see later in this chapter, though, achieving positive results to historical questions can indeed have an important role to play, but only as a starting point for further work.

One well-known evaluation was undertaken of two Neighbourhood Watch schemes in London (Bennett, 1990). It did not find any impact to speak of. Though technically this is a very skilful piece of work, it is not clear what lessons follow from this other than that the

Neighbourhood Watches in question did not produce the hoped-for impacts, perhaps because there wasn't much of a problem or because they were not implemented very energetically. However, from this and from a host of other studies of neighbourhood watch, we were able to construct a forward-looking account of Neighbourhood Watch, drawing together what was known from diverse research sources (Laycock & Tilley, 1995).

The constant conjunction questions, including:

- What always works?
- What side-effects are always produced?
- What always works effectively and efficiently?

At a meeting of the then Home Office Retail Action Group, discussing an apparently effective intervention in Eastbourne, it was said by one member that, 'If it works in Eastbourne, it will work anywhere on the planet', and that was the rationale for the evaluation. As claimed here, it is often implicitly understood that if a high quality evaluation asking the historical question comes out with positive findings, it follows that the same impact will be found anywhere and any time that the same measures are introduced. Constant conjunction between scheme and impact is sought, and it is assumed that it will be delivered through the verdict on the historical question. As many philosophers have pointed out, there is a logical error in this. If an association was found in the past, it does not mean that the same will always be found.

An instructive crime prevention example can be found in Sherman's substantial overview of evaluations of initiatives introducing mandatory arrest for domestic violence (Sherman, 1992). Different high quality historical evaluations have evidently come up with contradictory conclusions: according to some, perpetrator arrest reduces repeat domestic violence; according to others, it increases repeat domestic violence. What are we to make of this? Do the evaluations cancel each other out? Are they all inconclusive, so we need more research? Were some conducted poorly, and are hence unreliable? It turns out that perpetrator arrest may reduce domestic violence in some circumstances, and increase it in others. Amongst the unemployed, especially in areas of concentrated unemployment and single parenthood, perpetrator arrest seems to increase repeat domestic violence, presumably by increasing anger where little shame will follow from arrest. Contrariwise, amongst the employed living in stable neighbourhoods, perpetrator arrest seems to reduce repeat domestic violence, presumably by creating shame for the offender. In different circumstances, the same measure appears to work in different ways to produce contrary outcomes. Real variations in contexts mean that measures work differently to produce differing effects. We cannot, thus, conclude that just because a particular initiative was once associated robustly with a particular effect, it will always and everywhere be so.

Indeed, a moment's thought would lead us to realise that what goes for Eastbourne would not necessarily go for Brixton, Bradford or Buxton, much less for places further afield on the planet: Bombay, Beirut, or Bangkok.

Plain 'What works?' questions, premised on simple constant conjunction assumptions, are doomed to disappoint and to produce misleading answers. It is foolhardy to ask them. Nothing works all the time. It is simply a mistake to believe that this must be the case. The worst assumption, sadly held by many, is that, if the historical question comes out with a positive answer, it follows that the same positive result will be found whenever the same measure is introduced. It won't.

The prophetical questions, including:

- What will work?
- What side-effects will be produced?
- What will work most effectively or efficiently?

Schemes which have been successful in the past are often replicated in the expectation that similar effects will be achieved in the future. Here, then, constant conjunctions are anticipated. The future will reproduce the past. The mandatory arrest for domestic violence example has already shown how ill-conceived this view can be. Let me mention another: The Kirkholt Burglary Prevention Project was multi-faceted (see Forrester *et al.*, 1988, 1990). The following comprise a selection of its attributes:

- 'Kirkholt' was conceived and undertaken as a well-resourced demonstration project;
- 'Kirkholt' was about developing crime prevention measures in a high crime area;
- 'Kirkholt' was about tackling high crime areas, which are clearly circumscribed and can thus be treated as identifiable communities;
- 'Kirkholt' was about the removal of highly attractive targets (coin meters), which had rendered the area, in which such 'money boxes' could confidently be expected, a popular one with burglars;
- 'Kirkholt' was about carefully diagnosing the particular crime problems (burglary in an estate) and tailoring responses to these;

- 'Kirkholt' was about developing an effective inter-agency response to crime;
- 'Kirkholt' was about harnessing the community to protect itself from crime (through cocooning);
- 'Kirkholt' was about focusing on multiple victimisation and reducing it;
- 'Kirkholt' was about clarity of initial research, clarity of crime prevention method tailored to research findings, and clarity of leadership in implementing measures;
- 'Kirkholt' was about burglary prevention and was offence specific.

In practice, differing groups trying to replicate Kirkholt focused on different features (see Tilley, 1996). In principle, it was not self-evident which they had to follow. A mixed bag of impacts were felt in the replications, which is not surprising given that different measures were applied and the areas in which the replications were tried were in most cases quite different from Kirkholt.

In practice, it is, of course, important to ask predictive questions. They are, however, complex and always conditional.

The realistic questions, including:

- What works for whom in what circumstances?
- What will produce which side-effects in what circumstances?
- What will work most effectively and efficiently in what circumstances?

The previous questions have assumed that the 'What?' of 'What works' is unproblematic. It is the measure that works – for example, the property marking, neighbourhood watch, CCTV, or target hardening. Unfortunately, matters are rather more complicated than that. We need to know what it is about a particular measure which makes it work. Moreover, we also need to know what conditions are needed for the realisation of its potential to bring about change.

Gloria Laycock (1997) conducted a classic study of property marking and burglary. She raised the question, 'What is it about property marking which has (or may have) an effect on burglary?' Property marking certainly does not comprise a physical barrier preventing goods from being taken. What is it, then, that makes it work as a crime prevention measure? Is it that burglars are caught and punished, because they are found in possession of stolen goods that police can trace back to the owners because they find marks? Is it that prospective burglars think they will be caught and punished when the police find the marks? Is it that the sticker on the window puts burglars off? Or what?

In her evaluation, Laycock comes up with compelling evidence that it was credible publicity, persuading prospective burglars that burglary was being taken seriously, which led them to change their behaviour. Laycock asked what realists call the 'mechanism' question: 'What is it about the measure which made it work?' Laycock also goes one step further than this: she also shows that the publicity mechanism is contingent on conducive conditions. It will not always work in all circumstances and in this way inoculate householders against burglary. The measure has to be implemented to the crashing of cymbals and the banging of drums in a concentrated way and with high take-up by residents for the publicity mechanisms to work. In addition, the burglars themselves needed to be local, and, possibly by participating in the scheme, they had themselves to believe in its efficacy. This is what happened in the South Wales villages in which Laycock's demonstration project took place. She thus asks, not only the mechanism question, but also about what realists call the 'context' for the mechanism to be triggered to have the effect. Laycock shows that it is not simply a case of property marking directly stopping burglary.

Property marking had its impact in the South Wales study area because of the way it affected the reasoning of the would-be offenders in the circumstances in which it was brought in. Laycock formulates what realists call a 'context-mechanism-outcome pattern configuration': she shows how property marking worked, in the context in which it was introduced, to generate an identifiable effect. She began with one theory as to how this might have occurred, tested it, refined it, and came out with a more refined theory which can be used, and is also open to further refinement.

What goes for property marking goes for any crime prevention work. We need to know how it works where it is being used. Unless we do so we cannot learn usefully for the future. We need to be able to figure out how our proposed action will work in the conditions in which it is contemplated and we need good quality realistic evaluations to help us in that thinking. And good quality realistic evaluations will only emerge if they begin with the realistic questions and go about data collection to answer them.

I should add that the realistic question does not necessarily entail the adoption of any particular research techniques. Laycock's study was an experiment. Case studies, sifts through historical data, ethnographies and so on might all be undertaken in the course of realistic evaluations (see Pawson & Tilley, 1997; Pawson, 2006).

The options questions, including:

- What can work?
- What side-effects may be produced?
- What can work effectively and efficiently?

Things that can work are normally worth taking forward. The historical question ('Did this work?') can be useful if showing that a measure has potential. Unfortunately, any particular failure will not be sufficient to show that a measure cannot be effective. It might be that it was tried in the wrong place or implemented in the wrong way. Once enough evidence has been produced to show that an effect can be brought about, there is little to be gained from repeating the same question. If in any subsequent study the consequence does not follow, it is not shown that the impact cannot be created through the measure, only that the conditions were not conducive to its being effective.

The aircraft industry would never have emerged had historical failure been taken to mean permanent failure! Once we had learned that we could build flying machines, the ensuing problem was that of doing so reliably, cheaply and safely. In crime prevention, we are attempting to engineer safer communities. The raw material of human life is clearly different from that of physical objects, and our task is thus in many ways rather different from that of the physical engineer. Yet we can usefully take a leaf out of the inventive engineer's book. We can look at what can work, work through ways of making things work better, and learn to overcome problems with things that ought to work: (on illuminating models from engineering, see Petroski [1992]).

In the case of CCTV, for example, we do by now have some studies that show that CCTV can play a part in crime prevention (for example, Poyner, 1997; Armitage *et al.*, 1999). Other findings find that it does not always do so (Ditton & Short, 1999). The trick is to find out where it can and cannot have a positive impact, so as to use it appropriately (Phillips, 1999; see also Gill, 2003). This entails a realistic approach, difficult though this may be (see Gill & Turbin, 1999).

The practical questions, including:

- What will work for this problem here?
- What side-effects will be produced here, if this is done?
- What will be most effective and efficient here?

Practitioners implement policies and make use of evaluation findings, applying them as intelligently as they are able within the constraints facing them. In their decisions about advice to potential victims, in their encounters with offenders, in their interventions in planning and so on, their concern is to prevent crimes that would otherwise be committed, and to do so without provoking unwanted, unintended consequences. They have an interest in a developing knowledge-base that will permit them to anticipate the impact of their interventions. They want to be able to make good judgments about what will work in the circumstances facing them. They require habits of thought shaped by education in principles derived from systematic research. They need to know what can work and they need to be able to make informed judgments about the conditions in which that potential will be activated when they meet them. The *savoir faire* or 'tacit knowledge' (Polanyi, 1958; see also Tilley, 2006) that practitioners use is an inescapable part of any successful project implementation. It can usefully be informed by realistic evaluations. In so far as it goes beyond this into unspoken 'personal knowledge', there is a role for eliciting the assumptions, articulating and formalising them, and subjecting them to test and refinement.

What practitioners want to learn is what will or what could work to address the problem they are concerned with in their circumstances. They need realistic evaluations.

Conclusion

We can summarise our conclusions about 'What Works' questions with the following seven rules:

1. Always avoid opportunist questions.
2. Do ask historical questions, but as precursors to realist questions.
3. Do not ask or expect meaningful answers to constant conjunction questions.
4. Do ask prophetical questions, but making sure you are sensitive to specific conditions.
5. Always ask realist questions.
6. Ask options questions, and answer them drawing on a wide range of literature that helps identify

variations in outcomes produced by the same measure.
7. Ask practical questions and answer them drawing on refined theory, informed by realist evaluations and realist reviews.

I began by highlighting the parlous state of crime prevention evaluations, and the reasons for them. A broadly realist approach could help elicit better evaluations. Realist evaluations bring a range of distinctive advantages:

- They are more interesting to undertake than other types of evaluation, since they delve into the theory behind the intervention and its effects;
- They attend to practitioners' and policy-makers' thinking about how schemes could bring about their impact;
- Measurement efforts are targeted at points where impact is most expected – the specific expected signature of effects is identified and focused on;
- There should be less scope for practitioner and policy-maker resistance to the evaluator, since their thinking is build into the evaluation;
- They bring the added benefit that practitioners and policy-makers, knowing that they face realistic evaluation, may learn to plan interventions whose method of working to bring about the intended impact is thought through fully in advance. And that may improve crime prevention work itself (see Tilley & Laycock, 2002).

Finally, the 'what works' agenda is obviously attractive, because it looks as if it is hard-nosed and is rooted in common sense. By now we have quite a large volume of research that has been undertaken in its wake. Some is technically poor by any standards, and can on its own provide little insight. Some follows rather rigid methodological notions about what does and what does not constitute robust evidence of effectiveness. There is currently a major concern with capitalising on past research, to bring together findings to distil lessons. This is welcome, because there are risks in trusting the findings of single studies – there is too much scope for error, and the particular conditions in specific studies may make any generalisation very risky. There are two major approaches to drawing together findings. One tries to catalogue 'What works' lessons for policy-makers and practitioners by summing findings that meet specified methodological standards that purport to exclude threats to internal validity. This is associated with the Campbell Collaboration (www.campbellcollaboration.org). Another tries to distil what can be learned from rather a wide range of studies that use different techniques, in order to inform policy-makers about how to deal with problems through the intelligent application of tested theory. Ray Pawson has illustrated this and developed a review methodology (Pawson, 2002, 2006; Pawson & Tilley, 2001; Tilley, 2006). The general approach is reflected in the problem-specific COPS guides published by the US Department of Justice (for example, Clarke, 2002).

Readers are advised to look at both. It seems to me, though, that individual evaluation studies adopting realist, 'What for whom in what circumstances?' questions will be most useful. Moreover, realist reviews of past research, which can certainly draw on experimental 'What did work' studies, also most usefully try to draw together what is known of 'What works for whom in what circumstances?' It is this that will be best suited to informing answers to practitioner and policy-maker questions about options for policies and practices that will bring about intended consequences, whilst avoiding unintended and unwanted ones.

Even here, we should be aware that much skill and judgment (wisdom, *savoir faire* and tacit knowledge) will be needed by the informed policy-maker and practitioner to maximise the chances of success (Tilley, 2006). There are many sources of uncertainty. As the title of a recent book that catalogues many sources of uncertainty in many fields of human economic and social activity indicates, '...Most Things Fail' (Ormerod, 2005).

References

Armitage, R., Smyth, G., & Pease, K. (1999). Burnley CCTV evaluation. In K. Painter and N. Tilley (eds), *Surveillance of Public Space: CCTV, Street Lighting and Crime Prevention.* Crime Prevention Studies Vol. 10. Monsey NY: Criminal Justice Press.

Bennett, T. (1990). *Evaluating Neighbourhood Watch.* Aldershot: Gower.

Clarke, R. (2002). *Thefts of and From Cars in Parking Facilities.* Problem-Oriented Guides for Police Series No. 10. Washington: US Department of Justice.

Ditton, J., & Short, E. (1999). Yes, it works, No, it doesn't: comparing the effects of open-street CCTV in two adjacent Scottish town centres. In K. Painter and N. Tilley (eds), *Surveillance of Public Space: CCTV, Street Lighting and Crime Prevention.* Crime Prevention Studies Vol. 10. Monsey NY: Criminal Justice Press.

Ekblom, P., & Pease, K. (1995). Evaluating crime prevention. In M. Tonry and D. Farrington (eds), *Building a Safer Society*. Crime and Justice Vol 19. Chicago: University of Chicago Press.

Forrester, D., Chatterton, M., & Pease, K., with the assistance of Robin Brown. (1988). *The Kirkholt Burglary Prevention Project, Rochdale*. (Crime Prevention Unit Paper 13.) London, UK: Home Office.

Forrester, D., Frenz, S., O'Connell, M., & Pease, K. (1990). *The Kirkholt Burglary Prevention Project, Phase II*. Crime Prevention Unit Paper 23. London: Home Office.

Gill, M. (ed.) (2003). *CCTV*. Leicester: Perpetuity Press.

Gill, M., & Turbin, V. (1999). Evaluating "Realistic Evaluation": Evidence from a study of CCTV. In K. Painter and N. Tilley (eds), *Surveillance of Public Space: CCTV, Street Lighting and Crime Prevention*. Crime Prevention Studies Vol. 10. Monsey NY: Criminal Justice Press.

Laycock, G. (1997). Operation Identification, or the power of publicity? In R. Clarke (ed.) *Situational Crime Prevention: Successful Case Studies, Second Edition*. New York: Harrow and Heston

Laycock, G., & Tilley N. (1995). Policing and Neighbourhood Watch: Strategic Issues. *Crime Detection and Prevention Series Paper 60*. London: Home Office.

Mark, D. (2005). Village postie pays price for first-class friendliness. *Yorkshire Post* December 2nd.

Ormerod, P. (2005). *Why Most Things Fail*. London: Faber and Faber.

Pawson, R. (2002). Evidence-based policy: the promise of "realist synthesis". *Evaluation*, 8: 340-58.

Pawson, R. (2006). *Evidence-Based Policy: A Realist Perspective*. London: Sage.

Pawson, R., & Tilley, N (1997). *Realistic Evaluation*. London: Sage.

Pawson, R., & Tilley, N. (2001). Realistic evaluation bloodlines. *American Journal of Evaluation*, 22, 317-324.

Petroski, H. (1992). *The Evolution of Useful Things*. New York: A. Knopf.

Phillips, C. (1999). A review of CCTV evaluations: crime reduction effects and attitudes towards its use. In K. Painter and N. Tilley (eds), *Surveillance of Public Space: CCTV, Street Lighting and Crime Prevention*. Crime Prevention Studies Vol. 10. Monsey NY: Criminal Justice Press.

Polanyi, M. (1958). *Personal Knowledge*. London: Routledge.

Poyner, B. (1997). Situational crime prevention in two parking facilities. In R. Clarke (ed.), *Situational Crime Prevention: Successful Case Studies, Second Edition*. New York: Harrow and Heston

Sherman, L., (1992). *Policing Domestic Violence*. New York: Free Press.

Sherman, L., Gottfredson, D., MacKenzie, D., Eck, J., Reuter, P., & Bushway, S. (1997). *Preventing Crime: What Works, What Doesn't, What's Promising. A Report to the United States Congress.* Washington: US Department of Justice.

Tilley, N. (1993a). Understanding Car Parks, Crime and CCTV. *Crime Prevention Unit Paper 42.* London: Home Office.

Tilley, N. (1993b). The Prevention of Crime Against Small Businesses: The Safer Cities Experience. *Crime Prevention Unit Paper 45.* London: Home Office.

Tilley, N. (1996). Demonstration, Exemplification, Duplication and Replication in Evaluation Research. *Evaluation,* 2, 35-50.

Tilley, N. (2000). The evaluation jungle. In S. Ballantyne, K. Pease and V. McLaren (eds), *Crime Prevention: What Works?* London: IPPR, pp. 115-130.

Tilley, N. (2006). Knowing and doing. In R. Clarke and J. Knuttson (eds), *Crime Prevention Studies* Vol xxx, pp. 217 ff. Monsey, NY: Criminal Justice Press.

Tilley, N., & Laycock, G. (2002). Working Out What to Do: Evidence-based Crime Reduction. *Crime Reduction Research Series Paper 11.* London: Home Office.

Tilley, N., & Webb, J. (1994). Burglary Reduction: Findings from Safer Cities Schemes. *Crime Prevention Unit Series Paper 51.* London: Home Office.

'SAFER HOMES': AN INNOVATIVE APPROACH TO TACKLING DOMESTIC BURGLARY

Jeremy Warren and Graeme Gerrard

Introduction

Domestic burglary has for some time, and still remains, a government priority for crime reduction. The Association of Chief Police Officers recognised in 2002 that, whilst there were some models of good practice being accomplished across the country in respect of domestic burglary, there was no single source of good practice which forces could refer to when developing their own response to domestic burglary. The consequent development of the National Good Practice Guide and Tactical Options Guide by members of Cheshire Constabulary, which the implementation team referred to as a Business Process Analysis of the Force's response to domestic burglary, led them to question the processes which the Force had in place to deal with incidents of domestic burglary. The process of implementing the collective guidance within 'The Guide' became known within the Force as 'Safer Homes'. This implementation involved a comprehensive review of existing policies and procedures, with a mapping exercise to the good practice contained in 'The Guide'. This mapping and comparison exercise led directly to the creation of the 'Safer Homes' project, as Cheshire Constabulary changed policies and practices in line with the good practice collected. Whilst this project was not designed specifically as a community safety improvement initiative, the project implementation team felt that, at a 'common-sense' level, any improvements they managed to achieve against the key objectives would also have a beneficial effect on perceptions and levels of community safety in Cheshire.

This chapter will examine in some detail the background that led to the development of the 'Safer Homes' Initiative, both within Cheshire and also nationally. It will then consider why it was deemed important and necessary to develop a National Good Practice and Tactical Options Guide for tackling domestic burglary within the different force areas. This becomes significant as it has long been recognised within the police service that a 'one-size fits all' approach to the policing of particular problems does not work and that forces have to be free to respond to the crime problems of their local area in a way which best matches the manifestation of the problem on 'their patch' and the resources they have available to deal with the issue. This was recognised by Hirschfield (2004), when developing a typology of characteristics for projects arising from the Reducing Burglary Initiative.

The Development of the Domestic Burglary Good Practice and Tactical Options Guide

Within a short period of time of agreeing to lead the ACPO Burglary Reduction Working Group, one of the authors was presented with one of those rare opportunities that one initially wishes one had avoided. He was asked to write a good practice guide on how to investigate and reduce domestic burglary. At the time (December 2002), domestic burglary accounted for about one in 10 recorded crimes committed in England and Wales each year, a total of approximately 434,000 offences, and costs to society were estimated at over £2 billion per year in stolen property, damage and criminal justice system resources. The costs of burglary were examined by Brand and Price in 2000 and then again in 2005 (Brand & Price, 2000, 2005), when the identified costs were comparable to the Cheshire Constabulary estimates reported here.

The police service in England and Wales was struggling to meet the Public Service Agreement Target set by the Home Office to reduce domestic burglary by 25% by 2005, the baseline being set in 1998-99. The ten police forces involved in the Street Robbery Initiative (Tilley, 2004) had recently produced a Good Practice and Tactical Options Guide and it was thought that a similar guide focused on domestic burglary would assist forces in combating this form of criminal activity. Although there was a significant amount of research associated with domestic burglary and numerous tactical options, there was no single document that captured all available good practice.

A small project team was established, partly funded by the Home Office Police Standards Unit. The initial approach by the project team was to write to all Chief Constables in England and Wales and request examples of good practice in relation to burglary investigation and reduction. Unfortunately, only three forces responded to the initial circulation. Forces were either not prepared to share their good practice or they didn't feel that what they were doing constituted 'good practice'. Either way, the Project Team had to adopt a different methodology in order to gather material for the Guide.

Monthly data in relation to burglary investigation and reduction performance was examined and those police forces that appeared to be performing well were visited by members of the Project Team. This direct approach was more successful and every Force that the project team visited was prepared to share details of their strategic and operational policy, as to what they were doing. Operational tactics were examined and collated and the Project Team soon became adept at spotting an approach that was different and appeared to be effective.

Evaluation of the different tactical options was an issue that was considered by the Team in the early stages of the Project. If they were to label the practice as 'good' and include it within the National Guide, some form of evaluation as to its effectiveness needed to be undertaken. Anyone involved in the detailed examination of policing within the UK will know that comprehensive evaluation of new initiatives is not something the Police Service is particularly good at. Reasons as to why this may be the case include the dynamic nature of policing and the complexity of the environment within which the initiative is operating (Tuffin et al., 2006). It is almost impossible to isolate a new initiative from the surrounding changes that are constantly taking place, which makes it difficult to determine what works. Added to this is an organisational culture that perceives the need to 'get on with it', and produce immediate or at the very least early results.

Not surprisingly, the 'get on with it' culture also impacted upon the production of the Guide, in that there was pressure to produce the document as soon as possible. The project team therefore made a decision that they would not undertake any independent evaluation of each tactical option or example of good practice, but instead rely on the evaluation by the supplying force together with our own professional judgement. If it worked for them, then there was a likelihood that the initiative would work elsewhere. This approach no doubt horrifies those who insist on an academically rigorous evaluation involving control areas and a well defined methodology.

The visits to the Forces by members of the project team produced a wealth of information and by the time the document was finalised, 32 out of the 43 police forces in England and Wales had contributed by providing examples of good practice or tactical options. This information was collated with academic research on the subject of burglary, Home Office sponsored research studies and contributions from a number of agencies such as Trading Standards, the Forensic Science Service and Crime and Disorder Reduction Partnerships. The project team also examined developments in burglary investigation and reduction outside the UK.

Traditional approaches to the investigation of domestic burglary have either tended to focus on the activities of those officers that have been allocated the crime for investigation or have focused on one element of the overall process: i.e. repeat victimisation, crime scene examination, intelligence gathering, etc. (Jacobson, 2003). The approach used by the Project Team was different in that they adopted a holistic approach to the problem and viewed the investigation of domestic burglary as a series of business processes, starting from the initial call from the victim through to the final disposal of the case within the Criminal Justice System.

The adoption of a business process model extended the nature of the Project, in that it required each element of the process to be examined, current performance to be assessed and good practice established (Alderman, 1998; Darnton & Darnton, 1997; Mitchell, 1999). The Project Team recognised that, if the overall process was to be successful, all elements must operate to minimum standards, complement other elements of the model and perform as an integrated business process. To the best of the authors' knowledge, this 'cradle to grave' review of a crime type where every element of the business process was identified and then examined had not been undertaken before.

Mapping the business process highlighted the complexities of burglary investigation and identified that performance in certain areas of the model was poor and, on occasions, not even subject to any form of measurement. It was apparent that minimum standards did not always exist and some processes operated in a manner that did not enhance the overall performance. Certain elements of the business process were devoid of examples of good practice or tactical options and it was necessary for the Project Team to try and fill these gaps by designing and documenting business processes and developing forms of performance measurement.

After several months of consultation, collation and analysis, the *Domestic Burglary: National Good Practice & Tactical Options Guide* was published by the Home Office Police Standards Unit in October 2003. The written Guide was 70 pages in length and provided the headline information. An accompanying CD-ROM provided access to over 350 source documents, allowing the reader to explore each topic in more depth.

Cheshire Constabulary 'Safer Homes' Initiative

From the outset it was recognised that not all the tactical options featured within the Report would be applicable to every force, due to the differences between forces in terms of geography, demographics, the nature and extent of the crime problem, policing problems and current tactics employed. It was for each individual force to determine what was relevant and applicable to them, following an analysis of the nature and causes of burglary in their area.

Since the Cheshire Constabulary was writing the Guide on behalf of the Association of Chief Police Officers (ACPO) and the Home Office Police Standards Unit, the project team had an opportunity to examine and compare Cheshire's business processes and performance as the good practice was being gathered. As the Project Team uncovered a new tactical option or a more effective way of doing things, it would immediately prompt the Chief Officer in charge of the project to question what they were doing and whether our own approach was the most effective. This comparison against what was considered to be 'best in class' highlighted significant differences in approach and performance.

An example that illustrates this concept is related to the recovery and processing of DNA evidence from burglary scenes. The Project Team identified one force that had altered its business processes; they adopted a courier service to transport DNA samples and were paying the Forensic Science Service to provide a rapid analysis. The entire process took forty-eight hours from recovery at the crime scene to the results being presented to the investigating officer. Speeding up the process of DNA recovery allows for earlier arrests, which in turn can reduce the incidence of crime, particularly if the suspect is a prolific offender. Although the enhanced performance was achieved at increased cost, it did indicate what was possible by developing more innovative and creative approaches.

When the question was posed as to how long it took Cheshire Constabulary to turn around DNA evidence, the managers responsible were initially unable to provide an answer. The fact that the force didn't even measure the length of time was revealing in itself. When the process was finally mapped out, the answer was between five and seven weeks! This was reduced to five days by changing delivery schedules and placing an emphasis on speed of return. The improved performance was achieved with minimal expense and the review process was also applied to fingerprint evidence recovered from burglary scenes. Performance improvements were achieved, again with little or no cost.

The 'Safer Homes' Initiative evolved out of this ongoing analysis of Cheshire's burglary performance. Having gathered good practice from around the country, the project team was keen to implement as much of the Guide as was relevant to policing in the county. A number of the tactical options were implemented as and when we became aware of them, whilst others took time to plan.

An implementation team consisting of representatives from the Call Handling Department, Crime Recording Bureau, Forensic Investigations, CID, Community Partnerships, Press and Public Relations, Criminal Justice Department, Training and the Project Team came together to consider the Guide and determine how we could change our approach to burglary investigation. Every department ended up changing some element of its approach and for some the changes were fundamental. An implementation plan was developed, with regular updates provided to the implementation team, which was chaired by one of the current authors. The change programme was given the title 'Safer Homes', which became a generic title for the overall approach to burglary reduction and detection. Marketing material and a formal launch in April 2004, assisted by Sir Bobby Charlton, marked the official start of the Initiative, although in reality many of the changes had been implemented over the preceding months.

Once the business processes had been changed, there was a need to train members of staff and monitor the development of the initiative. Changing so many elements of the business at one time was challenging for both individuals and the organisation, particularly as many of the processes had been in place for years.

Sustaining a new initiative, particularly in the face of competing demands, is often a challenge for the police service. With new demands appearing to arrive on a weekly basis and operational priorities pulling resources from one initiative to another, it is often difficult to maintain focus and ensure that the organisation does not revert to the traditional (and sometimes easier) way of doing things. The development of a clear business process model with associated performance standards is necessary if the initiative is to survive the initial implementation phase and become an embedded and accepted way of doing things. In addition, there is a need to audit compliance and reinforce certain elements of the process where non-compliance is detected.

In addition to the compliance auditing, there was also a need to monitor the effectiveness of the various elements of the initiative and adjust the model as and when better practice was identified as a better way of doing things. 'Safer Homes' was constantly changing as the force identified better methods and adapted to the changing nature of policing. Although the Project Team has long been disbanded and the staff moved to other things, the force has retained one individual at Detective Inspector level who acts as burglary co-ordinator and has responsibility for the ongoing assessment of good practice from around the UK and the auditing of the business processes.

The organic nature of the initiative and the fact that 'Safer Homes' was more of a concept than a set of defined processes made evaluation of its effectiveness very difficult. The nature of those difficulties and the extent to which 'Safer Homes' impacted on the work of Cheshire Constabulary is what will concern us for the remainder of this chapter.

Evaluation of the 'Safer Homes' Initiative

The evaluation utilised the Ellis & Hogard 'Trident' model (2005), as this methodology is ideally suited to *post hoc* evaluations of this type. As may be surmised from the name of the model, it is formed from three components:

1. Outcomes
What did the project set out to achieve?

2. Process
How did it meet the objectives set?

3. Multiple Stakeholder Perspectives
What did people think about the project?

The project had already been in existence for some time before the evaluation team was brought in to assess the effectiveness of the initiative. This meant that in order to

Tackling Domestic Burglary

show some degree of 'distance travelled' the evaluation team was reliant upon previously collected data from the period before the introduction of the 'Safer Homes' Initiative. Whilst it was fortunate that such data existed, it had been collected with a different set of research questions in mind and detailed data were not available for some of the questions to which the research team would have like to have provided a more in-depth response: for instance, the affect of the 'Safer Homes' Initiative on levels of fear of crime within Cheshire.

Summary of Key Objectives

The implementation team defined four key objectives, which the project was designed to meet and by which it could reasonably be judged.

1. Delivery of a better quality of service to victims of domestic burglary.
2. A reduction in the overall number of domestic burglary incidents across Cheshire.
3. A higher quality of investigation leading to a higher domestic burglary detection rate.
4. An improvement in the relationships between crime reduction agencies in Cheshire.

It will be noted from the list of key objectives above that each of the first four objectives has a community safety element to them, in terms of improving the service to victims and assisting them in reducing their chances of becoming a victim on another occasion, and improving police efficiency when dealing with domestic burglary (on the assumption that the earlier a repeat offender can be brought to justice, then a greater number of burglaries that they would otherwise have been free to commit could be prevented). The fourth objective, of improving the relationships between the crime reduction agencies in Cheshire, was at the same time *prima facie* the easiest to achieve and yet the one which proved to be the most difficult to achieve in practice.

The fifth key objective was defined by the Home Office Police Standards Unit.

5. Evaluation of the role played by the Force Burglary Co-ordinator.

The last objective, whilst not having a direct impact upon community safety, did have a facilitatory function in influencing the community safety impact of the preceding four objectives.

Summary of Evidence

The evaluation of the project by the Social and Health Evaluation Unit involved the collection and analysis of a variety of different sources of data in order to provide as complete a picture as possible of the extent to which the project had met its stated objectives. These data provided a description and analysis of the processes which the SHI had employed in meeting its objectives and sampling of the views of recipients and providers. Research methods employed by the evaluation team included the following:

- Face-to-face interviews with:
  Members of the project implementation team;
  Representatives of local Crime and Disorder Reduction Partnerships;

A departmental manager whose area was particularly affected by the project;
A representative of the Basic Command Unit Superintendents;

- Telephone interviews with victims of domestic burglary;

- Survey of Basic Command Unit Superintendents;

- Survey of Crime and Disorder Reduction Partnerships within Cheshire;

- A survey of all Cheshire Constabulary staff, examining their knowledge of and response to, the Safer Homes project;

- Focus groups with Cheshire Constabulary departmental managers and Cheshire Constabulary staff;

- An ethnographic account of the work of a police officer who was delivering the 'Safer Homes' package to victims of domestic burglary;

- Analysis of pre-existing data sources:
  Victim of crime surveys conducted by Cheshire Constabulary in the years 2003/2004 and 2004/2005;
  Published data from the Police Statistics Branch at the Home Office.

Community Safety: Innovation and Evaluation

Outcomes of the 'Safer Home' Initiative

Delivery of a better quality of service to victims of domestic burglary

The comments made by victims of crime to the researchers conducting the evaluation and the responses given to Cheshire Constabulary's own victim satisfaction surveys both support the fact that the service given to victims as a result of the 'Safer Homes' Initiative is a significant improvement over the levels of service provided prior to the introduction of 'Safer Home' (see Figure 1, p. 343).

A reduction in the overall number of domestic burglary incidents across Cheshire

Views expressed to the researchers during the evaluation process from members of Cheshire Constabulary at all levels of the organisation suggested that there was a belief within the Force that the reduction of 1,500 incidents from 2003/2004 to 2004/2005 was a direct consequence of the 'Safer Homes' Initiative (see Figure 2, p. 344). Whilst this could not be substantiated from the data available, in terms of being able to identify the amount of reduction attributable to the project against the background of a falling trend in the numbers of domestic burglaries recorded, it does indicate the degree of pride which was felt by members of the Force towards the project.

A higher quality of investigation leading to a higher domestic burglary detection rate

The quality of investigation proved to be difficult to measure. However, the perceptions of police officers was that the project had given them the capacity to deal with a particular incident of domestic burglary in a way which

Tackling Domestic Burglary

they had always wanted to, but previously had not had the time (see Figure 3).

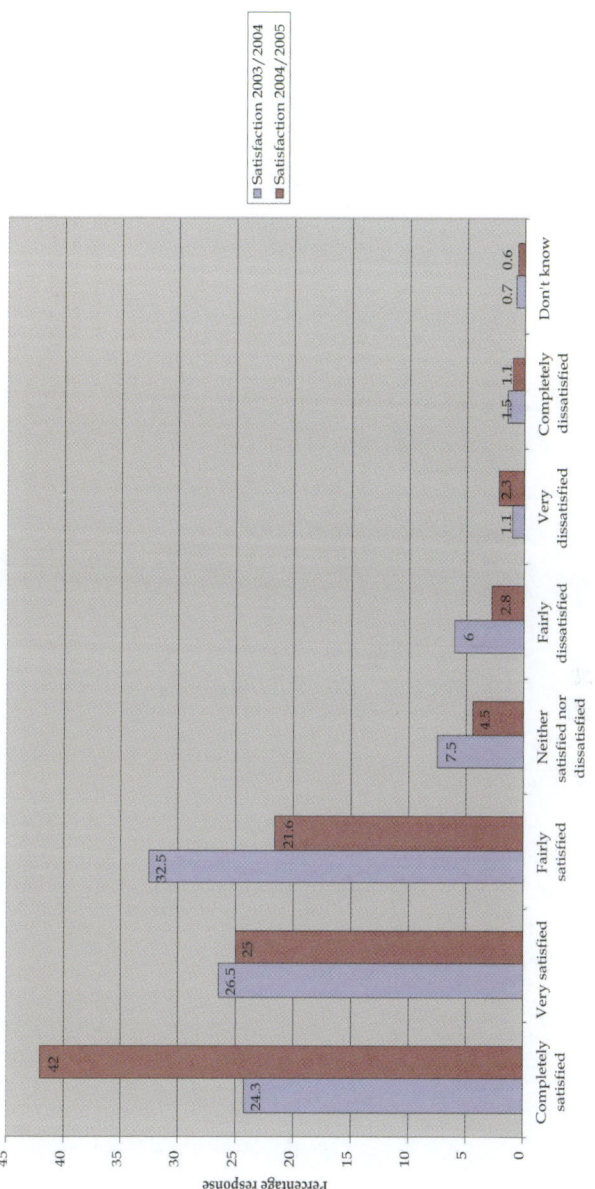

Community Safety: Innovation and Evaluation

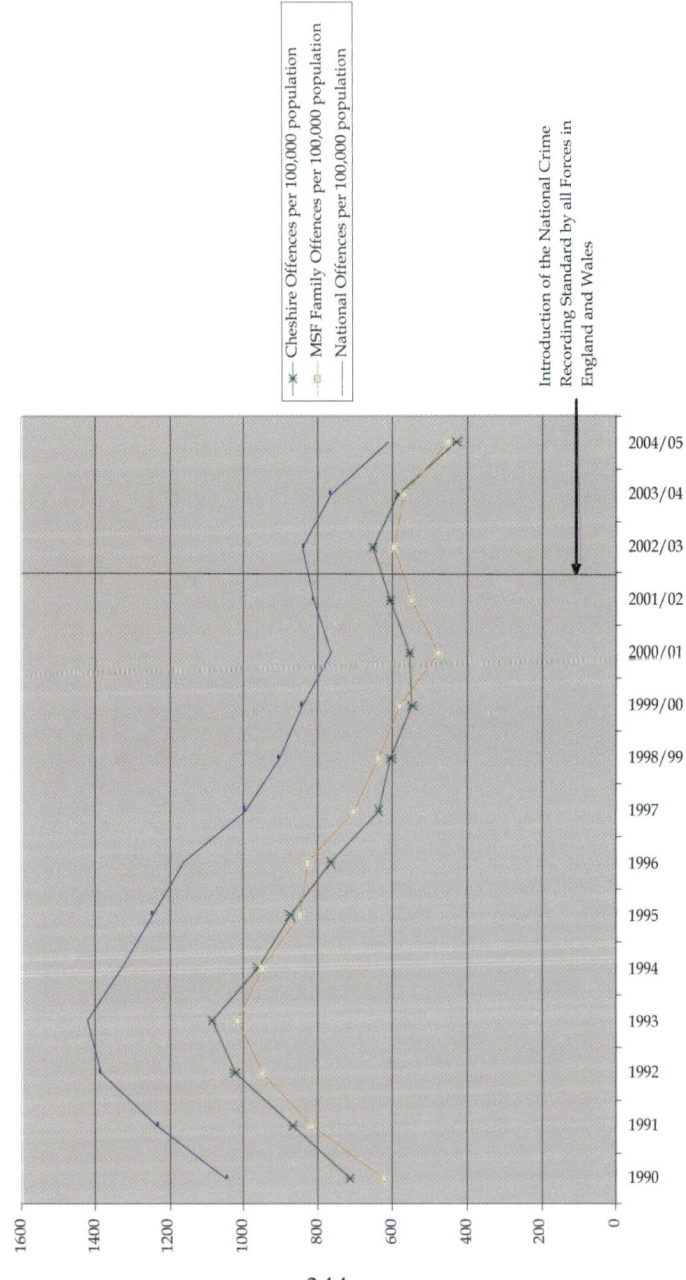

Tackling Domestic Burglary

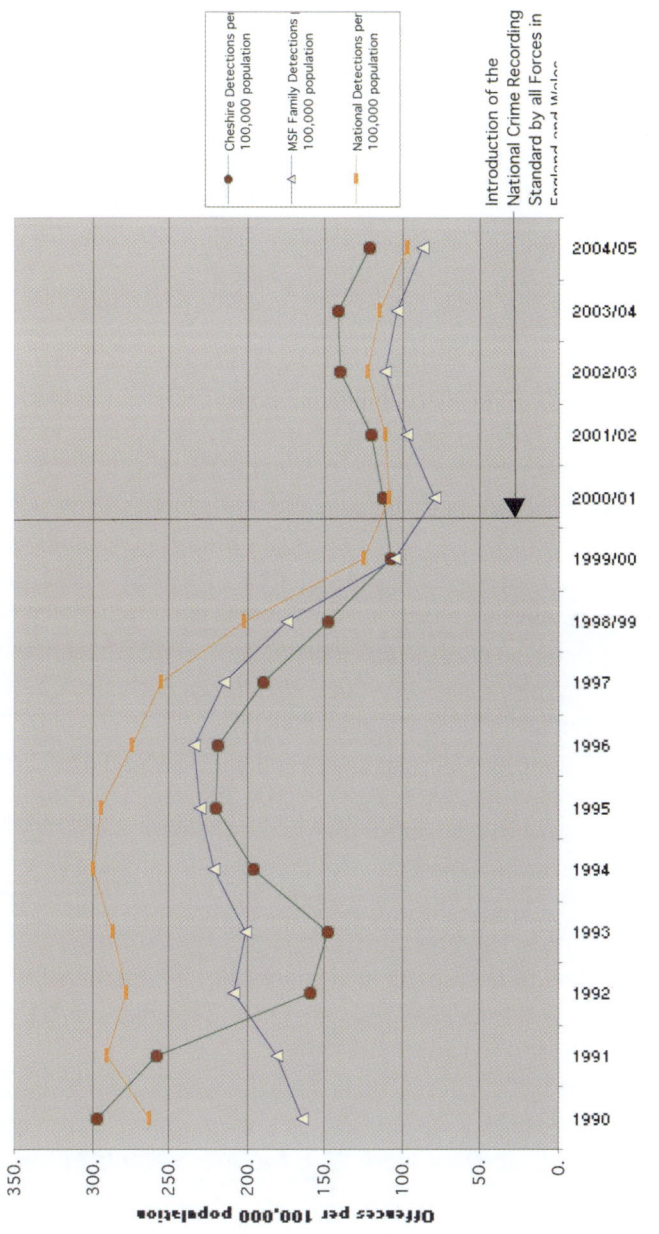

Figure 3.

Over the period of implementation of the 'Safer Homes' Initiative, the domestic burglary detection rate rose within Cheshire from 24.2% in 2003/2004 to 28.3% in 2004/2005, an increase of 4.1%. During the same period the rise for Cheshire's Most Similar Family of Forces was 1.3%, whilst the rise for all forces nationally was 0.9%.

An improvement in the relationships between crime reduction agencies in Cheshire
The project team achieved mixed degrees of success against this outcome measure. Considerable benefits of increased partnership working were seen at an operational and practitioner-based level, including the training of care staff in basic crime reduction methods so that they could inform the clients they supported, as well as increased co-operation between the police and trading standards officers. However, less success was seen at the more strategic CDRP Practitioner Group level, where the project was seen very much as a police initiative, with the CDRPs being used merely as sources of funding.

Evaluation of the role played by the Force Burglary Co-ordinator
The role played by the Force Burglary Co-ordinator (FBC), acting as a link between the ACPO officer in charge of the project and the departmental managers and BCU Commanders who had the responsibility for delivering 'Safer Homes' to their staff and the public, was essential for the success achieved by the project. This was achieved through a successful process of engagement and consultation, which Force senior staff were happy to take a role in as it meant that their views were being taken into account and that they were not having a solution forced

upon them with the instruction to implement it. The FBC therefore acted in part as a conduit for information to flow through the Force, giving departments and sections that had not previously had formal lines of communication between them the opportunity to see how changes made to their part of the domestic burglary process could have a significant impact on the work of another department. This improvement in communication would have been more difficult to achieve without an individual in the FBC role having the support of an ACPO officer.

Evaluation of the delivery of the 'Safer Homes' Initiative

The processes involved in the project can be summarised under two separate headings, as below: the process involved with the development of 'The Guide' and the process of implementing the good practice contained within 'The Guide' as the 'Safer Homes' Initiative. The process by which 'The Guide' was developed has already been covered in this paper and so this section will be concerned with the implementation of the good practice within 'The Guide', in a project that became known within Cheshire Constabulary as the 'Safer Homes' Initiative.

The Initiative adopted a corporate approach to a particular crime type; it was intended that, wherever in the Force area the incident occurred, the victim would receive the same high degree of professional service – not just a visit to record the bare essentials of the crime. The 'Safer Homes' Initiative (SHI) provided a solid body of evidence for what can be achieved by police forces in relation to efficiency and public satisfaction, without the addition of significant extra sums of money or additional resources.

Community Safety: Innovation and Evaluation

Implementation of the good practice within 'The Guide'

Once 'The Guide' had been produced, the project team turned their attention to the way in which that good practice could be implemented within Cheshire Constabulary. The following points represent a summary of that process:

- The 'ownership' of the Force response to domestic burglary sat at ACPO Officer level and this gave the project the weight which was required in order to undertake the necessary reviews and changes to policies and procedures;

- The appointment of a Force Burglary Co-ordinator, line managed by the ACPO Officer with responsibility for domestic burglary, had a significant positive impact on the way that the project was implemented and the way in which it was received by other members of the Force;

- The planning stages of the Initiative involved extensive consultation with all departments, operational and support, that had an interest in domestic burglary. This consultation process provided dividends in terms of the levels of commitment later shown towards the Initiative. The process of mapping existing procedures to the good practice contained within 'The Guide' was made very much more straightforward by the sequential nature of the way in which the good practice was presented. Changes within individual departments were made as a result of the ACPO lead officer presenting the relevant departmental manager with the section of 'The Guide' which was relevant to their area and asking them to come up with an implementation plan;

- The changes made to the internal processes for dealing with incidents of domestic burglary led directly to large increases in efficiency, particularly in relation to the handling of forensic evidence. These process changes included:
  - Ensuring that crime scene investigators were aware of a burglary incident as soon as possible, so as to maximise the opportunities for the collection of forensic data;
  - The prioritisation of finger-print evidence from burglary scenes by the forensic investigation department;

- The 'Safer Homes' Initiative provided various different departments and business areas of the force with the opportunity to work together on a common agenda and thus significantly improve the lines of communication and the flow of information for the organisation;

- The completion of paperwork in relation to incidents of domestic burglary, whilst an improvement on previous practice, was not as good as it might have been. An example of this was the completion of Modus Operandi forms and criminal incident forms which, if not completed satisfactorily, make it much more difficult to assign a crime incident to a series committed by a prolific offender;

- There were several excellent examples of direct contact with community-based organisations and individuals; e.g. the involvement of Sure Start in reducing the risk of burglary for vulnerable families by the provision of door and window locks. The Registered Social Landlords (RSLs) in Cheshire were very supportive of the 'Safer Homes' Initiative and provided funds for improving the security of the properties which they were responsible for managing;

- The 'Safer Homes' Initiative gave Cheshire Constabulary an opportunity for closer working with partner agencies, improving lines of communication and relationships between organisations. See examples below:
  - There was an increased linkage between the Police and the Trading Standards Agency, with the appointment of specific police liaison officers to improve lines of communication between the two organisations;
  - The Fire Service also recognised that the same homes which they were going into to install fire safety equipment, such as smoke alarms, would also benefit from increased security advice and equipment. Therefore, the 'Safer Homes' fitters who were going into homes to install additional security were trained by the fire service in the conduct of fire safety checks for properties and the correct placement of fire safety equipment;

- There appeared to be a lower level of engagement with the Crime and Disorder Reduction Partnerships within Cheshire, who saw the 'Safer Homes' Initiative as being a police-led initiative, in which they were asked to provide support through the provision of funding;

- In addition, there appeared to be a lack of understanding amongst some members of Cheshire Constabulary about the way in which their role contributed to the investigation and detection of domestic burglary incidents. Those closely associated with the Initiative seemed to have a good understanding of the role they played; however, individuals who were not so close to the centre or whose departments were only peripherally involved did not seem to feel that they had a role to play in the domestic burglary process.

Evaluation of Multiple Stakeholder Perspectives on the 'Safer Homes' Initiative

The views of those associated with, and affected by, the project are essential for any complete evaluation of an initiative. The following represents a summary of those views expressed to the evaluators:

- The extra capacity created by the changes to the domestic burglary response process within Cheshire had a considerable positive effect on the levels of satisfaction with the police response reported by victims of burglary;
- The greater time which the Initiative allowed attending officers to spend with victims had a direct effect on improving levels of victim satisfaction with the service provided by Cheshire Constabulary. This level of service exceeded that which was expected by the victims who were interviewed as part of the evaluation;
- The considerable levels of victim satisfaction with the initial police response noted above were somewhat ameliorated by the lower levels of satisfaction seen with the way in the police kept victims informed of the progress of the investigation;
- The project did not have a cohesive identity across the Force; different stakeholders had varying views on what the 'Safer Homes' Initiative was, depending on their role and level of seniority within the Force.

Community Safety: Innovation and Evaluation

Recommendations

These main recommendations have been drawn from the body of evidence collected during the evaluative process:

- As the creation of the Force Burglary Co-ordinator role was supported by a grant from the Police Standards Unit, it is our recommendation that this function be 'mainstreamed' and supported on an ongoing basis from within existing budgets; the financial savings delivered by the SHI and the application of the SHI approach to other crime types would be sufficient in our opinion to justify such an appointment;

- The business process analysis model utilised in the 'Safer Home' Initiative could be applied to other types of burglary and also to other crime types. Whilst there would almost certainly not be the resources in place to support all crime in this way, if forces were to concentrate this approach on the high volume and priority crimes which have been identified by the Home Office and the ACPO, then significant efficiency savings could be made, as each process does not operate in isolation and savings made in one area of police activity may result in opportunity savings in another part of police activity; in particular, if those changes occur in a centralised department which deals with many different types of crime, such as the Call Management Bureau or the Forensic Investigations Department.

In addition, the following recommendations can be drawn from the evidence collected in extending the operational impact of the 'Safer Homes' Initiative:

Tackling Domestic Burglary

- Training of Community Fire Prevention Officers in the undertaking of Home Security Assessments;

- Training of Crime Scene Investigators in the skills required to conduct preliminary investigations when visiting the scene of a burglary, as well as in the delivery of crime prevention advice to the victim. This could be complemented by the training of Burglary Officers in the collection of forensic evidence as well as Crime Scene Investigation techniques, the two groups of trained personnel then providing a one-visit service to the victim of a domestic burglary. This good practice comes from 'The Guide', but was not implemented as part of the 'Safer Homes' Initiative;

- Extension of the 'drop-down-menus' within the NSPIS Command and Control system, used by the Call Management Bureau to manage calls relating to incidents of domestic burglary, to other types of burglary and other crime types, when the ability to give appropriate advice to the caller/victim in a consistent manner would aid in the evidence preservation and recovery process and possibly lead to a greater number of offenders being brought to justice.

Implementation Checklist

One of the aims of the evaluation was the identification of those characteristics of the 'Safer Homes' Initiative which another Force would need to consider if they wanted to replicate the work which has been undertaken in Cheshire. Whilst it is the belief of the evaluation team that another Force could achieve improvements in relation to the domestic burglary process by implementing the good practice contained within 'The Guide', that document is not sufficient on its own and a Force would fall short of Cheshire's success if they did not take the following factors into account in the early planning stages of their initiative:

- Organisation of the ACPO management team so that an individual takes responsibility for the domestic burglary process, from initial call through to case disbursement within the Criminal Justice System;

- Appointment of a Force Burglary Co-ordinator (FBC) who sits within the Force Headquarters and is line-managed by the ACPO team member responsible for domestic burglary;

- Personal characteristics of the FBC:
    - A senior rank holder with the authority to deliver the aims and objectives of the project; preferably an officer of not less than Superintendent rank;
    - Passionate and enthusiastic about the aims of the project;
    - An ability to work with staff at all levels of the organisation;
    - Knowledge of, and commitment to, effective partnership working;
    - Tenacity and confidence in delivering the aims and objectives of the project;
    - An ability on the part of the post holder to work with both the crime reduction and police tactical delivery aspects of the service;

- The post holder would need a high level of credibility with colleagues inside the police service and with partners external to the police organisation – credibility based on an expert level of knowledge of the issues surrounding the investigation and prevention of burglary;

- Definition of the key outcomes that the Force wants to achieve from an implementation of the good practice within 'The Guide';

- Establishment of a project implementation group which includes the ACPO lead officer for domestic burglary within the Force, the FBC, the key departmental managers and representatives of the Basic Command Unit (BCU) Superintendents;

- Root-and-branch assessment of the domestic burglary process within the Force;

- Comparing existing practice with the good practice contained within 'The Guide';

- Prior to the project being implemented, it would be of benefit to engage with and secure the commitment of the Crime and Disorder Reduction Partnerships as well as other crime prevention partners. This will give the project a degree of shared ownership and avoid issues of partners viewing the project as simply a police initiative, with themselves being merely used as a source of income;

- Training inputs for all staff involved with the domestic burglary process, irrespective of their role, ensuring that staff are aware of the reasons for the changes to their role and the Force as a whole.

- The planning and implementation of a rigorous performance management system that can be applied at the individual, departmental and Force level – ensuring that improvements made as a result of implementing the good practice within 'The Guide' are maintained;

- Ensuring that the project team engages with, and secures commitment from, community safety and crime reduction organisations within their Force area. The project needs a measure of shared ownership, so that it is not seen as simply a police initiative, but a multi-agency approach in which each organisation has a role to play in reducing domestic burglary.

References

Alderman, N. (1998). *Business Process Analysis: a system-wide perspective.* Coventry: University of Warwick Business Processes Resource Centre.

Brand, S., & Price, R. (2000). *The Economic and Social Costs of Crime.* London: Home Office.

Brand, S., & Price, R. (2005). The economic and social costs of crime against individuals and households 2003/2004. *Home Office Online Reports* Retrieved 23/04/2006, from: http://www.homeoffice.gov.uk/rds/pdfs05/rdsolr3005.pdf

Darnton, G., & Darnton, M. (1997). *Business Process Analysis.* London: International Thomson Business Press.

Ellis, R., & Hogard, E. (2003). Two deficits and a solution? Explicating and evaluating clinical facilitation using consultative methods and multiple stakeholder perspectives. *Learning in Health and Social Care,* Volume 2, Number 1, pp. 18-27.

Hirschfield, A. (2004). *The Impact of the Reducing Burglary Initiative in the North of England.* Home Office Online Report 40/04. London: Home Office. Retrieved from: http://www.homeoffice.gov.uk/rds/pdfs04/rdsolr4004.pdf

Home Office, & Association of Chief Police Officers. (2003). *Domestic Burglary: National Good Practice & Tactical Options Guide.* London: Home Office Police Standards Unit.

Jacobson, J. (2003). *The Reducing Burglary Initiative: planning for partnership.* Home Office Development and Practice Report Number 4. London: Home Office.

Mitchell, P. (1999). *An Analysis of Business Process Re-engineering in the Public Sector.* Manchester: UMIST.

Tilley, N. (2004). *Problem-solving street crime: Practical Lessons from the Street Crime Initiative.* London: Home Office.

Tuffin, R., Morris, J., & Poole, A. (2006). *An Evaluation of the Impact of the National Reassurance Policing Programme.* London: Home Office Research Development and Statistics Directorate.

MAPPING THE FEAR OF CRIME – A MICRO-APPROACH

Chris Williams

Introduction

The Fear of Crime: "... *an anticipation of victimisation, rather than fear of an actual victimisation*" (John Howard Society, 1999).

Reducing the fear of crime has become a cornerstone of British social policy in recent years. The new National Community Safety Plan has the reduction of the fear of crime at the heart of its message:

> The Government's key priorities for 2006-09 are to: ... continue to develop, evaluate and disseminate good practice on reducing crime and the **fear of crime**" (Home Office, 2005. Emphasis added).

With a recorded reduction in crime rates of 35% since 1997 (Blears, 2005), one might expect to have observed a corresponding fall in the fear of crime. However, this appears not to be the case. In Merton, South London, residents' concern about crime actually rose 6% between 2004 and 2005, according to the Merton Annual Resident's Survey (TNS Social Research, 2005). While this could be due to many factors – media images, a rise in environmental and so-called "signal" crimes - one cause that can be discounted is an actual rise in reported crime; in Merton this fell by 7.8% over the same time period (Wood, 2005). As Innes and Ditton (2005) state:

Mapping the Fear of Crime

There has never been much relationship between levels of crime and levels of fear, and ... reductions in crime have rarely led to reductions of fear of it.

This anomaly is known as the "Reassurance Gap", and is one which government and police services are determined to plug; a population believing that crime is increasingly prevalent is likely to think unfavourably of its elected representatives and those funded from general taxation with the expressed purpose of ensuring their safety.

Whilst it is, somewhat paradoxically, important to maintain a certain amount of fear in a society – for example, in order to ensure that a certain amount of care is taken over one's possessions in order to prevent theft – there is obviously an "optimal or ideal level of positive fear" (Garofalo, 1981), though quite how this can be quantified is uncertain. After all, reducing fear may have a negative side-effect – namely, increasing victimisation. Fattah (1995) makes the point that:

> Our approach to fear of crime is ... problematic because we have no qualms about exploiting it when it suits our purposes but we are quick to condemn it when it becomes a source of public concern or complaint.

Process

Within this context, in Merton a partnership between the local Borough Command Unit of the Metropolitan Police and the Local Authority's Crime and Disorder Reduction Partnership (CDRP) sought to tackle the issue of fear of crime in one particular area of Abbey Ward, where traditionally burglary had been common. This particular group of eight streets is sandwiched between a run-down area of council housing containing three tower blocks and an area of extremely expensive, privately owned, terraced housing.

The area had been selected for use in a trial of a property-marking scheme (known as Smartwater), in order to attempt to reduce the number of burglaries within these eight streets. As the beat officers would be required to visit each occupied property on each street, it was realised that a written questionnaire, completed by the residents whilst the police were in attendance, could be carried out simultaneously in order to ascertain the fear of crime accurately in each household – and indeed, a 98% response rate was obtained from 309 households. There is a potential confounding bias with this approach: the very questioning of an individual about crime can negatively affect their feelings about the subject; the so-called "Hawthorne Effect". However, for these purposes, internal rather than external validity is the key.

In effect, we are seeking to complete a "Fear of Crime Census".

In order to establish some rationale above and beyond the quantitative approach, we were able to examine the free text responses on the questionnaires. The data they were able to provide – though largely anecdotal – has assisted with the interpretation of the results of the mapping process.

The process involved runs as follows:

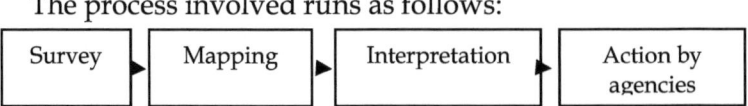

Mapping the Fear of Crime

Literature Review

A great deal of work has been done on understanding the fear of crime (Innes & Ditton, 2005; Williams & Pate, 1986; Cordner, 1986; Garafolo, 1981; Fattah, 1995; Jackson, 2004; John Howard Society, 1999), yet rather less has been undertaken on actually mapping fear. Where work has been done, it has tended to be around one of two themes:

1. Spatially, e.g. where fear is most prevalent; and
2. Thematically, e.g. how an area feels about different crime types.

Spatial Approaches

An example of the spatial mapping of fear of crime can be seen in the maps produced by Martin Innes and his team during the qualitative interviews undertaken for Signal Crimes Research for the National Reassurance Policing Programme (Innes *et al.*, 2004).

Here, residents were interviewed about the localities in their neighbourhood within which they felt unsafe – and what crimes or disorders they felt went on there. Safer Neighbourhood teams in South London, who bring maps to public meetings and invite members of the public to affix different-coloured stickers to areas in which they feel unsafe, use a simplified form of this mapping.

Whilst this process is comprehensive, the in-depth interviews required to obtain such detail are lengthy and perhaps beyond the skills of the everyday beat officer. The time required to transcribe and analyse the interviews, before capturing them in graphical format on a map, is equally likely to be beyond the capabilities of most neighbourhood policing teams.

A similar method was utilised at the University of British Colombia (UBC), where students were invited to highlight areas on the campus at which they felt both safe and unsafe.

During a partnership between Leeds University and Bradford Council, Evans and Waters (2005) designed an internet-based tool enabling residents to "spray" on to a map areas where they felt fear – and allowed them to intensify those parts where they felt most afraid.

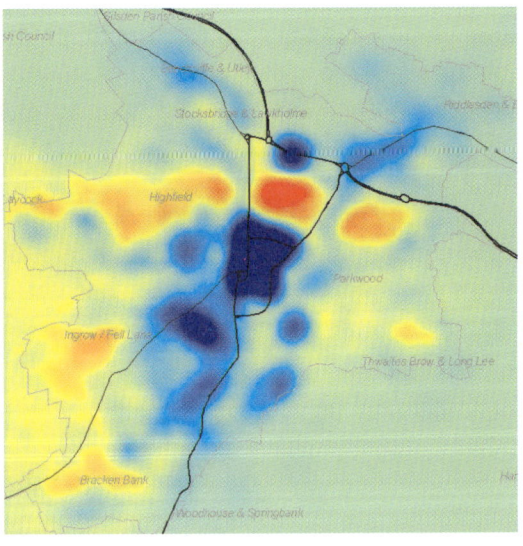

Figure 1. Leeds University and Bradford Council.

Mapping the Fear of Crime

The results were then compared with recorded crime figures to develop the map of perceptions you can see opposite (Figure 1). Areas of blue are where perceptions of crime are much higher than the reality; areas of red are where crime is higher than the perception.

This approach is useful in outlining the difference between perception and reality in terms of crime (and educating the public as to this difference), but this approach relies on sophisticated technology, requiring large amounts of technical expertise on behalf of the organisation – and, indeed, a certain amount of expertise on behalf of the resident (not to mention access to computers and the internet). There is likely to be a high start-up cost involved, and it is probable that only a small – and almost certainly highly unrepresentative - sample of the population will participate.

Thematic Approaches

In 2004, Robin Gawlik of Barrow-in-Furness Borough Council produced a series of interactive Fear of Crime maps based upon survey responses that also provided numerical outcomes to postal questionnaire replies. The responses were broken down to Super Output Area level[1] to develop a representation of fear of crime for the smallest possible layer for which data was available (the Super Output Areas, which have populations of about 1,000).

---

[1] Super Output Areas were introduced by the Office of National Statistics in order to produce a small-scale geographical area whose boundaries were resistant to political change (unlike wards).

However, the actual response rate was only about 26% (870 respondents from 3200 distributed questionnaires).

This approach is useful for work that aims to identify vulnerable or fearful communities – and perhaps for assistance in the targeting of medium or long-term resources – but tells us little about the experiences of residents at a micro-level.

We felt that there was a requirement for the creation of a set of maps indicating the levels of fear of crime for various crime types on a street-by-street basis, to provide a tool for beat managers and Safer Neighbourhood teams to target actively individual roads with high fears of particular crime types.

Method

In our survey of Abbey Ward, we used a variant of Gawlik's approach. By asking each householder a similar question and offering the same responses, we were able to attach a numerical value to the level of "fear".

We distributed a questionnaire to each of the 309 households in the selected eight streets, and these were completed whilst the police were in the property, informing the residents of the availability to them of the Smartwater scheme.

We asked, "How do you feel about ..." the topics listed below, which are historically the main concerns outlined to us by residents in public meetings and surveys.

Mapping the Fear of Crime

We used the above scale to ascertain people's levels of concern about each crime type. We weighted each response, so that a major problem was worth 3 points, a minor problem 2, and no problem 1, then divided it by the number of respondents, using the algorithm below:

$$FOC = \frac{(1a + 2b + 3c)}{X}$$

where a = no problem, b = minor problem and c = major problem, and x is the number of respondents.

	Size of problem			
	Major	Minor	Nil	Don't know
Crime	1	2	3	4
Youth anti-social behaviour	1	2	3	4
Burglary	1	2	3	4
Robbery Mugging or pick pocketing	1	2	3	4
Car crime Stealing cars or from cars	1	2	3	4
Drugs	1	2	3	4
Alcohol-related problems	1	2	3	4
Hate crimes Crime motivated by a hatred of difference: e.g. the colour of someone's skin, sexual preference, religion or disability	1	2	3	4
Traffic problems Speeding, parking, dangerous driving, etc.	1	2	3	4
Vandalism and Graffiti	1	2	3	4

There are, of course, issues about deriving means from ordinal data: however, the assumption underlying this analysis is that the fear of crime ratings are an approximation of an interval scale; in other words, the ordinal scale used to measure fear of crime has set intervals to which a numerical scale can be applied.

However, as the means produced in each instance were very close to both the mode and median, we can state that they are normally distributed and we can use the means on an interval scale.

Previous analyses have shown little difference between the mean and the median, and for illustrative purposes the mean has been used here to show levels of fear of crime. This was the same methodology used by Gawlik and applied, in his work, to Super Output Areas, with the prime differences being:

- Greater coverage – we are able to attain a much higher response rate;
- Greater accuracy – we are able to bestow a sense of "feeling" to individual streets;
- More meaningful results – by demarcating levels of fear on a street-by-street basis, we are able to target intervention on a local basis.

The results of this were collated on a street-by-street basis, and then mapped using the Thematic-mapping tool on MapInfo™, before being produced in the format seen below (Figures 2, 3, 4 and 5). In each map, levels of fear are articulated by darkening gradations of red; so the darker the colour, the higher the level of fear. The gradations themselves are those automatically designated by the software, generally dividing into four blocks of two streets each.

Results

All Crime

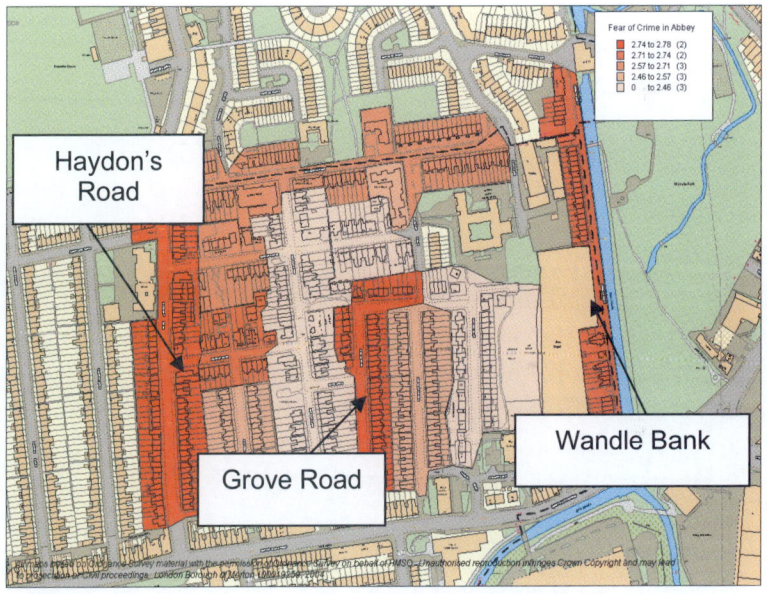

Figure 2. Fear of all Crime.

Figure 2 shows the overall Fear of Crime (FOC) for the eight streets selected for the pilot. The streets with the highest FOC are Haydon's Road, Wandle Bank and Grove Road.

Haydon's Road is a main thoroughfare linking Merton with Earlsfield; it has a lot of traffic (both foot and vehicle) and this may contribute to an overall unsteady feeling. Wandle Bank is rather exposed, with the river forming one side of the road. Grove Road, however, is contained in the midst of the housing block, so why should it have a higher fear of crime?

Interpretations can come from the comments made by the residents in the free text section of the questionnaire:

> The street lighting is poor on Grove Road - it makes me feel unsafe at night.

> The streets are dirty – rubbish bags are left out for days.

These two responses tell us, firstly, that poor lighting contributes to fear of crime (see Ramsey, 1991); and that environmental indicators contribute to fear (see Innes *et al.*, 2004). This interpretation by the residents can now be used to drive action: by contacting the Street Management team of the Local Authority to examine street lighting and improve rubbish collection (perhaps in a problem-solving framework), we hope to have a positive effect on fear of crime in Grove Road.

Youth Anti-Social Behaviour (ASB)

Fear of Youth ASB seems to be centred on the primary school (Figure 3) – maybe older children use the facilities out of hours? Hotham Road also appears to be a relative hot-bed of fear. We asked the resident's panel for some clarification on this matter:

Mapping the Fear of Crime

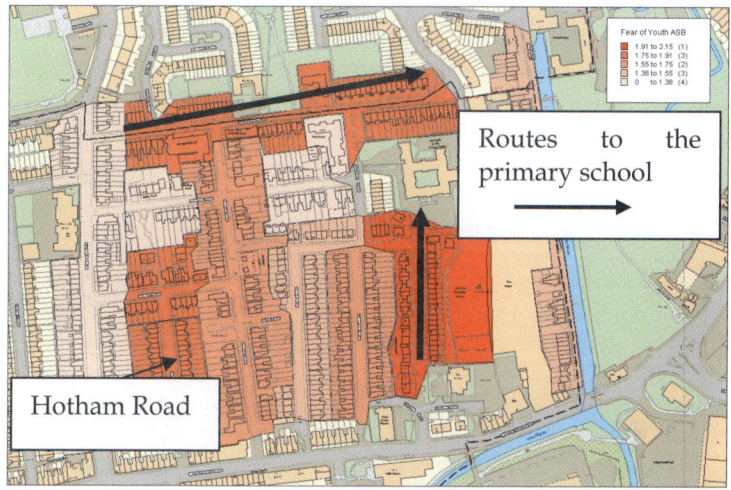

Figure 3. Youth Anti-Social Behaviour.

Gangs of older kids hang around the primary school and play football on the field after school has finished. They graffiti the cars too.

Kids mess around in the street on their way to and from the school.

Two kids in Hotham Road make our lives hell.

This small amount of insight helps greatly with the interpretation of the maps; essentially, key individuals act as "interpreters" of the knowledge we have on a quantitative level. Both the primary school and Hotham Road were mentioned, and detail was added which the mapping could not possibly have afforded – thus reinforcing the importance of a multi-faceted method.

In these three short extracts we see "Kids" mentioned in each and the school in two – strengthening the theory that the school is the centre of the Youth ASB problem in the area.

Burglary

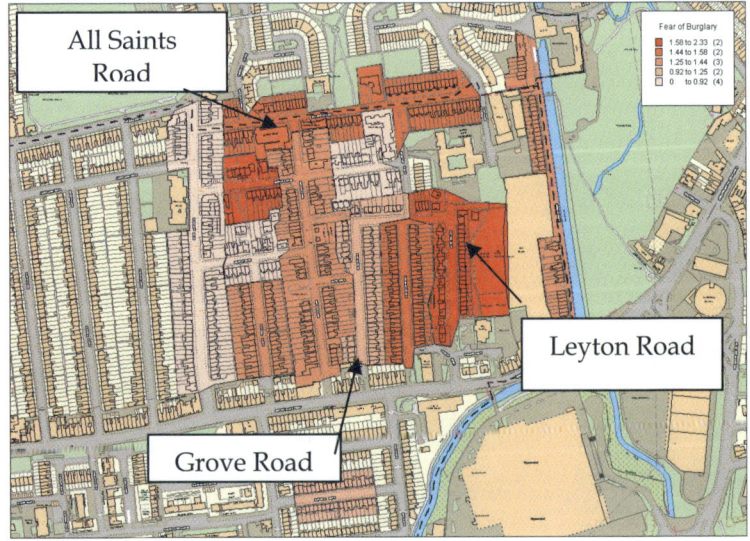

Figure 4. Burglary.

Burglary is traditionally high in these streets, and was indeed the initial motivation for carrying out the work. It is possible that the high fear in Leyton Road is due to the proximity to the Bus Depot, and therefore easy access to the housing and an easy escape route, with limited natural surveillance. All Saints Road again features highly (Figure 4); perhaps because it borders an area of different housing types – a 1970s estate with lots of open spaces between the properties, which again could potentially make residents feel vulnerable. Houses on the outskirts of neighbourhoods are more likely to be burgled (Weisel, 2003).

A resident said:

> There were three burglaries on Grove Road in a week. A man wrote a message on his door to the burglars – so now we all know what's happening!

This is very interesting, as the Grove Road resident actively raised the fear of crime in his immediate vicinity (perhaps rightly so, given that there were three burglaries in a week); yet as we can see, Grove Road is in the middle ranking of the roads for fear of burglary. Perhaps there are some other factors more telling than the Grove Road story? Perhaps not everyone on Grove Road had as much access to the knowledge of the resident who fed us this information?

Drugs

Fear of drugs is an issue in some of the same locations as previously established – Leyton Road, All Saints Road and Hotham Road. It is perhaps notable that the areas with high fear of drugs, youth ASB and burglary are areas close to open land.

The residents said: "There are dealers working over the river."

The number 1 on Figure 5 signifies this. There is a playground here that, according to the residents, is being used by local drug dealers: "We find syringes in our drains."

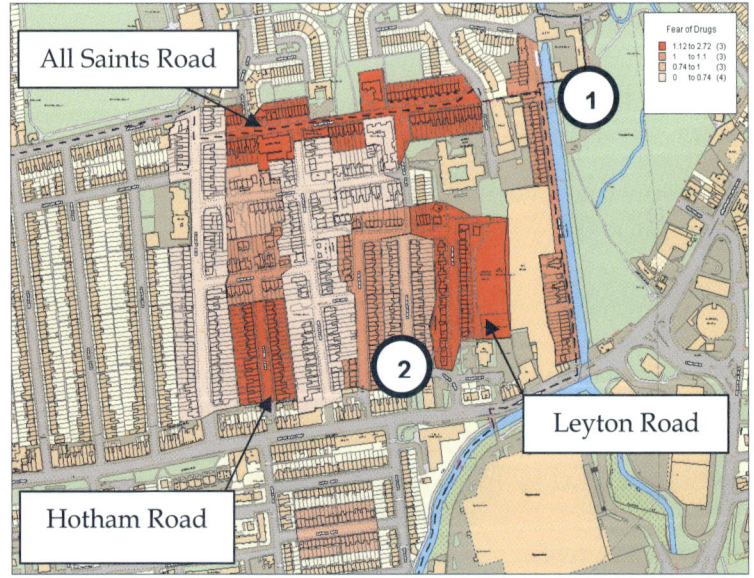

Figure 5. Drugs.

The number 2 on Figure 5 signifies the location of this. Here we are using a mixture of this method and the Signal Crimes methodology shown earlier. Both these locations are nearer to Wandle Bank, yet the residents of that street have a lower concern about drug use than Leyton Road or All Saints Road. Why might this be?

There are only thirty-seven houses on Wandle Bank, of which thirty-three were sampled. The actual number of residents who actively observe goings-on immediately outside their window is probably very small – most people's observations about their environment are made during their regular journeys (Brantingham & Brantingham, 1981), and only a small portion of those journeys is along their own street. On streets with more residents we would hope that those who are more active in their local area (traditionally the young and the old are the most active) would balance out these community non-participants. Wandle Bank is possibly the most salubrious of the streets surveyed (a three bedroom terrace is on the market in November 2005 for £385,000, a price well above those of the other streets, probably due to a slightly older housing stock and a riverside setting), which may mean it attracts more professionals, who tend to spend less time in a community setting. These people are, in the language of Experian, "New Urban Colonists": that is, "young professionals quite content to trade access to the city for a higher density of population"; therefore it is likely that these residents are less aware of their surroundings in general than those in other streets – perhaps their cosseted position, insulated from the community around them, serves to maintain a low fear of crime?

Methodological Issues

There are several issues arising with the maps. Firstly, does a heightened police presence in the area (and, indeed, in people's houses during the survey) serve to intensify fear of crime artificially, by the simple fact of reminding people that crime is occurring outside their door – the Hawthorne Effect? Could it be that a "reassurance" visit could be counter-productive – that although respondents regularly complain about the lack of police on the streets, this could be construed as being a *positive* sign about a neighbourhood ("If there are no police, then there can't be anything bad happening?")?

There are ways of improving the method. Only one member of each household – generally the head of the household – completed the survey (309 in total). For a true reflection of people's perceptions of the area, we should try to interview every resident, especially the young, who are typically without a voice yet, as previously mentioned, often have a greater knowledge of their immediate environs than anyone else.

There have been issues in the past in community safety surveys when respondents have exaggerated the extent of problems in their areas; or such exaggeration may occur when they are recounting the most threatening of the events and base their response on the intensity of feeling that occasion produced – and then over-estimate the frequency of these events (Jackson, 2004). This is the inherent danger in placing a numerical responsibility on an emotional response.

It is also clear that the use of interpretation by the resident's themselves is a vital part of the process – otherwise we are hypothesising blindly. The use of the key individuals to inform the work is essential; a little bit of local knowledge can go a long way.

This pilot scheme tests the value of the method, and the findings here would indicate that, for the value of results to be enhanced, some form of qualitative research must be carried out in addition to the questionnaires – perhaps in the form of focus groups or semi-structured tape recorded interviews. As the method is designed to be used easily by neighbourhood police teams, the teams could use the consultative process already in place with Resident's Panels or Key Individual Networks to inform this.

Mapping the Fear of Crime

Methodological Applications

With the advent of Safer Neighbourhood policing in London (and Reassurance Policing across the UK), an in-depth knowledge of levels of residents' fear and hotspots of those fears for differing crime types, throughout a small urban geographical area, can aid greatly in the reassurance process, be it for tasking purposes (perhaps to send foot patrols down one road with a particular fear of crime), or for publicity reasons (to send a positive message to a fearful area), or even for target-hardening schemes to help reassure an area with a high fear of burglary.

Eventually, a series of thematic maps could be made up of an entire ward or even borough, where at a glance areas with high levels of fear could be identified. Further qualitative work could be done in those streets to break this down more; perhaps fear of crime is being fostered by an overhanging bush or dark alleyway which, with a simple application of multi-agency working, perhaps in a problem-solving framework, could be cut back or lit up, helping to narrow further the Reassurance Gap.

Conclusion

The method described above is designed to provide a relatively simple framework for neighbourhood police officers or ward teams to produce easy-to-use graphical representations of the fear of various crimes at street level, thus enabling the targeting of resources to be made to try to reduce that fear.

References and Other Publications

Blears, H. (2005). Foreword. *The National Community Safety Plan 2006-9*. London: Home Office.

Brantingham, P.J., & Brantingham, P. L. (1981). *Environmental Criminology*. Beverly Hills, CA.: Sage Publications.

Cordner, G. (1986). Fear of Crime and the Police: an evaluation of a fear-reducing strategy. *Journal of Police Science and Administration*, 14, 223-33.

Evans, A., & Waters, T. (2005). *Mapping the Fear of Crime: A web-based GIS solution to capturing "fuzzy" geography*. Leeds. Retrieved from: http://www.geocomputation.org/2003/Papers/Waters_Paper.pdf

Fattah, E. (1995). Victimisation and Fear of Crime among the elderly – a possible link? Australian Institute of Criminology, Canberra. Conference paper. Retrieved from: http://www.aic.gov.au/conferences/olderpeople/fattah.pdf

Garofalo, J. (1981). The fear of crime: causes and consequences. *Journal of Criminal Law and Criminology*, 72, 839-857.

Gawlik, R. (2004). *Report on Fear of Crime in the Borough*. Barrow-in-Furness.

Home Office. (2005). *The National Community Safety Plan 2006-9*. London: Home Office.

Innes, M., & Ditton, J. (2005). The role of perceptual intervention in the management of fear of crime. In N. Tilley (ed.), *Handbook of Crime Prevention and Community Safety*. Cullompton: Willan Publishing.

Innes, M., et al. (2004). *The Signal Crimes Perspective: Interim Findings*. Guildford: Surrey Police. Retrieved from: http://www.reassurancepolicing.co.uk

Jackson, J. (2004). Validating New Measures in the Fear of Crime. *International Journal of Social Research Methodology*, 8 (4), 1-19.

John Howard Society of Alberta. (1999). *Fear of Crime*. Retrieved from:
http://www.johnhoward.ab.ca/PUB/C49.htm

Office of the Personal Security Co-ordinator. (2000). *Personal Security Mapping Project*. University of British Colombia Department of Health, Safety and Environment. Retrieved from:
www.safety.ubc.ca

Ramsey, M. (1991). The effect of better street lighting on crime and fear. *Crime Prevention Unit, Paper Number 29*. London: Home Office.

TNS Social Research. (2005). *Merton Annual Residents' Survey*. London.

Weisel, D. L. (2003). *Burglary of Single-family Houses*. Center for Problem-Oriented Policing. Retrieved from: http://www.popcenter.org/Problems/problem-burglary-family.htm

Williams, H., & Pate, A. (1986). Returning to first principles: reducing the fear of crime in Newark. *Crime and Delinquency*, 33, 3-70.

Wood, M. (ed.) (2005). *Merton Borough OCU Policing Plan 2005/6*. London.

INDEX

anti-social behaviour (ASB)
  a 1-day survey of 263
  Chiltern Vale case study
    analysis 269-271
    events 265-269
  definition 262
  micromapping project in Merton Borough 368-370
  recognising 260-261
  relation to drug lifestyles 271-275
    Chiltern Vale case study
      analysis 277-279
      events 275-277
    victims 263-265

behaviour *see* anti-social behaviour (ASB)
Birmingham Reducing Gang Violence (BRGV) group 55
  survey results 57-59
  use of REA methodology 56-57
burglary 329
  costs of 330-331
  micromapping project in Merton Borough 370-371
  patterns in Cornwall 218-222

property marking schemes
  evaluation 318-319
  Smartwater Scheme 360
  see also Kirkholt Burglary Prevention Project
Burglary Projects 153-154
Burnley (Lancs), i-NSI case study 195-202

Campbell Collaboration 70
CCTV (redeployable)
  defined 128
  effectiveness 129-130
  evaluation 321
  use in ASB cases 266-267
  use in DAT initiatives 131
    methods of survey 131-132
    survey results 132-143
    survey results discussed 143-145
Cheshire Constabulary *see* Safer Homes Initiative
Chiltern Vale ASB case study
  analysis 269-271
  events 265-269
  relation to drug lifestyles
    analysis 277-279
    events 275-277
clinical facilitators, case

study 110-111, 113-114, 118-122
Community Against Drugs (CAD) initiatives 131
community intelligence (commtel)
  capture 192-193
    CWAP 193-194
    i-NSI 194-195
      case study 195-202
  cf. evaluative data 185-186
  defined 187-188
  methodologies evaluated 190-192
  role of police 185
  use of strategic contacts 189-190
community safety
  defining the concept 184
  role of police 184-185
  see also community intelligence
Community Safety Partnerships 242
commuters and crime 216-222
Conjunction of Criminal Opportunity (CCO) framework 91
contestability 156, 158
contextual intelligence 188
conversation with a purpose (CWAP) 193-194
Cornwall CDRP audit
  introduction 209-214
  summary 229-232
  victim categories

    commuters 216-222
    domestic violence 214-216
    tourists 222-229
Covert Human Intelligence Sources (CHIS) 188, 189-190
Crime and Disorder Act (1998) 2, 238
Crime and Disorder Reduction Partnerships (CDRPs) 2-3
  auditing 208-209
  complexity 163-165
  Cornwall case study
    introduction 209-214
    summary 229-232
    victim categories
      commuters 216-222
      domestic violence 214-216
      tourists 222-229
  establishment 208
  evaluation of success 239-240
  extending 241-243
  funding 243-244
  future options 171-174
  introduction 238-239
  knowledge management 159-162
    Government approach 167-168
  local agenda setting 206-207
  Merton Borough 359-360
  modernisation agenda 155-159

Index

consequences of 163
obstacles 150-151
options in crime
  prevention 168-169
  impact on partnerships
    169-170
  performance 152-155, 170-171
  management of 166-167
  populist pressures 165-166
  set up 148
  shortcomings 240-241
crime intelligence 188
Crime Triangle 86, 91
criminal intelligence 188
CWAP 193-194

Derbyshire *see* Safer
  Derbyshire Project
deviant lifestyles 260-261
Domestic Burglary Good
  Practice and Tactical
  Options Guide 329
  performance in Cheshire
    335-336
  preparation 330-334
  publication 334
domestic violence 214-216
  mandatory arrest
    initiative 314-315
Drug Action Teams (DAT)
  239
  use of redeployable
    CCTV 131
    methods of survey 131-132

survey results 132-143
survey results
  discussed 143-145
drug use 271-273
  Chiltern Vale case study
    analysis 277-279
    events 275-277
    link to ASB 274-275
drugs, micromapping
  project in Merton Borough
    371-373

effect signatures 285-286
  treatment *v.* regression
    effects 288-294
  where to look for 287-288
environment, role in fear of
  crime 368
evaluation 109
  complexity 96-99
  growth of 306
  impact shortcomings
    delivery 78-80
  performance
    framework 72-78
  selecting interventions
    69-71
  and knowledge 66
    knowledge and know
      how 67-79
  process 80-82
    knowledge
      requirement 83-85
  new framework 87-95
  practice guidance 85-87
  public leadership 31-36
    setting the standards

Community Safety: Innovation and Evaluation

31-36
testing the standards 37-42
purpose of 64-65
role of appropriate questioning 309-310
constant conjunction 314-316
historical 312-314
opportunist 310-312
options 320-321
practical 321-322
prophetical 316-317
realistic 317-320
role in crime prevention 307-308
weaknesses of 308-309
summary 322-325
summary of requirements 99-100
and the Trident tool 110
  components
    addressing outcomes 110
    delivery process 110
    multiple stakeholder perspectives 110-111
  context 117-118
  methods of data gathering 112
    multiple stakeholder perspectives 116-117
  outcomes 112-114
  process 115-116
  in use
    clinical facilitator

case study 118-122
safer home initiative 122-124
evidence
  role in social policy decision making 50
  see also rapid evidence assessment (REA)

fear of crime
  defined 358
  mapping
    spatial 361-363
    thematic 363-364
  Merton Borough micromapping project 364-367
    all crime 367-368
    burglary 370-371
    drugs 371-373
    evaluation 373-374
    youth ASB 368-370
  partnership approach 359-360
  relation to reported crime 358

gang violence *see* Birmingham Reducing Gang Violence (BRGV) group

Hawthorne Effect 360

Index

i-NSI 194-195
  in operation 195-202
impact, in the context of evaluation 89
implementation, in the context of evaluation 89
information
  importance of 183
  police as providers of 184-185
  see also community intelligence
intelligence
  cf. evaluative data 185-186
  in the context of evaluation 89
  deficit and surplus 189
  types of 187-188
  see also community intelligence (commtel)
intelligence based neighbourhood security interview (i-NSI) 194-195
  in operation 195-202
intervention, in the context of evaluation 89, 93-95
involvement, in the context of evaluation 89, 93-95

Kirkholt Burglary Prevention Project 316-317

leadership
  attempts to define 9-14
  collective 17-19

evaluation of
  setting standards 31-36
  testing the standards 37-42
  new model for 8-9, 19-21
  building capacity 25-28
  leading delivery 23-25
  managing the organisation 28-31
  shared vision 21-23
  role of individual in 14-16
  role in partnership 8
  summary of challenges 44-46
lifestyles, deviant 260-261
lighting, role in fear of crime 368
Local Area Agreements (LAA) 244

mass-media communication 165-166
mental illness, role in ASB 264
Merton Borough 359-360
  fear of crime
  micromapping project 364-367
    all crime 367-368
    burglary 370-371
    drugs 371-373
    evaluation 373-374
    youth ASB 368-370
Morgan Report 2, 238

National Community Safety

Plan (2005) 3, 247-248, 358
National Reassurance Policing Project (NRPP) 192
Neighbourhood Watch, evaluation 313-314
New Public Management 156

outcome measurement 110, 112-114, 310
outputs v. outcomes 310

partnership working
  effect of leadership on 8
  expansion 244-248
  extension of 241-243
  funding 243-244
  history of approach 237
  obstacles to 150-151
police and policing
  CWAPing 193-194
  role in community safety 184-185
  see also Chiltern Vale ASB case study
Police Reform Act (2002) 239
process of intervention 110, 115-116
Prolific Offenders initiative 245
property marking and burglary
  evaluation 318-319
  Smartwater Scheme 360

purchasers and providers 158

randomized control trials (RCT)
  practicalities 285, 286-287
rapid evidence assessment (REA) 50
  case studies on gang violence 55-59
  future of 60-61
  history 51
  literature v. systematic reviews 51-54
  methodology 54-55
  practicalities 59-60
Reassurance Gap 359
regression v. treatment effects 288-298
  asymmetric censoring 301
  crime risk and crime spates 300
  survival modelling 301
rubbish, role in fear of crime 368

Safer Cities Programme 307
  evaluation 312
Safer Derbyshire project
  evaluation 258-259
  objectives 256-257
  problems 250-251
    causes of 251-254
  products 257-258
  solutions 255-256
  stakeholders 250

Index

Safer Homes Initiative 122-124, 329
  evaluation with Trident 338-341
    multiple stakeholder perspectives 351
    outcomes 342-346
    process 346-351
    recommendations 352-356
  implementation 334-337
  launch 337
  preparatory work 330-334
  training and development 337-338
Safer and Stronger Communities Fund (SSCF) 243
safety, defined 1
SARA (Scanning, Analysis, Response and Assessment) 45-46, 86, 91
  evolution of 89-90
schools, role in fear of crime 370
Smartwater Scheme 360
stakeholders, documenting perspectives of 110-111, 116-117
survival analysis 288-294
Sustainable Community Strategy 242

Tackling Violent Crime Programme 244
TOGETHER Campaign 246
tourists and crime 222-229

travel to offend patterns 218-222
Trident: an evaluation tool 110
  components
    addressing outcomes 110
    delivery process 110
    multiple stakeholder perspectives 110-111
  context 117-118
  evaluation of Safer Homes Initiative 338-341
    multiple stakeholder perspectives 351
    outcomes 342-346
    process 346-351
  methods of data gathering 112
    multiple stakeholder perspectives 116-117
    outcomes 112-114
    process 115-116
  in use
    clinical facilitator case study 118-122
    Safer Homes Initiative 122-124

victimisation and victims 263-265
  study in Cornwall
    commuters 216-222
    domestic violence 214-216
    tourists 222-229